"The 21st century capitalist economy is marked by globalization but also globalization backlash. It features radical technological change but also stagnant productivity. Above all it is defined by the rise of China and Asia and their challenge to the prevailing order. Donghyun Park in this book does an admirable job of navigating this complex landscape."

Barry Eichengreen
George C. Pardee & Helen N. Pardee Professor of Economics and
Political Science
University of California, Berkeley

"This insightful and timely book provides an interpretation of the backlash against capitalism in the 21st century. Dr Donghyun Park, a seasoned economist with ample field and research experience in applied economics and finance, overviews the dynamics of this backlash with the help of several examples, and outlines possible remedies. Capitalism is far from perfect and must bear some blame for global problems. But the book's central argument is that it is not capitalism per se but the grotesquely deformed capitalism of the 21st century that is failing. More specifically, capitalism has been hijacked by the financial industry, which is no longer the valuable tool of capitalism that channels capital to entrepreneurs and companies. Instead, it has become a self-serving leviathan whose blind pursuit of profit almost wrecked the world economy in 2008. This book should provide an essential reference for scholars, graduate students, and practitioners."

Joshua Aizenman
Robert R. and Katheryn A. Dockson Chair in Economics and
International Relations and
Professor of International Relations and Economics
University of Southern California

"*Capitalism in the 21st Century* is a frank, provocative and passionate discussion of fundamental strengths and deficiencies of modern capitalism. Dr Donghyun Park argues that while capitalism is not functioning as well as we would like it to, the solution is to fix it rather than to throw it away — the alternatives are much worse. This is much needed and timely analysis of market failures — and of government failures — which brings about the conclusion that in some cases we need more rather than less capitalism."

Sergei Guriev
Chief Economist
European Bank for Reconstruction and Development

"Capitalism is currently under siege in the battlefield of public opinion. Capitalism is widely blamed for virtually all of the major problems plaguing the world today, from inequality to environmental degradation to inhumane poverty. Wide and growing inequality in particular is undermining the foundations of democratic, socially beneficial capitalism by undermining popular belief in equality of opportunity. However, this eloquent and perceptive book by Dr Donghyun Park, a well-published research economist, cogently argues that entrepreneurial capitalism remains a central part of the solution to humanity's most pressing challenges. The argument is supported by a wide array of interesting and relevant real-world examples. Returning capitalism to its Adam Smith-ian roots of private self-interest promoting the social good requires reforming the role of the government and financial system in the economy. The book concludes that there is every reason for a better capitalism and a better tomorrow."

Otaviano Canuto
Executive Director
Executive Board of Directors of the World Bank Group and its Affiliates

"Dr Donghyun Park is a prominent and rare economist in Asia who can combine frontline economic theories, lively data, and real-time policy analyses. *Capitalism in the 21st Century* is a masterful book by Dr Park, providing a comprehensive understanding of heterogenous trajectories of economies around the globe and more fundamental mechanisms of the modern capitalistic system. This is a 'must-read' for those who are interested in comparative economic systems, global economy, and international development."

Yasuyuki Sawada
Chief Economist, Asian Development Bank
Professor of Economics, University of Tokyo

"Donghyun Park makes clear that capitalism gets a bad rap, in large part because of too much emphasis on capital as in financial engineering, and too much emphasis on capitals as in government protectionism. Park argues a compelling case that genuine capitalism, which is about entrepreneurship, is necessary to solve the big problems most people face around the globe."

Adam S. Posen
President, Peterson Institute of International Economics

Capitalism

in the 21st Century

Why
Global Capitalism Is
Broken and

How It Can Be
Fixed

Other Related Titles from World Scientific

Seeking Adam Smith: Finding The Shadow Curriculum of Business
by Eli P Cox III
ISBN: 978-981-3206-72-4
ISBN: 978-981-3206-73-1 (pbk)

Inequality and Global Supra-surplus Capitalism
by E Ray Canterbery
ISBN: 978-981-3200-82-1

State Capitalism in Eurasia
by Martin C Spechler, Joachim Ahrens and Herman W Hoen
ISBN: 978-981-3149-37-3

Why
Global Capitalism Is
Broken and

How It Can Be
Fixed

Donghyun Park

Asian Development Bank, Philippines

World Scientific

NEW JERSEY · LONDON · SINGAPORE · BEIJING · SHANGHAI · HONG KONG · TAIPEI · CHENNAI · TOKYO

Published by

World Scientific Publishing Co. Pte. Ltd.

5 Toh Tuck Link, Singapore 596224

USA office: 27 Warren Street, Suite 401-402, Hackensack, NJ 07601

UK office: 57 Shelton Street, Covent Garden, London WC2H 9HE

British Library Cataloguing-in-Publication Data
A catalogue record for this book is available from the British Library.

CAPITALISM IN THE 21ST CENTURY
Why Global Capitalism Is Broken and How It Can Be Fixed

ISBN 978-981-3274-23-5
ISBN 978-981-3275-29-4 (pbk)

For any available supplementary material, please visit
https://www.worldscientific.com/worldscibooks/10.1142/11098#t=suppl

Desk Editor: Jiang Yulin

Typeset by Stallion Press
Email: enquiries@stallionpress.com

Printed in Singapore

Lovingly dedicated to the memory
of my beloved late mother
Young-Sook Chung and my beloved father
Chang-Nam Park, who gave me the gift of
clear thinking and good writing

About the Author

Dr Donghyun PARK is currently Principal Economist at the Economic Research and Regional Cooperation Department (ERCD) of the Asian Development Bank (ADB), which he joined in April 2007. Prior to joining ADB, he was a tenured Associate Professor of Economics at Nanyang Technological University in Singapore. Dr Park has a Ph.D. in economics from UCLA, and his main research fields are international finance, international trade, and development economics. His research, which has been published extensively in journals and books, revolves around policy-oriented topics relevant for Asia's long-term development, including population aging, service sector development, and financial sector development. Dr Park plays a leading role in the production of *Asian Development Outlook*, ADB's biannual flagship publication on macroeconomic issues, and leads the team that produces *Asia Bond Monitor*, ADB's quarterly flagship report on emerging Asian bond markets.

Global capitalism is currently suffering from an unmistakable malaise, epitomized by wide and growing inequality that is eroding popular support for capitalism. Such anti-capitalist sentiment, coupled with a growing anti-globalization mood, delivered Brexit in a UK referendum and swept Donald Trump to the US presidency. In *Capitalism in the 21st Century*, internationally well-regarded economist Dr Donghyun Park articulately explains why more capitalism is needed to tackle global problems such as climate change and inhumane poverty. While defending capitalism against its unfair demonization, the author makes a positive case for entrepreneurial capitalism, which creates wealth and jobs as well as drives human progress. According to the author, reforming the financial industry, which has become a self-serving leviathan, and more fundamentally, tweaking the economic role of the government, which stifles growth-promoting entrepreneurship, are critical to restoring the vitality of capitalism. The book is explicitly written in such a way that the general reader without any background in economics or finance can easily understand it.

About the Book

Contents

Contents

Contents

Contents

Contents

CAPITALISM IN CRISIS?

Without a shadow of a doubt, capitalism is the single greatest invention in human history. The impact of capitalism on the material progress of mankind dwarfs the impact of the steam engine, electricity, combustible engine, and all other technological breakthroughs combined. Indeed it was raw capitalism, epitomized by larger-than-life titans such as Cornelius Vanderbilt, John Rockefeller, Andrew Carnegie, J.P. Morgan, and Henry Ford, that produced such game-changing breakthroughs.[1] Yet the central role of capitalism in expanding the sheer amount and variety of goods we enjoy, and in lifting our living standards beyond all recognition, is often underappreciated, if not forgotten altogether. Perhaps this is because we take capitalism for granted, like oxygen, especially after it defeated socialism and became the dominant global economic system. Or, perhaps the lack of appreciation is due to the intangible nature of capitalism, which is not something we can see, touch and feel, unlike the mobile phone, laptop, or internet.

Furthermore, even the most articulate supporters of capitalism usually define their support for capitalism in terms of what they are against — e.g. socialism, excessive government

[1] The extraordinary exploits of these giants of capitalism are chronicled in the excellent, entertaining, and informative TV documentary *The Men Who Built America*, produced by History Channel in 2012.

interference, stifling bureaucracy — rather than what they are for. Advocates of capitalism usually cite something vague like freedom or liberty, which implicitly refers to freedom or liberty from the government. But there is, in fact, a crystal-clear intellectual, moral, and common-sense positive case for capitalism. That positive case is that capitalism is ultimately a supremely fair economic system. The essence of capitalism is that each of us is rewarded according to the quality and quantity of our work. Under capitalism, the amount of pie we get to eat depends on the amount of crust and fillings we add to the pie. What can be fairer than that? From this angle, the popular criticism of capitalism as an unfair system is unfounded and puzzling.

Notwithstanding its invaluable contribution to human progress, there is currently a torrential global backlash against capitalism, along with a gathering sense of disillusionment about capitalism. To a large extent, the backlash and disillusionment reflect the public's legitimate concerns about the wide and growing income gap between the rich and the poor, crystallized in Thomas Piketty's bestseller *Capital in the Twenty-First Century*. It is only natural to blame growing inequality on an economic system that is widely seen as inherently unfair. More generally, there is a disturbing tendency to blame capitalism for all the ills of today's world, from climate change to youth unemployment to Third World poverty. But the capitalist malaise runs much deeper than just unfair perception. Capitalism is, in fact, suffering from an unmistakable loss of momentum — a malaise — and it is no longer the dynamic wealth- and job-creating engine of human progress that it used to be.

Linked to the rise of anti-capitalist sentiment across the world is the rise of anti-globalization

> **"**
> But there is, in fact, a crystal-clear intellectual, moral, and common-sense positive case for capitalism. That positive case is that capitalism is ultimately a supremely fair economic system. The essence of capitalism is that each of us is rewarded according to the quality and quantity of our work.
> **"**

sentiment. A dramatic example of the growing popular anger was Brexit, or the shocking decision of British voters to leave the European Union (EU) in a national referendum held on 23 June 2016.[2] A number of factors contributed to Brexit, including Britain's traditional reluctance to fully embrace Europe.[3] But a big factor behind Brexit was the British voters' hostility to immigration and a popular belief that the EU was responsible for immigration.[4] In other words, Brexit was ultimately a vote against globalization.[5] Anti-globalization sentiment is by no means limited to Britain. Xenophobic, immigrant-bashing parties such as the National Front in France, led by Marine Le Pen, and Party for Freedom in the Netherlands, led by Geert Wilders, have become major political forces across Western Europe. In Eastern Europe, which ironically receives very few refugees from Syria or other developing countries, refugee-bashing has become a surefire recipe for political success, as evident in the enduring popularity of Hungary's populist nationalist leader Viktor Orbán. The frontal assault against globalization is further tightening the full-scale siege of capitalism in the battlefield of public opinion.[6]

Even more shocking than Brexit was the election of Donald Trump as the 45th president of the United States on 8 November 2016. Notwithstanding its significance, Brexit is a tiddling wave compared to Trump's election, which is a gigantic tsunami that sent shock waves throughout the world. Trump, a real estate mogul and former reality TV show star with no political or government experience won a completely unexpected electoral victory over Hillary Clinton, a highly experienced politician with a wealth of government experience. Despite being a rich millionaire, Donald Trump campaigned on an unabashedly populist platform, and claimed to be the champion of

[2] See, for example, "Europe's crisis of faith," TIME magazine, 11/18 July 2016, or "An aggravating absence," The Economist, 2 July 2016, for analysis of Brexit. While the long-term consequences of Brexit are uncertain, the short-run effects were clearly negative, especially for Britain. For example, the pound fell to its lowest level in almost 31 years in the immediate aftermath of the referendum. Prime Minister David Cameron, who staked his political future on the referendum, promptly resigned.

[3] Britain has traditionally looked across the Atlantic to America rather than across the English Channel to the EU, dominated since its inception by France and Germany, as its closest ally and partner.

[4] The EU mandates freedom of movement for EU citizens within the EU. Paradoxically, although significant numbers of citizens from poorer EU countries such as Poland and Slovakia did migrate to Britain for work, the majority of immigrants to Britain are from non-EU countries although the share of EU immigrants has been rising in recent years.

[5] See, for example, "The politics of anger," The Economist, 2 July 2016. Tellingly, London and its suburbs, the most prosperous area of Britain which gained the most from globalization, voted solidly in favor of remaining in the EU. London is one of the world's greatest international financial centers. In stark contrast, the run-down industrial cities of northern England, hit hard by imports from China and elsewhere, voted heavily in favor of leaving the EU.

[6] Almost invariably, anti-capitalism and anti-globalization go hand in hand together. But capitalism and globalization are fundamentally different concepts. Capitalism is a system for organizing the economy while globalization refers to the free flow of goods, services, capital, people, and knowledge and ideas across borders. Of course, there are many close links between the two — perhaps the most visible symbols of global capitalism are large multinational companies like McDonald's and Coca-Cola which operate across the world. Nevertheless, in this book, we will look first and foremost at capitalism. Indeed a meaningful discussion of the pros and cons of globalization would require another entire book! A clear global trend in recent years is the rise of often virulent anti-globalization popular sentiment. This points to a need for governments to make a stronger case for globalization, which benefits the economy and society as a whole, and to make a more concerted effort to help those who lose out from globalization — for instance, workers who lose their jobs due to cheaper imports. See, for example, "The new political divide," The Economist, 30 July 2016.

3

the common man forgotten and ignored by the elite. His upset victory was due to a number of different factors, including a widespread sense of alienation among working-class white Americans, shift of the popular mood against immigration and free trade, and hostility at the political establishment in Washington, D.C., personified by Clinton. Since his inauguration in January 2017, President Trump has gradually begun to pursue the anti-free trade and anti-immigration policies he stridently advocated during the election campaign.[7] It still remains to be seen whether his anti-globalization bite will ultimately match his anti-globalization bark during his presidency, but the signs so far give plenty of cause for concern.

A powerful common undercurrent linking the various ingredients of Trump's success is popular disillusionment about capitalism. America has traditionally been the undisputed leader and bastion of global capitalism. Capitalism, in the best, Adam Smith-ian sense of the word as well as in the entrepreneurial, risk-taking, value- and job-creating sense of Steve Jobs and Silicon Valley, has long been identified with America. A defining feature of America has been broad, deep, and genuine support for capitalism among ordinary Americans, not only rich Americans. That support rested on the popular belief that America was a land of opportunity, where anybody with talent, drive and determination, can succeed and move up the social and economic ladder. However, in recent years, worsening inequality and declining social mobility are eroding the very foundations of people's capitalism or democratic capitalism or best-man-wins capitalism. What explains Trump's rise is his ability to capitalize on such disillusionment with capitalism. Increasingly, capitalism is seen as benefiting only a self-perpetuating, hereditary elite while

[7] On 1 March 2018, the Trump administration imposed a 25% tariff — i.e. tax on imports — on imported steel and 10% tariff on imported aluminum. On 22 March, the administration announced tariffs on up to US$60 billion of Chinese imports, including parts and components used in the aeronautics, technology, and energy industries. China responded to the US actions in kind, imposing new tariffs on agricultural and other US imports. A full-fledged trade war between America and China, which may still be averted, will be catastrophic for the world economy. Tellingly, stock markets across the world, including US markets, fell visibly on 23 March 2018, although they subsequently recovered. The Trump administration is re-negotiating the North American Free Trade Agreement (NAFTA), which links the economies of the US, Mexico, and Canada. In addition, it has re-negotiated the US's trade deal with South Korea. At the same time, the Trump administration is making concerted efforts to impose a blanket ban on travel to the US by citizens from six largely Muslim countries, on the grounds that they posed a serious risk to US national security. The ban has been challenged as unconstitutional by US courts but on 4 December 2017, the US Supreme Court ruled that the ban can go into effect, paving the way for implementation. The Trump administration is threatening an end to DACA, or Deferred Action for Childhood Arrivals, a program established by President Barack Obama that protects 690,000 people who arrived illegally in the US as children from deportation. Those immigrants are known as Dreamers. More broadly, the overall environment in the US has become much less welcoming to immigrants and would-be immigrants, including highly skilled ones, since the advent of the Trump administration.

impoverishing the masses. Trump's political genius was to tap into this revolt of the masses against a capitalism of the elite, by the elite, and for the elite.

Capitalism is, no doubt, far from perfect and must bear some blame for global problems. But our central argument is that it is not capitalism per se but the grotesquely deformed capitalism of the 21st century that is failing. More specifically, capitalism has been hijacked by the financial industry, which is no longer the valuable tool of capitalism that channels capital to entrepreneurs and companies. Instead it has become a self-serving leviathan whose blind pursuit of profit almost wrecked the world economy in 2008. Critically, that greed-crazed frenzy, more frightening than a school of Amazon River piranhas devouring a fish to its bare bones within seconds, was made possible by cozy ties between the financial industry and the government, whose implicit guarantees encourage banks to take undue risk, safe in the knowledge that tax payers will bail them out if things went wrong.[8] Instead of serving entrepreneurs and firms, many of the financial industry's so-called innovations fatten its own pockets, but add little value to the economy and jeopardize financial stability. The US subprime mortgage crisis of 2008, which morphed into the Global Financial Crisis, underlined the industry's unlimited potential for damage.

But the good news is that there is still plenty of hope for capitalism to return to its roots. Capitalism's current woes do not begin and end with the financial industry. In fact, reforming the financial industry is a good place to start reforming capitalism. The twisted 21st-century capitalism of the financial industry dominating the real economy must give way to the original, benign, socially desirable

[8] And, sure enough, things went spectacularly wrong when Lehman Brothers went bankrupt in September 2008, triggering the Global Financial Crisis. As it rightly turned out, the US government honored its guarantee with a multibillion-dollar bailout package for the banks.

5

capitalism of the financial industry serving the real economy. Good capitalism is vibrant capitalism in which greed and the profit motive encourage innovative, risk-taking, profit-seeking entrepreneurs to create new and better products, to invest in new and better technologies, and to hire more workers and devote in their training and re-training. Therefore, reinstating the weakened links between the financial industry and the real economy is vital to restoring the health of capitalism. A healthy capitalism, in turn, is crucial to tackling humanity's greatest contemporary challenges, like environmental destruction, youth unemployment and chronic poverty.

At a deeper level, the root cause of capitalism's current slump is stifling government regulation and interference that stands in the way of private enterprise and entrepreneurship. Revamping the financial industry so that it serves the real economy rather than itself is, for sure, a major priority for fixing capitalism. But the bigger priority is to get government and government bureaucrats off the back of private business so that entrepreneurs can take risks and go about doing what they do best — creating useful new products and technologies, jobs, and wealth. Paradoxically, the government was asleep at the wheels when it came to regulating the financial industry, which needs to be tightly regulated, while it was overregulating the real economy and the risk-taking entrepreneurs who create wealth and jobs. In other words, governments were giving a free pass to the likes of hedge funds, which create little social value, while handcuffing the likes of Steve Jobs, who generate plenty of social value.

In truth, capitalism is not even remotely in any slump. What passes for capitalism today, the same capitalism that is widely and unfairly criticized

"

In other words, governments were giving a free pass to the likes of hedge funds, which create little social value, while handcuffing the likes of Steve Jobs, who generate plenty of social value.

"

as the root cause of all of mankind's problems, is not capitalism at all. Today's capitalism is so far removed from the benign original vision of Adam Smith — individual greed promoting the social good and driving human progress — that he would barely recognize it if he came back to life.[9] The visible, meddling, and corrupt hand of the government has pushed aside the invisible, entrepreneurial, and wealth-creating hand of the market. Across vast swathes of the world, the only growth industry is the government industry. But notwithstanding the wishful self-delusion of politicians and bureaucrats, the government industry does not create useful new products and technologies, and it most certainly does not create wealth and jobs. Far worse, government interference suffocates wealth- and job-creating entrepreneurship and brings economic progress to a rude stop.

The runaway growth of the government industry, which squeezes the very life out of the private sector, is indeed cause for deep concern and alarm about the future prospects of capitalism and mankind. No country ever got rich by expanding the government, and no country ever will. Conversely, no country ever got rich by suffocating its private sector. Moreover, the world will not solve its myriad urgent challenges — from climate change and environmental destruction which threaten us and our children and grandchildren, to the inhumane poverty which still enslaves far too many of our fellow global citizens, to the bleak employment prospects of millions of youths in both rich and poor countries — by adding yet more foot soldiers to its already-bulging army of government bureaucrats. Tackling global problems requires less, not more, government, and what the world needs is more, not less, capitalism. Capitalism is not part of the problem, but a central part of the solution.

[9] His hugely influential 1776 masterpiece *The Wealth of Nations* is considered the first modern work of economics, and eloquently explains how rational self-interest and competition fosters economic prosperity.

Above all, government officials need to get out of the way and allow dynamic, creative entrepreneurs (think of Steve Jobs and his friends starting Apple in a suburban California garage) to work their capitalist magic — taking risks, inventing useful new products and technologies, creating wealth and jobs in the process, and finding innovative solutions to mankind's biggest challenges. For example, environmental destruction and global warming are giving rise to an increased demand for environment-friendly technologies and products. Green demand is growing not only in rich America but also in much poorer China, where millions of people are suffering from some of the worst air quality in the world. Where there is demand, there are profit opportunities. And where there are profit opportunities, there are profit-seeking, risk-taking entrepreneurs. Elon Musk is a prime example of a visionary green entrepreneur and his Tesla electric car is the kind of innovative green product which will move us toward a greener, better future.

At a broader level, much of the blame for capitalism's current malaise lies with the government. Capitalism at its best requires the government to be an honest and competent referee of a fierce but fair, never-ending contest among entrepreneurs and firms. If the government did this well, the winners will be entrepreneurs and firms that create socially valuable products and technologies. Yet far too often, the government does a terrible job of refereeing the competition. For one, unhealthily close ties between government and business mean that the winners are those who are good at cozying up to politicians and bureaucrats, not those who are good at creating social value. The unholy alliance is good for corrupt politicians and bureaucrats, and good for corrupt businessmen,

"

For example, environmental destruction and global warming are giving rise to an increased demand for environment-friendly technologies and products.... Where there is demand, there are profit opportunities. And where there are profit opportunities, there are profit-seeking, risk-taking entrepreneurs.

"

but bad for everybody else and the entire economy. Even worse, the government produces far too many goods and services, even though it tends to be terrible at making things. Last but not least, as already alluded to, bureaucrats often suffocate the private sector with mind-numbing overregulation. Therefore, tweaking the role of the government in the economy must be at the front and center of reforming capitalism.

❝

Capitalism at its best requires the government to be an honest and competent referee of a fierce but fair, never-ending contest among entrepreneurs and firms. If the government did this well, the winners will be entrepreneurs and firms that create socially valuable products and technologies.

❞

9

WORLD'S WORST CARS, NORTH KOREA, BIGGEST MAN-MADE DISASTER IN HISTORY, AND ENTREPRENEURIAL CHINESE DNA

The superiority of capitalism over alternative economic systems is so self-evident that it requires no explanation. For starters, the collapse of the Soviet Union and socialism has left the world with no alternative system for organizing the production of goods and services. The victory of capitalism over socialism in the Cold War was, in the final analysis, the triumph of a vastly superior economic system which delivered far superior living standards to the masses. The level of material comfort enjoyed by an average middle-class family in, say, New York City in 1980 far exceeded that of their counterparts in Moscow in 1980. In fact, the difference was night and day. For sure, there were a large number of non-economic factors which played a role in the defeat of socialism. These include growing popular resentment at stifling political repression, omnipresent intrusion of the government into daily life, and lack of individual freedom. But the failure of socialism was ultimately due to its utter flaw as an economic system.

The bewildering variety and dazzling quality of goods and services seen in the West could not even remotely compare with the monolithic, drab junk mindlessly churned out by Soviet

"

The victory of capitalism over socialism in the Cold War was, in the final analysis, the triumph of a vastly superior economic system which delivered far superior living standards to the masses.

"

factories. The iconic tragicomic — tragic if you lived in a socialist country, comic if you didn't — image of the socialist economy is the long queue of frustrated consumers, bending around the street corner, standing in line for hours for basic necessities such as bread or toilet paper. Lada, Trabant, and Yugo — from the Soviet Union, East Germany, and Yugoslavia, respectively — rank right up there in the pantheon of worst automobiles ever produced, and are a vivid testament to the inability of communism to deliver economic progress. When communism fell, socialist countries were flooded with far superior imports from the West, and many factories that churned out Ladas and the like were shuttered for good. Good riddance. Socialist production destroyed rather than added value. That is, the steel used to build Ladas was arguably worth more than the cars themselves! This is the sad but predictable result of government bureaucrats, instead of the market, calling the shots in the economy.

Perhaps the most striking illustration of the colossal gulf between the productivity of capitalism and socialism comes from the Korean Peninsula. The peninsula is inhabited by a single people who share a common history, culture, and language, and are a hardworking, talented, and resilient lot. The peninsula was divided into a socialist North and a capitalist South in the aftermath of the Second World War. Both countries were poor at that time and, to make things worse, they were devastated by the fratricidal Korean War of 1950–1953. Since the end of the war, the South achieved an economic miracle which catapulted the country from rubbish-scrounging Third World poverty to wine-sipping First World affluence within one generation. In stark contrast, the North, which had higher income than the South until the early 1970s, has degenerated into a Somalia with

> **"** Perhaps the most striking illustration of the colossal gulf between the productivity of capitalism and socialism comes from the Korean Peninsula.... Since the end of the war, the South achieved an economic miracle which catapulted the country from rubbish-scrounging Third World poverty to wine-sipping First World affluence within one generation. In stark contrast, the North, which had higher income than the South until the early 1970s, has degenerated into a Somalia with nuclear bombs. **"**

11

nuclear bombs. That the North was ahead less than five decades ago seems astonishing today. In 2017, the average South Korean made around US$40,000, close to the UK and Japan figures, while the average North Korean made less than US$2,000, roughly equal to the figure for Haiti, the poorest country in the Western Hemisphere, and Sierra Leone, a country that is poor even by African standards.[1]

Today South Koreans enjoy living standards comparable to those of the West and their country exports high-tech manufactured goods all over the world. Samsung mobile phones, Hyundai cars, and LG television sets are top-notch products produced by world-class companies. In stark contrast, north of the border, socialism has succeeded in reducing the same energetic, hardworking, talented people into one of the poorest nations in the world, eating grass for lunch, and fleeing desperately across the Yalu River to China for survival. The country's main export is to blackmail the South, Japan and the US for economic aid with its nuclear bomb-making capability.[2] North Korea is, in short, a poster child for the unparalleled destructive capacity of socialism as an economic system. Socialism's power to impoverish, immiserize, and dehumanize is equivalent to a million nuclear bombs. Socialism is, without any doubt and by a long distance, the single biggest man-made disaster in the history of mankind. Bar none.

A striking example of the transformative power of capitalism comes from the recent rise of the Chinese economy, undoubtedly the most significant trend in the global economic landscape during the last 40 years. The market reforms initiated by Deng Xiaoping in 1978 jumpstarted decades of world-topping growth which vaulted China from the sidelines of the world economy

[1] The GDP (gross domestic product) per capita figures are what economists call purchasing power parity (PPP) incomes. Simply put, the figures adjust for the fact that goods that cannot be traded internationally, such as haircuts or domestic help, are cheaper in poor countries than in rich countries. In other words, a dollar goes further in poor countries than in rich countries, and hence we need to adjust for the purchasing power of a dollar in different countries to get a more accurate comparison of living standards in different countries.

[2] North Korean leader Kim Jong-un and South Korean leader Moon Jae-in held a summit meeting on 27 April 2018, giving rise to optimism that North Korea would give up its nuclear bombs in exchange for economic assistance. It remains to be seen whether Kim is serious about his purported plan to focus his efforts on improving the economy. If this is true, it would be fantastic news for the North Korean people.

to its front and center. A large number of factors help to explain the phenomenal rise of China, which has grown at around 10% per year over the last 30 years, by far the fastest pace among major economies. China overtook Japan in 2010 to become the world's second biggest economy and it can knock the US off its top spot as early as 2025 under reasonable assumptions. China's average income rose by more than 40-fold, from US$400 in 1978 to more than US$16,000 by 2017.[3] Furthermore, poverty rate, defined as the share of population living on US$1.25 or less a day, dropped from 85% in 1981 to single digits by 2017. Massive foreign investment, a huge supply of industrious workers, and good roads, electricity and other infrastructure were some of the secrets of China's meteoric economic rise.

But one key factor that is often overlooked is that the Chinese are by nature a highly entrepreneurial lot. It is in the Chinese DNA to start new businesses, take risks, and pursue profits. That kind of optimistic, get-up-and-go spirit sounds awfully similar to another big country, on the other side of the Pacific. In fact, entrepreneurial zeal is the vastly under-appreciated common bond between America and China. For every Apple, Microsoft, Google, Amazon, and Facebook, there is a Baidu, Alibaba, Tencent, NetEase, and Xiaomi. And for every Steve Jobs, Bill Gates, Larry Page, Jeff Bezos, and Mark Zuckerberg, China has its Robin Li, Jack Ma, Pony Ma, William Ding, and Lei Jun. Another hint of China's entrepreneurial DNA comes from the headlong rush of Chinese companies into high-risk frontier markets such as Africa, shunned by companies from rich countries. To some, this reflects a questionable tolerance for doing business with corrupt, unsavory governments. But more fundamentally, it shows a hearty Chinese appetite for taking risk in adventurous pursuit of profit. After all, it

13

[3] Again, these are PPP figures.

is no picnic to do business in such rough and tumble countries, let alone turn a profit.

In short, China's economic resurgence owes a great deal to unleashing the genie of entrepreneurial energy, which had been bottled up for decades under socialism. The predictable result was a massive tsunami of entrepreneurship and private enterprise. The whole country has become a startup! Strikingly, the government still controls large swathes of the Chinese economy, evident in the dominant role of state-owned enterprises in many industries and state control of big banks. In other words, China's capitalist revolution still has some distance to run. That is good news for China as it implies that China can continue to grow at a healthy pace for years to come as it shakes off the remaining shackles of socialism. It is also positive news for the world economy as China is already an important market and driver of growth, both for advanced economies — e.g. machinery from Germany and Japan — and developing countries — e.g. soya beans, minerals and oil from Africa, Asia, and Latin America.

"

In short, China's economic resurgence owes a great deal to unleashing the genie of entrepreneurial energy, which had been bottled up for decades under socialism. The predictable result was a massive tsunami of entrepreneurship and private enterprise. The whole country has become a startup!

"

CUBAN DOCTORS, COMMUNISM VERSUS SOCIALISM, AND NORTH KOREA VERSUS INDIA

3

To be fair, socialism is not without its attractions. Otherwise, an economic system as inefficient, dehumanizing, and morally bankrupt as socialism could not last for decades and enslave a good share of humanity. For sure, the secret police — for example, the infamous Stasi of East Germany, which spied on the entire population, primarily through a vast network of ordinary citizens turned informants — and a general political climate of fear and intimidation — for political prisoners, being sent to Siberian gulags or forced labor camps was a relatively mild form of punishment — played a major role in stifling dissent and sustaining the system. But even so, one has to admit there were some material benefits to living in a socialist country, as paradoxical as this sounds. More specifically, a sense of economic security — the universal provision of housing, health care, education, pension, and other basic social services — was largely responsible for the puzzlingly long survival of socialism.

For example, a high priority on social services explains why socialist Cuba, despite its crushing poverty, had one of the best health care systems in Latin America, and why doctors and

> **"**
> But even so, one has to admit there were some material benefits to living in a socialist country, as paradoxical as this sounds. More specifically, a sense of economic security — the universal provision of housing, health care, education, pension, and other basic social services — was largely responsible for the puzzlingly long survival of socialism.
> **"**

15

other medical personnel became a top Cuban export. The main destinations of Cuba's medical personnel exports were Latin America, Africa, and Pacific Ocean island states. The top market was oil-rich Venezuela; Cuba provided over 30,000 medical personnel plus medical training for Venezuelan students in exchange for 100,000 barrels of oil per day under an "oil for doctors" program. Furthermore, in some parts of Eastern Europe and the former Soviet Union, free or heavily subsidized provision of basic services and a guaranteed minimum standard of living help to explain the genuine, heartfelt nostalgia for the good old days of socialism. The nostalgia is especially strong among older residents who feel insecure about the extensive disruption brought on by the onslaught of capitalism.

Overall, however, the benefits of socialism pale in comparison to its monstrous shortcomings. Above all, socialism is a supremely unfair ideology and economic system. The irony here is, of course, that socialism claims to be the most humane, decent, fair system that treats everybody equally and gives a sense of dignity to even the most downtrodden. Nothing could be further from the truth. At the end of the day, in a socialist economy, the self-important, risk-averse government bureaucrat arbitrarily dictates the economy rather than the market. What is fair about that? Under capitalism, the winners of the economic game are entrepreneurs who survive the tough competition of the market. There is a clear moral, intellectual, and common-sense case for their victory. They won fair and square because they delivered the best value — superior products at competitive prices — and captured the hearts and dollars of consumers.

Under socialism, in contrast to capitalism, the winners of economic competition are determined by the government rather than the consumers.

" Overall, however, the benefits of socialism pale in comparison to its monstrous shortcomings. Above all, socialism is a supremely unfair ideology and economic system. The irony here is, of course, that socialism claims to be the most humane, decent, fair system that treats everybody equally and gives a sense of dignity to even the most downtrodden. Nothing could be further from the truth. "

But then what gives the bureaucrats the right to determine winners? Pray tell me, just what do those bureaucrats deliver, other than harassing entrepreneurs and extorting bribes on the side? Socialism is, in short, an elitist ideology in which a self-important, all-knowing elite spells out "what is good for the masses". Defenders of socialism like to believe that socialism and Soviet-style communism are fundamentally different. But there is one gigantic common bond between the two — ownership of major industries by the government rather than private individuals. The defining characteristic of both socialism and communism is the omnipresent, meddling, arbitrary, corrupt, bribe-extorting hand of the government in the economy. That deadweight, rather than the dynamic, innovative, risk-taking, wealth- and job-creating energy of the entrepreneur, determines the quantity and quality of goods and services that firms produce and households consume, with predictably disastrous consequences for the economy.

Socialism is, in effect, communism minus the dictatorship, secret police, and forced labor camps. It may seem grossly unfair to compare socialist democracies with brutal communist dictatorships. And, politically, such comparisons are indeed preposterous. One-party dictatorships that keep the population in line through fear and intimidation, such as North Korea or Cuba, share nothing in common with vibrant democracies with free elections and free press, such as India. But as economic systems, socialism and communism are one and the same. The same sterile economic philosophy — i.e. the economy dictated by pompous, risk-averse government bureaucrats sitting in their cozy offices with lifetime job security and generous pensions — wrecks socialist and communist countries alike, and delivers poverty and misery for everybody. Equality of sorts, but

> **"**
> But as economic systems, socialism and communism are one and the same. The same sterile economic philosophy — i.e. the economy dictated by pompous, risk-averse government bureaucrats sitting in their cozy offices with lifetime job security and generous pensions — wrecks socialist and communist countries alike, and delivers poverty and misery for everybody.
> **"**

17

the worst kind. That explains why, for example, India's pre-1991 socialist economy was every bit as lethargic and lifeless as the Soviet economy and grew at a glacial pace, widely ridiculed as the Hindu rate of growth. It was only when India began to shake off its socialist chains in 1991 that its private sector and economy finally began to breathe and grow, and it has now become one of the world's fastest-growing and most dynamic economies.[1]

[1] In response to an economic crisis, in 1991 the Indian government, led by Prime Minister Narasimha Rao and Finance Minister Manmohan Singh, took various measures to open up and liberalize the economy. Those measures reduced government intervention and increased the role of the private sector. More recently, the government of Prime Minister Narendra Modi, who took office in May 2014, has taken further measures to improve the business climate and promote private enterprise.

INEQUALITY, THE CANCER AT THE HEART OF CAPITALISM

A t the same time, it should be acknowledged that capitalism is far from perfect and saddled with major problems of its own. The single biggest flaw with capitalism is the staggering inequality that it often breeds. Even in the world's most affluent countries, abject squalor exists side by side with luxurious abundance. Run-down and decaying inner cities, epitomized by the surreal ghost town of Detroit, once the automobile capital of the world, are ringed by leafy, affluent suburbs. Such stark contrasts between the haves and have-nots are a hallmark of urban America. The decaying slums of inner city America and pleasant middle-class American suburbia might as well be different countries. For sure, they are different worlds. Similarly, grim and grimy banlieues — low-income suburbs populated by Arab and African immigrants — are a world away from chic, elegant Champs Elysées and the scintillating splendor of central Paris.

The gap between the haves and have-nots is even more glaring within developing countries, if not downright scandalous. In those countries, the poor scrounge for food at rubbish dumps, while the rich fly off to the French Riviera, to enjoy champagne and caviar at a five-star

> " The single biggest flaw with capitalism is the staggering inequality that it often breeds. Even in the world's most affluent countries, abject squalor exists side by side with luxurious abundance.... The decaying slums of inner city America and pleasant middle-class American suburbia might as well be different countries. For sure, they are different worlds. "

19

resort hotel. The rich elite of the world's poorest countries are richer than most people in the world's richest countries while most of their fellow citizens do not even have the basic necessities of life. And, many of the rich in those countries did not get rich because of their entrepreneurial talent or hard work. They got rich by plundering their countries to the bone. The international income gap between rich countries and poor countries is equally outrageous. While the average middle-class American family debates at the dinner table about whether or not to buy a third car, the average family in, say, the Sahel region of Africa, seeks the answer to the much starker and more significant question of how to get their third meal of the day.

There have been many explanations for the ever-widening income gap between the rich and the poor. Thomas Piketty, for example, produces evidence which indicates that wealth grows faster than economic output over time. This implies that the income gap between factory owners — i.e. capitalists or owners of capital — and factory workers — i.e. owners of labor — will widen over time. At a broader level, unfortunately, many factors that contribute to economic growth also lead to greater inequality. For example, technological progress is a powerful driver of economic growth but it benefits skilled workers more than unskilled workers. The former are better able to work with new technologies than the latter. Likewise, international trade and globalization benefit some groups more than others. Firms and industries that can compete in the global marketplace will thrive, while those that do not will wilt.

Much more fundamentally, capitalism is an intrinsically unequal and unfair economic system, and there is no two ways about it. No apologies needed, and no apologies forthcoming. The

At a broader level, unfortunately, many factors that contribute to economic growth also lead to greater inequality. For example, technological progress is a powerful driver of economic growth but it benefits skilled workers more than unskilled workers.

basic tenet of capitalism is that each of us earns according to one's ability and enterprise. Some of us are more talented than others. It can also be that some of us work harder and/or are luckier than others. Hence, it is only natural that some of us are richer than others. As much as we like to pretend otherwise, let us face it; men are not created equal, at least not in terms of their ability. This is not a politically correct or incorrect statement. Political correctness has nothing to do with it. It is an obvious and self-evident fact of life. To the extent that we are unequal in our ability and how well we fare depends on our ability in a capitalist economy, then, well yes, capitalism is, by its very nature, an unequal and unfair system.

Of course, this is not to say that inequality is a good thing. To the contrary, most people would agree that inequality is a bad thing, especially if it is extreme and getting worse, as it is around the world today. For one thing, vast income gaps between the rich and the poor fuel discontent and resentment among the poor, who see the rich feeding steaks to their pet dogs while they fight starvation. The resulting social instability, which sometimes fuels social explosions such as violent riots, sours the business climate, discourages investment, and harms economic growth.[1] Furthermore, severe inequality is bad even for the rich. A few millionaires surrounded by a sea of desperate, destitute masses are bound to feel a paranoid sense of insecurity and anxiety, constantly looking over their shoulders. In fact, many developing countries that suffer from high inequality suffer from rampant crime, including an epidemic of kidnapping for ransom. In those countries, the fearful rich protect themselves with an army of private bodyguards.

Inequality is a classic example of what economists call "market failure". Left to

[1] Indeed, some in-depth studies by economists find that greater inequality reduces economic growth. See, for example, https://www.imf.org/external/pubs/ft/sdn/2015/sdn1513.pdf

themselves, the markets sometimes fail to produce socially desirable outcomes, such as tolerable income gaps between the rich and the poor. Market failures are grounds for government intervention and in fact, redistributing income from the rich to the poor through taxation and income transfers to reduce income inequality is one of the key roles of the government in market economies. For example, Western European countries, especially Nordic countries such as Finland and Sweden, impose very high tax rates on the rich, which enables them to transfer large amounts of income to the poor.

But more often than not, government intervention to correct a market failure makes the failure even worse, not better. This can be in the form of government efforts in fighting inequality. Take, for example, South Africa's Black Economic Empowerment (BEE) program. Under the racist apartheid regime, which lasted from 1948 to 1994, when the inspirational Nelson Mandela took office, South Africa was ruled by a white minority, which systematically discriminated against the black majority. To reduce the huge income disparity between whites and blacks, in 2003 the black-majority government implemented BEE, an economic affirmative action program which favored blacks. In principle, BEE's goal was sensible and desirable — to redress past imbalances and help blacks catch up with whites. In practice, BEE only benefited a small elite of politically well-connected blacks, rather than the broader black population, which remain mired in poverty, unemployment and hopelessness.[2]

Another example of misguided and ineffective government intervention to reduce income inequality comes from Malaysia, a multiracial middle-income country in Southeast Asia. The Chinese minority was visibly better off

[2] http://www.economist.com/news/briefing/21576655-black-economic-empowerment-has-not-worked-well-nor-will-it-end-soon-fools-gold

than the indigenous Malay majority, and this inequality was the root cause of the race riots which erupted in May 1969. In response to the riots, and with the broader aim of reducing inequality between the Chinese and the Malays, the Malaysian government implemented the New Economic Policy (NEP) in 1971. The policy, which subsequently became the New Development Policy (NDP) in 1991, was an economic affirmative action program that discriminated in favor of Malays and against the Chinese and Indians. In principle, as with South Africa's BEE, the goal was desirable, but in practice, as with BEE, the results were dubious. In particular, NEP–NDP failed to create a large, self-sustaining class of Malay entrepreneurs and businessmen who build new businesses and contribute to Malaysia's economic dynamism. In fact, NEP–NDP is widely seen by the business community as a costly tax, and it is a major barrier to economic growth.

"

In response to the riots, and with the broader aim of reducing inequality between the Chinese and the Malays, the Malaysian government implemented the New Economic Policy (NEP) in 1971.... In particular, NEP–NDP failed to create a large, self-sustaining class of Malay entrepreneurs and businessmen who build new businesses and contribute to Malaysia's economic dynamism.

"

23

EQUALITY OF OPPORTUNITY, BARACK OBAMA, BEN CARSON, DAYMOND JOHN, BLACK LIVES MATTER, AND PUBLIC EDUCATION

5

However, there is indeed a critical contribution that the government can make to reduce income inequality on a sustainable basis, without harming economic growth but instead fostering growth. That contribution is to promote equality of opportunity. In other words, the government can help level the playing field so that anybody with talent, ingenuity and drive can become another Steve Jobs, Elon Musk or Ted Turner. Equality of opportunity is a nice ideal, but in the real world, some of us have a head start over others. Somebody born with a silver spoon in his mouth in Beverly Hills, for example, will have an incomparably higher chance of a successful life than somebody born without a spoon at all in Watts. The silver spoon will have access to better home, better education, better nutrition, better health care, and better everything. Yes, there are inspirational no-spoons who overcame the odds to succeed in life — for example, the renowned neurosurgeon Dr. Ben Carson — but these are few and far in between.

Speaking of Ben Carson, it is puzzling why black Americans and liberal white Americans — their purported friends — do not celebrate the success of successful black Americans like

"

However, there is indeed a critical contribution that the government can make to reduce income inequality on a sustainable basis, without harming economic growth but instead fostering growth. That contribution is to promote equality of opportunity. In other words, the government can help level the playing field so that anybody with talent, ingenuity and drive can become another Steve Jobs, Elon Musk or Ted Turner.

"

Barack Obama, Ben Carson, Oprah Winfrey, Tyler Perry, Daymond John, Sean Combs, JayZ, Reginald Lewis, Condoleezza Rice, Colin Powell, and Magic Johnson with greater enthusiasm. In fact, it is downright disturbing. The feel-good life stories of these role models for black America suggests that anyone including members of America's supposedly most oppressed and disadvantaged minority can make it in America with determination and hard work. President Obama and the other luminaries are the positive role models that should inspire and motivate black Americans to aspire to a better life. In fact, the black middle class has expanded visibly in recent decades, and there are millions of black Americans who are as hardworking and aspirational as Americans of any other race.

Perversely and disturbingly, it seems that black Americans and their liberal white American friends are much more interested in protesting the injustices suffered by the black underclass than in celebrating and emulating the Barack Obamas, Ben Carsons, and Oprah Winfreys. Instead of looking up to, finding inspiration in, and learning from such success stories, too many blacks and liberal whites glorify and lionize the likes of Rodney King, Michael Brown, Trayvon Martin, Freddie Gray, and O.J. Simpson, whose only "achievement" is to be the alleged victims of American injustice. These characters may be many different things but they are no role models, not for young black Americans and not for young Americans of any color. For sure, police brutality against minorities is a serious American problem that must be addressed, along with the underlying problem of ingrained racism in some segments of the law enforcement community and society. Movements like Black Lives Matter have legitimate issues, but racism is not the be-all and end-all of black underperformance. After

> **"**
>
> Perversely and disturbingly, it seems that black Americans and their liberal white American friends are much more interested in protesting the injustices suffered by the black underclass than in celebrating and emulating the Barack Obamas, Ben Carsons, and Oprah Winfreys.
>
> **"**

all, racism in America has abated to the extent that the country had a black president!

The sooner that more black Americans get excited about strengthening their families and doing better in school, and joining millions of other black Americans who are working hard and aspiring to a better future for their children, the sooner the day will arrive when America becomes a truly color-blind society. What will definitely not get black Americans closer to such a society is unending whining and harping on racism as the source of all their problems. Certainly, the blacks are entitled to fight aggressively for their rights and resist against police brutality and other barriers to their progress. But whining incessantly about racism and blaming it for all their failures will not win them any sympathy from other Americans. More importantly, it will postpone the arrival of a color-blind society by distracting them from the hard work they must do to get their fair share of the American Dream, such as staying in school and becoming better parents.

Upon closer thought, the tendency of some blacks and liberal whites, even thoughtful ones, to explain black underperformance through racism and racism alone is grounded in a pernicious kind of racism — the worst kind. The kind that assumes blacks will never succeed and hence makes lame excuses for failure without even trying. The kind that implicitly accepts the stereotype of the young black man — either unemployed, a criminal locked up in prison, permanently on welfare, buying or selling drugs, fathered and abandoned a child, or all of the above. Closely related to this, there is a disturbing tendency to assume that the black urban underclass is the black mainstream. Perhaps this explains the puzzling under-celebration of black success stories.

> **"**
>
> Upon closer thought, the tendency of some blacks and liberal whites, even thoughtful ones, to explain black underperformance through racism and racism alone is grounded in a pernicious kind of racism — the worst kind.
>
> **"**

But while some segments of American society are probably hardcore racist, by and large Americans are not racist. If they were, Barack Obama would not have been the US president and Ben Carson would not have drawn so much enthusiasm from Republican voters despite his utter lack of political skills. Black America, if you are serious about a color-blind society, it is time to stop whining, roll up your sleeves instead, and start doing the hard work.

"

Black America, if you are serious about a color-blind society, it is time to stop whining, roll up your sleeves instead, and start doing the hard work.

"

THE BEST USE OF TAX PAYERS' MONEY AND THE BEST WAY TO HELP THE POOR

6

Inequality of opportunity perpetuates income inequality and passes income inequality from one generation to the next. The children of the rich become rich and the children of the poor become poor. But inequality of opportunity affects much more than just income gaps between the rich and the poor. Indeed, it weakens the very foundation of capitalism, as well as the intellectual, moral, and common-sense case for capitalism. That case is that capitalism is a fundamentally fair system. Inequality is a permanent fact of life, which means that the playing field can never be completely level. Nevertheless, some government intervention can help make the field more level, and improve the odds of a poor, single-parent black kid from inner-city Detroit becoming another Dr. Ben Carson. Such government action not only reduces inequality, it helps to promote healthy and vigorous competition, and thus strengthens the very foundation of capitalism.

In this context, the best way for governments to foster equality of opportunity is to build good public education and health care systems. Education is the most important avenue for upward social mobility, or moving up the

"

But inequality of opportunity affects much more than just income gaps between the rich and the poor. Indeed, it weakens the very foundation of capitalism, as well as the intellectual, moral, and common-sense case for capitalism. That case is that capitalism is a fundamentally fair system.

"

socio-economic ladder. If Dr. Ben Carson did not get a good education — he graduated from Yale University and University of Michigan Medical School — he might have suffered the sad fate that befalls too many young black men in inner-city Detroit — e.g. criminals who are shot dead before 30 or jailed for life. That would have been a terrible waste of a brilliant mind. But the cost of education can prevent bright but poor youngsters from going to school, which is why there is a strong case for the government to subsidize education. Good public schools are probably the single best use of tax payers' money. By equipping the poor to better compete with the rich, good public schools reduce inequality *and* strengthen capitalism. They expand the size of the pie *and* divide up the pie more fairly. Best of both worlds.

Another excellent use of tax payers' money is public health care. Health is as important as education in determining a person's chances of succeeding in life. We realize the importance of good health when we fall sick, as all of us do. When we are stuck in bed with a high fever, unable to do anything, we realize that everything is secondary to good health. If the rich had access to health care and the poor did not, the rich would have a decisive advantage over the poor since they will be healthier, more energetic, and more productive. Therefore, government support for health care, much like their support for education, helps to level the playing field between the rich and the poor, and enables the poor to compete with the rich. The field will never be completely level — let us face it, the rich will always have a big head start — but the poor have a much better chance of becoming rich themselves if they are healthier and better educated. Good public health care, like good public schools, boosts efficiency and promotes equity.

"

Good public schools are probably the single best use of tax payers' money. By equipping the poor to better compete with the rich, good public schools reduce inequality *and* strengthen capitalism. They expand the size of the pie *and* divide up the pie more fairly. Best of both worlds.

"

Economists view education and health as investments in human capital, which contributes to economic growth as much as investments in physical capital — e.g. factories, machines and roads. In plain English, education increases the skills and knowledge of the workers, which makes them more productive. Likewise, good health improves our mental and physical energy, and makes us perform better. But there is another critical but often ignored contribution of public education and health care to economic growth. By leveling the playing field, or at least making the field more level, they bolster the belief that anybody, not just the rich, can make it through hard work and effort. This strengthens the moral fiber of capitalism and popular support for capitalism, and hence the very foundation of capitalism, the greatest engine of growth in human history. What is more, public education and health care reduce inequality even as they foster growth. Not even anti-tax, anti-government extremists could argue against that.

There are, however, two major caveats about the role of public education and health care as instruments for promoting equality of opportunity, which is good for growth *and* fairness. First, governments face limited tax revenues and thus limited resources. Hence, they will have to make tough choices when it comes to supporting education and health care. Of course, irresponsible, populist governments spend left and right, much of the spending goes into their own pockets. Such spending is the surest path to fiscal bankruptcy and economic ruin. Unfortunately, examples of such governments are all too common. Good for votes, bad for country. More responsible governments that do care about their societies have to decide how much to spend on primary schools, high schools, and universities. At a broader level, government

“

But there is another critical but often ignored contribution of public education and health care to economic growth. By leveling the playing field, or at least making the field more level, they bolster the belief that anybody, not just the rich, can make it through hard work and effort. This strengthens the moral fiber of capitalism and popular support for capitalism, and hence the very foundation of capitalism, the greatest engine of growth in human history.

”

officials have to decide how much to spend on education versus all other government programs, including income support for the poor.

This brings us to the second caveat. While fostering equality of opportunity is by far the best use of tax payers' money, it is also the government's job to help the most disadvantaged and vulnerable members of society. Let us face it, there are always going to be people left behind in a capitalist economy. Even honest, hardworking people — not just the stereotypical lazy, criminal drug addicts on welfare — can become destitute through bad luck or other factors beyond their control. Unfortunately, the markets will not help such people. Therefore, there is a strong case for government intervention. But in light of the government's limited resources, that intervention should be limited to those most in need and it should take a distant back seat to public education, health care and other programs that promote the equality of opportunity. The best way to help the poor and tackle inequality is to help this group of individuals to catch fish, instead of hand-feeding them with fish.

"

Even honest, hardworking people — not just the stereotypical lazy, criminal drug addicts on welfare — can become destitute through bad luck or other factors beyond their control. Unfortunately, the markets will not help such people. Therefore, there is a strong case for government intervention. But in light of the government's limited resources, that intervention should be limited.

"

GATES FOUNDATION, GIVING PLEDGE CAMPAIGN, CARNEGIE LIBRARIES, AND PANAMA PAPERS SCANDAL

It is not entirely accurate to view inequality and poverty as market failures because in some instances, the private sector does play an important role in fighting inequality and poverty. That is, while the government must stand at the forefront of the fight against inequality and poverty, capitalists and entrepreneurs often make sizable contributions. Take, for example, the Bill & Melinda Gates Foundation, or the Gates Foundation. It is led by two of the world's most famous billionaires — Bill Gates of Microsoft fame and the legendary genius investor Warren Buffet — and is the world's largest private charity foundation. Its sheer scale — more than US$40 billion in assets in 2014 — and its mode of operation — more like a business than a government bureaucracy — have turned it into an innovative pioneer in private philanthropy. Tellingly, the foundation seeks to help the poor catch fish with its work on health care enhancements and extreme poverty eradication globally, and making education and information technology (IT) accessible in the US.

As generous as Bill Gates is — he gave almost US$30 billion of his own personal wealth to his foundation — he is hardly alone. For example, under the Giving Pledge campaign, Bill Gates

> **"** That is, while the government must stand at the forefront of the fight against inequality and poverty, capitalists and entrepreneurs often make sizable contributions. Take, for example, the Bill & Melinda Gates Foundation, or the Gates Foundation. **"**

and Warren Buffet recruited billionaires from America, Asia, Europe, and elsewhere to pledge to give away at least half of their wealth during or at the end of their lifetime. As of 15 January 2016, no fewer than 141 global billionaire individuals and couples joined the campaign.[1] One prominent pledgee is Facebook founder Mark Zuckerberg, who announced on 1 December 2015 that he will give away 99% of his Facebook stocks, worth US$45 billion then, to charitable causes. He and his wife Priscilla Chan created the Chan Zuckerberg Initiative as a focal point for their charity activities. Perhaps not surprisingly, the mandate of the initiative was learning and disease control, and more generally to "advance human potential and promote equality for all children in the next generation."[2]

Quite clearly, the kind of charity that Mark Zuckerberg has in mind is to help the poor to catch fish rather than to hand-feed fish to the poor. Given their entrepreneurial background, it is hardly surprising that Bill Gates and Mark Zuckerberg share the same charity philosophy — to help people help themselves. Many business moguls from earlier generations who gave away much of their wealth also donated heavily to education and health care. For example, donations from steel tycoon Andrew Carnegie, who benefited from free access to a rich man's personal library when he was a poor young man, built over 2,500 libraries in America and elsewhere. Oil magnate John Rockefeller gave billions to various causes, including eradication of hookworms and other public health endeavors. Coming from humble backgrounds themselves, men like Carnegie and Rockefeller probably appreciated that education and health, much more than handouts, help the poor compete and rise to greater heights.

[1] http://givingpledge.org/
[2] http://www.businessinsider.com/mark-zuckerberg-giving-away-99-of-his-facebook-shares-2015-12

Unfortunately, not all millionaires are as public spirited as Andrew Carnegie, Bill Gates, or Warren Buffet. Indeed there are plenty of wealthy individuals and powerful companies who give wealth and capitalism a bad name. The Panama Papers scandal that erupted in April 2016 and rocked global news headlines is a case in point.[3] While it is well known that many rich individuals and large multinational corporations squirrel away much of their income and wealth in offshore tax havens, the Panama Papers bombshell brought to light the colossal magnitude of the tax justice problem. The 11.5 million documents from 40 years leaked from Mossack Fonseca, a large Panama-based offshore law firm, indicate that for the affluent and powerful, using low-tax foreign jurisdictions to avoid taxes has become almost second nature. The scandal already forced the resignation of Icelandic Prime Minister Sigmundur David Gunnlaugsson, who cleaned up and strengthened his country's financial system,[4] and there may be other high-profile casualties to come. There are at least 12 national leaders, including their close family members, who have been named in the scandal.

The failure of rich individuals and large companies to pay their share of taxes is patently unfair. It is patently unfair because those individuals and companies earn the bulk of a country's income, but pay a visibly smaller share of the country's tax bills. As a result, ordinary folks and smaller companies, who do not have the luxury of shifting their income to tax havens like Switzerland or the British Virgin Islands, have to pay more than their fair share. More importantly, the loss of revenue due to tax avoidance deprives governments of the resources they need to provide education, health care, and other public services. Cracking down on tax evasion is one area in which

[3] http://www.theguardian.com/news/2016/apr/03/what-you-need-to-know-about-the-panama-papers

[4] Iceland's banks were devastated by the Global Financial Crisis. http://www.economist.com/news/europe/21696574-reformer-entangled-investigation-offshore-shell-companies-big-fish

governments around the world need to do more rather than less, for the sake of a healthier capitalism. Furthermore, given the ease with which individuals and companies can now move their money around the world, stronger international tax cooperation must complement stronger national-level tax enforcement efforts to ensure that the rich pay their fair share. Encouragingly, governments of the US, Europe, and other major economies have recently begun to apply heavy pressure on tax havens to become more transparent.[5]

Importantly, offshore tax havens grease the wheels of corruption because they enable powerful politicians to hide their ill-gotten wealth. This explains why much, if not most, of the global public ire about the Panama Papers is directed toward politicians, in particular national leaders. Offshore tax havens are not the be-all and end-all of corruption, and it would be naïve to believe that tackling offshore tax havens will end corruption around the world.[6] There are also more legitimate functions of offshore tax havens. For example, it is unfair to blame the individuals of an unstable country ruled by predatory government prone to arbitrary confiscation of private property for parking their hard-earned wealth in safe places. Overall, however, a healthy dose of transparency in offshore tax havens will make it much more difficult for the rich and the powerful to evade taxes and hide ill-gotten wealth. Global coordination is required to give teeth to efforts to promote transparency; otherwise, the illicit wealth will simply flow to the least transparent tax haven. Transparency will name and shame individuals and companies engaging in questionable activities.[7]

Inequality is not something that can be glossed over. In and of itself, inequality, especially

[5] For example, the US can threaten to cancel the US banking license of Swiss banks if they do not hand over information about the Swiss bank accounts of wealthy Americans or American companies. Since US is a big market for banking services, this would impose huge costs on Swiss banks. http://www.bbc.com/news/business-33628020

[6] http://www.economist.com/news/leaders/21696532-more-should-be-done-make-offshore-tax-havens-less-murky-lesson-panama-papers

[7] Transparency is important but more fundamentally, large multinational corporations have become adept at minimizing their tax burdens through perfectly legal, crafty global tax planning. (see, for example, http://www.economist.com/news/business/21696542-open-warfare-breaks-out-between-white-house-and-americas-tax-shy-multinationals-pfiasco) One common tactic for multinationals, which operate in many different countries, is to shift profits to countries with low tax rates. The culmination of such global tax planning is "inversions", takeovers of foreign companies with the goal of switching the purchasing company's nationality to a country with lower tax rate. In April 2016, US government opposition forced Pfizer, an American pharmaceutical giant, to cancel plans to buy Allergan, an Irish pharmaceutical company. The takeover, a classical example of "inversion", would have shifted Pfizer's tax domicile to Ireland, which has lower tax rates. Clearly, what is required to make large multinational companies pay their fair share of taxes is fundamental global tax reform, based on international cooperation and coordination.

35

the severe and growing inequality we see in the world today, is a bad thing. It is morally unacceptable for some global citizens, in Beverly Hills, to worry about what snacks to feed their dogs and cats while many of their fellow global citizens, in Africa, get by on one meal a day. Furthermore, inequality, especially inequality of opportunity which places the poor at a decided disadvantage in competing with the rich, seriously harms fair competition, which is the core essence and chief virtue of capitalism. Inequality, if left unaddressed, will grow like a virus to contaminate and eventually destroy capitalism. That, more than any sophisticated number-crunching statistical analysis by economists, is why inequality is bad for capitalism and hence bad for the economy. Therefore, inequality is something that cannot and should not be glossed over.

Governments can help to level the playing field — or at least make it less tilted against the poor — by investing in education and health care. Private charity — e.g. Gates Foundation — too can make significant contributions. In addition, governments can and do employ tax incentives to encourage the rich to donate their wealth to charitable causes. To sum up, inequality is indeed the cancer at the heart of capitalism. Thankfully, the government, working together with generous entrepreneurs, can move us closer to a world where every child can aspire to become another Steve Jobs. Inequality is definitely not something to gloss over and is certainly not an unsolvable problem. Complete equality is neither feasible nor desirable, but a combination of government investments in education and health care, private charity, and tax incentives to promote private charity can bring inequality down to more tolerable levels. The key is to foster the equality of opportunity that reduces inequality on a sustained basis.

"

To sum up, inequality is indeed the cancer at the heart of capitalism. Thankfully, the government, working together with generous entrepreneurs, can move us closer to a world where every child can aspire to become another Steve Jobs.

"

Capitalism has its faults and flaws, in particular inequality. But as an engine of growth and creator of wealth and jobs, it is unparalleled, unmatched, and unbeaten. It is driven by the most basic and powerful human instinct — greed and self-interest. The greatness of capitalism is crystal clear when juxtaposed next to the sterility of socialism. The stark contrast between dirt-poor North Korea and high-tech South Korea, and the phenomenal economic transformation of China since it ditched socialism and embraced capitalism, speak volumes about the superiority of capitalism as an economic system. However, highlighting the superiority of capitalism by comparing it with socialism is a useful but unsatisfying exercise. It is unsatisfying because socialism, a system in which arrogant, risk-averse bureaucratic elites create misery for all, is hardly a worthy competitor. That capitalism is far superior to socialism is hardly a ringing endorsement of capitalism, although the comparison does serve a powerful illustrative purpose.

"

The greatness of capitalism is crystal clear when juxtaposed next to the sterility of socialism. The stark contrast between dirt-poor North Korea and high-tech South Korea, and the phenomenal economic transformation of China since it ditched socialism and embraced capitalism, speak volumes about the superiority of capitalism as an economic system.

"

THE MYTH OF EUROPEAN SOCIALISM

8

Socialism is such a patently inferior economic system that highlighting the superiority of capitalism by comparing it with socialism may seem like a pointless, rigged exercise. But capitalism and socialism are, in fact, the two main alternative systems of producing goods and services. Moreover, communism is simply socialism plus political dictatorship, secret police and forced labor camps. There is a widespread but misguided tendency to view the rich economies of Western Europe — e.g. Germany, France, and Italy — as examples of an intermediate third way, somewhere between capitalism and socialism. The defining feature of these economies is a visibly lower level of inequality than America. Some names for this supposed alternative economic system are "mixed economy" and "social democracy". This is utter hogwash. There is nothing mixed or socialist about European economies. What creates wealth and jobs in Europe is, as in America, a dynamic and efficient private sector — in other words, capitalism. To be sure, government control of industries, for example health care, is greater in Europe than in America, but government-owned industries are not the main creators of wealth.

> There is a widespread but misguided tendency to view the rich economies of Western Europe — e.g. Germany, France, and Italy — as examples of an intermediate third way, somewhere between capitalism and socialism. The defining feature of these economies is a visibly lower level of inequality than America. Some names for this supposed alternative economic system are 'mixed economy' and 'social democracy'. This is utter hogwash. There is nothing mixed or socialist about European economies.

Germany has its Siemens, DaimlerChrysler (makers of Mercedes-Benz), Porsche, Bayer, and BASF; France has its Total, Carrefour, PSA Peugeot Citroën, Christian Dior, and Vivendi; and Italy has its Fiat, Ferrari, Eni, Benetton, and Salvatore Ferragamo. These companies are the reason that Western Europe enjoys one of the world's highest living standards. Germany is Europe's economic giant not because of its extensive welfare state but because it has a world-class manufacturing sector, which turned the country into the world's top exporter. In particular, Mittelstand, or small and medium-sized firms which produce high-quality machinery, auto parts, chemicals, and electrical equipment, help sustain Germany's export boom and economic prosperity. Europe's economic system, or at least its system for producing goods and services, is capitalism. Again, there is nothing mixed or socialist about how Europe produces goods and services.

These private sector companies are the sources of wealth and jobs of Western Europe, not the paper-pushing, risk-averse government bureaucrats sitting in their cozy offices in Berlin, Paris, Rome, or Brussels. Notwithstanding the wishful, deluded thinking of the anti-capitalist crowd, the splendor of Paris or the glory of Rome and the general affluence of Western Europe is not due to some mythical economic system that combines the best of capitalism and socialism. It is, in fact, due to the very system — capitalism — that they denounce so vociferously. The wealth that makes possible the lifestyles of many members of the anti-capitalist crowd — sitting for hours in cafes, debating 18th-century French philosophy — is generated by capitalism. They could not afford such idle, exorbitant lifestyle were it not for the wealth created by capitalism. Talk about ingratitude! If they were in the good old Soviet Union, they would have been hauled

"

Europe's economic system, or at least its system for producing goods and services, is capitalism. Again, there is nothing mixed or socialist about how Europe produces goods and services. These private sector companies are the sources of wealth and jobs of Western Europe, not the paper-pushing, risk-averse government bureaucrats sitting in their cozy offices in Berlin, Paris, Rome, or Brussels.

"

off to some wretched coal mine in Siberia and told to emulate Alexey Stakhanov.[1]

The Western European welfare state reaches its pinnacle in the Scandinavian countries — Denmark, Finland, Norway, and Sweden. The social and economic systems of these countries are far from uniform, but they do share some key common features — most importantly, world-topping living standards with low levels of income inequality. The Nordic model is widely admired across the world since it delivers high living standards while preserving social cohesion. But again, what creates wealth in those countries is not the government bureaucrats but dynamic private sector companies like Denmark's Bang & Olufsen, Maersk, and Royal Copenhagen, Finland's Nokia and Kone, Norway's Aker and Orkla, or Sweden's IKEA, Ericsson, Volvo, Electrolux, and Skype. They create the wealth that makes the generous welfare state possible. In the special case of Norway, vast oil wealth, managed much more efficiently than in other oil-producing countries, also makes a significant contribution.

The big difference between Europe and America is not the source of wealth and jobs. In both economies, it is the innovative, risk-taking, profit-seeking entrepreneurs of the private sector — i.e. capitalism. Government bureaucrats do a lot of good and useful things, but common sense alone tells us that they cannot and do not create wealth or jobs. Indeed taxes on the wealth created by the private sector pay for the government, including the salaries of bureaucrats. Instead the big difference is society's preferences on the tradeoff between efficiency and equity. Europe has visibly lower income inequality than America because European societies place a higher value on equity, and thus want their governments to

[1] Alexey Stakhanov, a legendary Soviet coal miner, inspired the infamous, tragi-comical Stakhanovite movement, which exhorted Soviet workers to follow his example and work hard, so the Soviet Union can surpass the West. In August 1935, he allegedly mined a record 102 tons of coal in a single shift, and a few days later, he was reported to have broken his own record by mining 227 tons. It is not clear what effect, if any, Stakhanov's stellar work ethic had on the morale and productivity of Soviet workers.

impose higher taxes and transfer more income from the rich to the poor. Conversely, American society places a higher value on efficiency. Neither is right nor better. They are just different. But crucially, the two societies differ on how to divide wealth once it is created, *not* on how to create wealth in the first place.

Europe's preference for equity comes at a cost. There is a palpably greater sense of dynamism and vibrancy in the American economy — epitomized by the Silicon Valley, the capital of the global tech industry — than in European economies, even successful ones such as Germany. Given the deafening silence of entrepreneurial buzz in Europe, it is altogether impossible to even imagine a European Silicon Valley. Overall, the government in America meddles far less in the affairs of doing business than that in Europe, which explains America's far louder entrepreneurial buzz. But if European societies are willing to sacrifice economic dynamism for the sake of less inequality, that is their prerogative. After all, America too pays a steep price for its social preference, in the form of greater inequality. Many Americans criticize European "socialism" while many Europeans ridicule America's "Anglo-Saxon" capitalism. Again, neither is right nor wrong. They merely differ.

What is much more harmful and dangerous is for developing countries to draw wrong lessons from the comparison between Europe versus America, which is irrelevant for them. That comparison is between two economies that already have the goose that lays the golden egg — dynamic, entrepreneurial private sectors that create wealth and jobs. For developing countries without the golden goose — which is to say, most developing countries — to even contemplate the European model is the surest

There is a palpably greater sense of dynamism and vibrancy in the American economy — epitomized by the Silicon Valley, the capital of the global tech industry — than in European economies, even successful ones such as Germany. Given the deafening silence of entrepreneurial buzz in Europe, it is altogether impossible to even imagine a European Silicon Valley.

way to economic ruin. Examples of such ruin are dime a dozen, in Africa, Middle East, Latin America, and parts of Asia. The European model is not a model for getting rich; it is a model for what to do with one's wealth when one is already rich. No country ever got rich by growing the government, and certainly not by expanding the army of incompetent, corrupt, and private sector-stifling bureaucrats that blight the economic landscape of far too many developing countries.

"

The European model is not a model for getting rich; it is a model for what to do with one's wealth when one is already rich.

"

LEBRON JAMES, LIONEL MESSI, AND SUPERSTAR SALARIES

I n Europe as in America, capitalism is the engine of economic progress. The biggest virtue of capitalism is that it is a fundamentally fair system. As noted earlier, under capitalism, how well one does depends on one's own ability and effort. Your income is determined by your contribution to the economy. In other words, under capitalism, you get what you deserve. What can be fairer than that? This does not contradict my earlier statement that capitalism is an inherently unequal and unfair system. The two definitions of fairness are completely different, and do not contradict each other at all. If we define fairness to mean that everybody should earn the same, regardless of their ability and effort, then capitalism is unfair, for sure. On the other hand, if we define fairness to mean that how much we earn should depend on how much we contribute, then capitalism is as fair as it gets.

Some simple sports analogies illustrate the stark difference between the two definitions of fairness. Under one definition, all members of a basketball team earn the same salary regardless of their contribution to team performance — i.e. points, rebounds, assists, overall offensive production, steals, blocks, altered shots, and

> **"**
> As noted earlier, under capitalism, how well one does depends on one's own ability and effort. Your income is determined by your contribution to the economy. In other words, under capitalism, you get what you deserve. What can be fairer than that?
> **"**

43

overall defensive contribution. This is like LeBron James and the last player on the Cleveland Cavaliers roster making the same money. Or, if we switch to football or soccer, all members of the team earn the same salary regardless of goals, assists, tackles, and other contributions to team success. It would be like Lionel Messi making the same money as the last player on the FC Barcelona roster. Or, like a major league baseball pitcher with a 1.58 ERA and a 20–5 win–loss record making the same money as a teammate with a 4.53 ERA and a 5–12 win–loss record.[1] This kind of compensation may be equal but very few reasonable people would consider it to be fair.

On the other hand, in the real world, in the capitalist world we live in, LeBron James and Lionel Messi earn much higher salaries than their teammates, and very few reasonable people would have any problems with that. In fact, such people would consider this kind of compensation system to be much fairer than the alternative of paying all players the same amount. For example, during the 2015–2016 season of the National Basketball Association (NBA), the main US professional league, Cleveland Cavaliers gave LeBron James a salary of around US$23 million.[2] During the same season, his teammate Matthew Dellavedova, a reserve point guard, will earn a salary of a little more than US$1 million. If you add endorsement income, the income gap becomes even more staggering. No disrespect to Dellavedova, a valuable role player who made an impact during the 2014–2015 NBA Finals, when he started in place of Kyrie Erving, the injured star starter, but nobody would think twice about the huge income gap.

While it is only fair that superstar athletes make more money than their less stellar teammates,

[1] In baseball, an American team sport that is also popular in parts of Asia and Latin America, the pitcher is the most important player in the team and largely determines how many points the opposing team scores. ERA or earned run average refers to how many points the pitcher gives up, which means that good pitchers have low ERA and bad pitchers have high ERA.

[2] http://espn.go.com/nba/salaries

many people still wonder whether they deserve their stratospheric salaries and endorsement income. We must admit that long time ago we too thought it was unfair that superstar athletes earned a large multiple of our lifetime earnings as, for example, an economist. But then it dawned on us that people are willing to pay top dollars to watch LeBron James play basketball and Lionel Messi play soccer, both live and on television. Certainly, the amount is much more than what they are willing to pay for our economics lectures and economics research papers. Furthermore, the immense popularity of superstar athletes means their faces can help move products off the shelves, which is why big corporations like Coca Cola, Apple and Samsung pay them millions of dollars to endorse their products.

Sports superstars give a huge amount of joy and happiness to billions of sports fans around the world. As big sports fan ourselves, we get plenty of thrills from James' thunderous, gravity-defying slam dunks or Messi's dazzling, as-if-the-ball-is-glued-to-his-feet runs past opposing defenders. However, not even the most fanatical sports fans would argue that LeBron James or Lionel Messi and the staggering salaries they command are the best advertisements for the virtues of capitalism. It is true that the colossal gap between their salaries and the salaries of their less illustrious teammates highlights the core essence and main virtue of capitalism — your pay depends on your relative contribution. And, for sure, James and Messi deserve their astronomical salaries because millions of sports fans will pay them to see them play. However, while sports excellence entertains, thrills and inspires us, it does not move mankind forward.

> **"**
>
> ... the immense popularity of superstar athletes means their faces can help move products off the shelves, which is why big corporations like Coca Cola, Apple and Samsung pay them millions of dollars to endorse their products.
>
> **"**

JOSEPH SCHUMPETER, CREATIVE DESTRUCTION, iPHONE, UBER, AND COMPETITION AS THE ESSENCE OF CAPITALISM

10

The likes of Steve Jobs, Bill Gates, and Larry Page make for much better advertisements for the virtues of capitalism. These Silicon Valley titans created entirely new products and industries through their visionary entrepreneurship. They are the modern-day Andrew Carnegies, John Rockefellers, and Henry Fords, the men who built America. Both groups of audacious, big-thinking, larger-than-life dreamers and risk takers embody the very best of capitalism — the dynamic, regenerative capitalism championed by Joseph Schumpeter. In his 1942 masterpiece *Capitalism, Socialism and Democracy*, the great Austrian economist envisioned capitalism as a process of creative destruction whereby new firms, industries and products arise to better serve human needs. In the process, they destroy old firms, industries and products, but overall that creative, regenerative destruction improves the quality of our lives and propels mankind forward.

For example, the mobile phone has emerged in recent years to replace the fixed-line phone as the world's dominant communication device. The mobile phone is an infinitely superior device since it allows you to communicate with

> **"** In his 1942 masterpiece *Capitalism, Socialism and Democracy*, Joseph Schumpeter envisioned capitalism as a process of creative destruction whereby new firms, industries and products arise to better serve human needs. In the process, they destroy old firms, industries and products, but overall that creative, regenerative destruction improves the quality of our lives and propels mankind forward. **"**

other people anytime, anywhere. The contrast with fixed-line phone, which allows you to communicate only when you are physically next to your phone and the other party is physically next to their phone, is night and day. Indeed while both the fixed-line phone and mobile phone serve the same basic human need — our need to connect with other human beings — it is difficult to even see them as the same product. The first commercially available mobile phone — the clunky DynaTAC 8000x — came onto the market only in 1983. Presently, mobile phones are a ubiquitous part of everyday life, all over the world, in rich countries and poor countries alike. Indeed by 2014, mobile phone subscriptions reached 7 billion, or one for every man, woman or child on Earth.

The process of creative destruction in the telecommunication industry in recent years did not end with mobile phones stealing the spotlight from fixed-line phones. New technologies and products constantly replaced existing products and technologies within the mobile phone industry. Second-generation (2G) digital cellular technology pushed out first-generation (1G) analog technology in 1991, only to be replaced by the more advanced 3G technology in 2001. Different versions of 4G first appeared in 2007 and 2009, and 4G is now spreading across the globe. It has to be noted that even 5G is already on the horizon. The main improvement from one G to another is the speed and amount of data that can be transferred to and from the phone. Data transfer brings us to another big jump in the evolution of the mobile phone, from dumb phone to smart phone, which allows the user to surf the internet and send emails — that is, exchange data, not just voice. The smart phone combines the telephone and the personal computer.

"

The process of creative destruction in the telecommunication industry in recent years did not end with mobile phones stealing the spotlight from fixed-line phones. New technologies and products constantly replaced existing products and technologies within the mobile phone industry.

"

Such constant technological upheaval predictably produces winners and losers. For example, Finland's Nokia, which produced the hip cellphone of the 1990s, failed to catch the smartphone wave early on and paid a steep price for its failure to keep up with the times. The company, a synonym for innovation in its heyday, suffered the humiliation of having its corporate bonds rated as junk by credit rating agencies in 2012.[1] On the other hand, Samsung and its iconic Galaxy smartphones, and Apple and its even more iconic iPhones, which are almost status symbols, rode the wave early and fully, and reaped enormous rewards as a result. The fallout from the smartphone revolution is not confined to the mobile phone industry. For example, its ripple effects — we can take good pictures, including selfies, with smartphones — contributed to the bankruptcy of Kodak, a camera maker which was once a household name, although the much bigger cause was its failure to switch from film cameras to digital cameras.

We can see the process of creative destruction all around us, even in 2018, when one might suspect that the scope for revolutionary technological breakthroughs is limited. In fact, creative destruction, or the emergence of new firms, industries, and products to better serve human needs, is entirely possible without any breakthroughs at all. All it takes is an original idea. Some examples of such innovative ideas are Uber, Airbnb, and Netflix. Uber, an app-based service which provides on-demand automobile transportation, is threatening to turn the taxi industry upside down. In 2015, Uber, which was founded in 2009, became the fastest ever start-up to reach a market value of US$50 billion.[2] Similarly, Airbnb, an internet-based service which allows people to rent their homes

[1] http://www.cnet.com/news/nokia-sinks-deeper-into-junk-status-with-new-s-p-downgrade/

[2] http://www.forbes.com/sites/lbsbusinessstrategyreview/2015/10/09/the-value-of-uber/#6f5f020f7dda

to visitors, is threatening to disrupt the hotel business and Netflix, which allows you to watch movies on your laptop, threatens the cinema industry.[3] Uber and Airbnb are widely cited as prime examples of the sharing economy — Uber lets you share your car and Airbnb lets you share your home. However, at a broader level, Uber, Airbnb, and Netflix are innovative applications of evolving technologies.[4]

As if all that is not enough creative disruption, technologies themselves are constantly evolving, pushing the frontiers of human knowledge and capability, even in 2018. In fact, some pundits argue that we are on the cusp of a fourth industrial revolution, which is driven by technological breakthroughs in a number of fields, including drones or unmanned aerial vehicles, artificial intelligence, big data, cloud computing, blockchains, machine learning, robotics, nanotechnology, 3D printing, genetics, and biotechnology.[5] Technological progress is always disruptive, and the ongoing fourth industrial revolution is no different. Indeed, according to some estimates, those new technologies may contribute to the loss of over 5 million jobs in 15 major advanced and developing countries by 2020.[6] Although such innovations tend to be disruptive in the short run — for example, the horse cart industry was destroyed by the invention of the automobile — they stimulate economic activity, create jobs, and improve our quality of life, and their benefits multiply over time.

Competition is the essence of Schumpeterian capitalism that creates socially useful new products and technologies, and moves mankind forward. This is so critical that it bears repeating and highlighting — **competition is the essence of capitalism**. Without Steve Jobs, there would have been no Bill Gates, and without Bill Gates,

[3] The market values of both Airbnb and Netflix also took off like rockets. For example, in 2015, Airbnb was worth more than the well-established Marriott hotel chain.

[4] For example, Netflix is benefiting from the improvement in internet connections, which allows for better online streaming of movies.

[5] An important new revolutionary technique in biotechnology is CRISPR-Cas9, which allows scientists to edit DNA. The technique has a wide range of potential applications, ranging from food to electricity generation and fueling cars to disease treatment. TIME magazine, "Life, the remix," 4 July 2016.

[6] http://time.com/4186599/davos-2016-technology-jobs/

there would have been no Steve Jobs. It is the intense and relentless competition between Gates and Jobs, between Microsoft and Apple, that transformed the information technology (IT) industry in the last few decades. More generally, the drive and determination of the likes of Gates, Jobs, and other Silicon Valley titans such as Bezos, Page and Zuckerberg to constantly outdo each other is what made Silicon Valley what it is today. The central importance of furious competition to healthy capitalism fueled by creative juice and entrepreneurial buzz is nothing new. Late 19th-century capitalist titans such as John Rockefeller, Andrew Carnegie, and J.P. Morgan competed just as furiously against each other as today's Silicon Valley titans. Competition is the lifeline of capitalism, and a government that referees competition honestly and competently is the lifeline of competition.

> **"**
>
> It is the intense and relentless competition between Gates and Jobs, between Microsoft and Apple, that transformed the information technology (IT) industry in the last few decades. More generally, the drive and determination of the likes of Gates, Jobs, and other Silicon Valley titans such as Bezos, Page and Zuckerberg to constantly outdo each other is what made Silicon Valley what it is today.
>
> **"**

ROCKEFELLER, ROBBER BARONS, AND BERNIE SANDERS

While Uber, Airbnb, and Netflix are very recent, IT-based examples of the process of creative destruction, that dynamic, never-ending process started long before the advent of the internet. For example, the period between the end of the US Civil War and the onset of the First World War marked a golden age of creative destruction. The five decades transformed the American economy, and firmly established America as the world's pre-eminent power.[1] The transformation was similar to the spectacular rise of China since 1978, except it was even more dramatic. It was driven by a group of visionary, larger-than-life capitalists, men like Cornelius Vanderbilt, John Rockefeller, Andrew Carnegie, J.P. Morgan, and Henry Ford. Each left a lasting imprint on the economy and indeed human life, and is associated with a game-changing innovation — railroads (Vanderbilt), oil (Rockefeller), steel (Carnegie), electricity (Morgan), and automobile (Ford). These men did not invent these products, but they brought them to the masses and made them a part of everyday life. They are kindred spirits and spiritual forerunners of Steve Jobs, Bill Gates, Larry Page, Jeff Bezos, and Mark Zuckerberg.

[1] The History Channel TV documentary *The Men Who Built America* provides a superb account of this transformation.

The post-Civil War wave of capitalist giants took enormous risks and reaped enormous rewards. For example, when Cornelius Vanderbilt sensed that railroads were the future of transportation, he boldly invested all his wealth in railroads even though he had been successful in the shipping business, so much so that his nickname was Commodore Vanderbilt. Andrew Carnegie built the first bridge across the mighty Mississippi River in St. Louis — an engineering feat thought impossible at the time — by using steel, and laid the groundwork for the skyline of urban America — and cities all over the world — by erecting skyscrapers with steel structures. The other titans achieved equally visionary and innovative breakthroughs in pursuit of profit. John Rockefeller used pipelines instead of trains to transport oil, J.P. Morgan brought electricity to the masses and lit up whole cities, and Henry Ford mass-produced automobiles and brought down their cost to within the reach of the common man. The sheer audacity of their imagination, and the guts and drive with which they transformed their dreams into reality, is every bit as bold and inspiring as the sagas of Silicon Valley tech titans.

But there was clearly a dark side to the game-changing, transformative capitalism of the Carnegies and Rockefellers. Indeed the popular press of the time coined the infamous nickname Robber Barons, which captured the public mood of the times — i.e. growing anger at the long litany of dubious business practices perpetrated by the capitalist titans. These included paying workers survival wages while making them work impossibly long hours, crushing smaller competitors with unfair business practices and buying them out at rock-bottom prices, and gouging consumers once they became monopolists by driving all other companies from

"

But there was clearly a dark side to the game-changing, transformative capitalism of the Carnegies and Rockefellers. Indeed the popular press of the time coined the infamous nickname Robber Barons, which captured the public mood of the times — i.e. growing anger at the long litany of dubious business practices perpetrated by the capitalist titans.

"

the market. There was an element of truth to such unsavory allegations, and the Robber Barons were no cuddly teddy bears but often merciless men who wanted to beat their competitors into submission. Even so, another popular nickname for the group, Captains of Industry, was a nod to their contribution to economic growth and progress.

In any case, the public's growing anger toward the excesses of the Robber Barons found a political voice in William Jennings Bryan, a populist Democratic political heavyweight who vowed to bring them down. A colorful, bombastic, oratorically gifted three-time Democratic nominee for the US president, in 1896, 1900 and again in 1908, his strident criticisms of big business frightened the rich and the middle class at a time of rising prosperity. As a result, he was defeated by colorless Republican candidates all three times. Big campaign contributions from big business also greatly helped the Republicans. If William Jennings Bryan sounds awfully similar to a contemporary politician, that is because he is. That would be Bernie Sanders, who fought Hillary Clinton for the Democratic nomination for the US presidency in 2016. Sanders, a self-proclaimed socialist, rails against the large and growing income gap between the rich and the poor, and claims to speak for the ordinary 99%, as opposed to the richest 1%.

Despite their excesses and the public anger they provoked, many of the Robber Barons embody the best of capitalism in the sense that they were born poor and owed every cent of their vast fortunes to their own efforts. Among the big five — Andrew Carnegie, Henry Ford, J.P. Morgan, John Rockefeller, and Cornelius Vanderbilt — only J.P. Morgan was born with

"

Despite their excesses and the public anger they provoked, many of the Robber Barons embody the best of capitalism in the sense that they were born poor and owed every cent of their vast fortunes to their own efforts.

"

a silver spoon in his mouth. For example, John Rockefeller had to work and help support his family from his teens because his father was a two-bit con artist who flitted in and out of their home. In addition, while the moguls accumulated astronomical wealth (for example, the wealth of John Rockefeller amounted to more than 1% of the US national economy!) they also gave away astronomical amounts to charity and good causes. In other words, while they may have done a lot of evil while they accumulated their wealth, they did a world of good with their wealth. But the single most definitive overall verdict in favor of the Carnegies and Rockefellers is that, as a result of their revolutionary innovations, the quality of life in America was incomparably higher in 1915 than in 1865, for all Americans, not just rich Americans. Verdict in and case closed.

"

But the single most definitive overall verdict in favor of the Carnegies and Rockefellers is that, as a result of their revolutionary innovations, the quality of life in America was incomparably higher in 1915 than in 1865, for all Americans, not just rich Americans. Verdict in and case closed.

"

GOOGLING, TED TURNER, AND JOB-CREATING ENTREPRENEURS

Entrepreneurial capitalism is necessarily disruptive, even destructive, since existing firms and industries are driven out of business, and thousands of workers lose their jobs. The arrival of the automobile destroyed the horse cart industry, but automobiles are an incomparably superior mode of transportation. Likewise, the invention of the airplane dealt a big blow to the railroad and ship industry, but revolutionized the long-distance transportation of both passengers and cargoes. More recently, Googling has replaced library card catalogs as sources of information, and fixed-line telephones have lost vast ground to mobile phones as communication devices. Creative destruction is not without its costs but on the whole, propels mankind forward and upward. Very few, if any, would argue for banning the internet to protect library catalogues or outlawing the automobile to preserve the horse cart industry. Better and cheaper products and technologies are the engines of mankind's material progress.

The profit motive is vital for motivating the likes of Steve Jobs, Bill Gates, and Larry Page to invent and develop the iPhone, Microsoft Office, and the Google search engine. What motivates entrepreneurs to create new products and technologies is to make as much money as

> **"**
> Entrepreneurial capitalism is necessarily disruptive, even destructive, since existing firms and industries are driven out of business, and thousands of workers lose their jobs. The arrival of the automobile destroyed the horse cart industry, but automobiles are an incomparably superior mode of transportation.
> **"**

possible. They would not risk their time, effort, capital, and their lives unless they could fully reap the rewards of their endeavors. Some of those entrepreneurs are visionary giants who are driven by more than just money — e.g. Steve Jobs and his vision of harmony between machine and man — but that does not dilute the importance of the profit motive. Most of us would not begrudge the fact that those innovative entrepreneurs are multi-billionaires. In fact, many of us would say that they deserve every penny of their vast wealth. They took big risks, those risks paid off, and the end products of their gambles are goods beloved by consumers and companies all over the world. Private profits thus go hand in hand with social good.

There is a misperception or perhaps a willful self-delusion, especially among those on the left, that the economy will be just as big under socialism as under capitalism, or at least that the economy will be nearly as big under socialism as under capitalism. If that were true, the only difference between capitalism and socialism is how the pie is divided, not the size of the pie. In fact, this is complete nonsense. This is also dangerous nonsense because some people actually believe it. Precisely because capitalism allows you to keep the fruits of your own enterprise and effort, whereas socialism gives everybody equal amounts of fruit regardless of enterprise and effort, everybody works much harder under capitalism than socialism. The predictable end result is an incomparably bigger and richer pie. It is difficult to imagine a Ted Turner, who created CNN (Cable News Network), an all-day news television network which was given little chance of survival, or Tony Fernandez, the founder of Air Asia, the pioneer of Asian budget airlines, arising in an economy bereft of the profit motive. The sterile, sclerotic, stultifying environment of a socialist economy is incompatible with, and hostile to, dynamic creative destruction.

"

There is a misperception or perhaps a willful self-delusion, especially among those on the left, that the economy will be just as big under socialism as under capitalism, or at least that the economy will be nearly as big under socialism as under capitalism. If that were true, the only difference between capitalism and socialism is how the pie is divided, not the size of the pie. In fact, this is complete nonsense.

"

In addition to pushing forward the material progress of mankind through creative destruction, capitalist entrepreneurship and risk-taking deliver a much more mundane but no less important social benefit. Everyday entrepreneurs far less glamorous and innovative than Steve Jobs or Ted Turner do society a big favor by creating jobs. Indeed job creation is probably the single most significant social good arising from profit-driven entrepreneurship. Those who have ever started their own business — I must admit I am not one of them — know all too well that paying workers and dealing with workers is one of the biggest costs, and often headaches, of going into business. Entrepreneurs invest a lot of time and effort in finding and hiring workers, and an equal amount of time and effort in firing workers who do not do their jobs.

A thriving private sector is the most reliable engine of job creation, just as it is the most reliable creator of economic growth. Entrepreneurs do not hire workers out of charity but because they need them for their business. Nonetheless, those jobs put food on the dining tables of workers' families, a roof over their heads, and their children through school. Stagnant economies with little or no economic or employment growth are often saddled with bloated public sectors that weigh on and stifle struggling private sectors. Many developing countries fit this description. The Arab world is a perfect example. In those countries, where the government serves, in effect, as the employer of last resort, redundant bureaucrats pester entrepreneurs with ever more pointless regulations, along with demands for bribes to bypass those regulations. The end result is a vicious cycle of a self-important, arrogant government growing ever bigger and progressively squeezing the very life out of an overwhelmed, demoralized private sector.

"

Everyday entrepreneurs far less glamorous and innovative than Steve Jobs or Ted Turner do society a big favor by creating jobs. Indeed job creation is probably the single most significant social good arising from profit-driven entrepreneurship.

"

57

ARAB SPRING, MOHAMED BOUAZIZI, AND EQUITY-EFFICIENCY TRADEOFF

13

> "

conomic sclerosis, anemic growth, and sky-high unemployment are a surefire recipe for social and political explosion, and one such explosion — the Arab Spring — engulfed much of the Middle East and North Africa in recent years. The flames of that explosion are still burning strong and show no signs of dying out anytime soon. From its inception, the Arab Spring was a natural and predictable reaction to the bleak despair and hopelessness that confront millions of youths in the Arab world, from Baghdad to Cairo to Algiers. The self-immolation of Mohamed Bouazizi, a 26-year-old Tunisian street vendor fed up with petty harassment by petty local officials, on 17 December 2010 set off widespread nationwide protests that eventually ousted a president who had run the country for 23 years. When the only way a young man can support himself and his family is to sell fruits from a wheel barrow, and small-time bureaucrats with plenty of time on their hands prevent him from doing even that, then the unfortunate actions of Mohamed Bouazizi may be unsurprising. There is no cure for utter hopelessness, bottomless despair, and broken spirits.

> The self-immolation of Mohamed Bouazizi, a 26-year-old Tunisian street vendor fed up with petty harassment by petty local officials, on 17 December 2010 set off widespread nationwide protests that eventually ousted a president who had run the country for 23 years. When the only way a young man can support himself and his family is to sell fruits from a wheel barrow, and small-time bureaucrats with plenty of time on their hands prevent him from doing even that, then the unfortunate actions of Mohamed Bouazizi may be unsurprising.
> "

Not surprisingly, the Tunisian revolution spread like a wildfire to the rest of the Arab world, from the Mediterranean Sea to the Persian Gulf, and from Mesopotamian Plains to the Sahara Desert. This phenomenon is anticipated because Arab countries outside Tunisia are beset by exactly the same set of daunting social, political, and economic problems: autocratic and unaccountable governments, political repression, lack of social cohesion, among many others. But the single biggest reason for why those countries and societies are rotting at their very core is the absence of economic opportunity which, in turn, owes a lot to the dearth of dynamic, job-creating, growth-promoting private sectors. There is not a single Arab country which is seen as an economic success story for other developing countries to aspire as a model. There are no Koreas or Singapores in the Arab world, not even any countries remotely resembling Korea or Singapore.

One might make a case for Dubai but it is not a country, but an emirate in the United Arab Emirates (UAE), a confederation of seven emirates. More fundamentally, notwithstanding its many bold impressive achievements, above all its emergence as a central hub of commerce, finance and transportation in the Middle East, Dubai still has a long way to go before it can be in the same league as Singapore or Hong Kong.[1] Dubai has the physical hardware — Dubai's world-class international airport and the iconic, sail-shaped, seven-star Burj Al Arab hotel are just two examples — but it is still very much in the middle of building up its human software — it has very little homegrown talent and relies almost entirely on foreigners for professional, managerial, as well as blue-collar work. One might make a stronger case for

[1] Unlike Korea or Singapore, Dubai is not known as a world-class producer of anything. Furthermore, during the Global Financial Crisis, Dubai avoided bankruptcy largely due to a massive bailout from Abu Dhabi, its oil-rich fellow emirate in the UAE. Nevertheless, to be fair, thanks to the visionary leadership of its ruling family, the Al Maktoum family, the emirate has become the leading business hub of the Middle East and a tourist mecca.

59

Morocco, which is a country with a population of around 35 million, rather than a city-state dependent entirely on foreign workers.[2]

The Arab Spring has taken on different contexts in different countries. For example, in Syria, it has evolved into a brutal sectarian civil war between a ruling Alawite minority and a numerically dominant Sunni majority. In Libya, it has degenerated into a lawless free-for-all after an odious dictator was toppled. Throughout all the different shades of the Arab Spring, the one common denominator that stands out is the vast army of unemployed youths with hollow lives devoid of any purpose or hope. These youths provide plenty of live ammunition for any number of armies, from the armed forces of beleaguered dictators to radical Islamic militias bent on waging jihads or holy wars. If there is no meaning in one's life, and it there is absolutely no hope that tomorrow will be better than today, then fighting and dying for a brutal dictator like Bashar Assad or blowing oneself up in the name of the Islamic State may not be such a bad option. It may even be the only option.

Our journey through LeBron James, Steve Jobs, and Mohamed Bouazizi makes a distinctly positive case for capitalism rather than a negative case based on comparison with socialism, a deeply flawed ideology and economic system. Whatever problems capitalism may have, they pale in comparison with those of socialism, which delivers the worst of all worlds — material misery and political tyranny — under the rule of a self-appointed bureaucratic elite class. The positive case ultimately rests on the idea of fairness. Capitalism is, in the final analysis, a profoundly fair system for determining how the economy produces goods and services as well as how those goods and services are divided among all of us. Those who contribute more to

[2] In addition to a thriving tourism industry, Morocco is building up a manufacturing sector. For example, Renault–Nissan and PSA Peugeot Citroën built car assembly plants in Morocco and are also trying to develop a network of local suppliers. Politically too, it is a relatively stable monarchy. http://www.economist.com/news/special-report/21698438-rentier-system-trouble-big-oil-producing-states-and-beyond-black-gold Two major advantages of Morocco as a manufacturing center are a large pool of low-wage workers and relatively good infrastructure. Other North African countries such as Algeria and Egypt share some of those advantages but they are politically less stable than Morocco. Foreign direct investment by big manufacturing companies from Europe, especially France, is playing a key role in the development of Morocco's manufacturing sector. In 2012, Renault–Nissan invested US$2.1 billion in a car plant in Morocco. The car plant is Africa's largest and employs 10,000 local workers. In fact, cars have become the world's largest single export, bring in some €4.8 billion in 2015. In addition, Morocco has been successful in attracting foreign investment into the aerospace industry, which employed around 11,500 local workers in 2015. "Factories in the sun," The Economist, June 2016.

the pie get a bigger share. That is about as fair as it gets, in anybody's dictionary, or at least in any reasonable person's dictionary.

Furthermore, it is that kind of fairness that makes capitalism such a productive economic system. Fairness — or more precisely, a popular belief that everybody and anybody can succeed with ingenuity and hard work — encourages everybody to work harder and smarter. The conventional wisdom that there is a tradeoff between efficiency and equity is a complete nonsense once we define equity as equality of opportunity — creating a level playing field where anybody can succeed with ingenuity and hard work — as opposed to taking money from the rich and giving handouts to the poor. If we define equity as a more level playing field, then equity goes hand in hand with stronger economic growth. We do not have to sacrifice equity for the sake of efficiency and growth, or vice versa. To the contrary, equity is vital for efficiency and growth.

If we define equity as a more level playing field, then equity goes hand in hand with stronger economic growth. We do not have to sacrifice equity for the sake of efficiency and growth, or vice versa. To the contrary, equity is vital for efficiency and growth.

COURAGEOUS OFFICE WORKERS WHO BECOME ENTRPRENEURS, RYANAIR, AND AIRASIA

The social value created by iconic heroes of capitalism such as Steve Jobs is self-evident, and most of us would agree that the millions they make are just reward for their visionary products. Even everyday capitalists — for example, the office worker who quits his job to start his own business — should be rewarded for the risks they take, and for the jobs they create if they succeed.[1] If everybody is content to be an office worker, and nobody has the guts to start his own business, then for sure, the economy would suffer. That economy would be like a pool of stagnant water, with vastly diminished capacity for creating wealth and jobs. The risks that the entrepreneurial few take greatly increases the size and richness of the pie, so that all of us — including the vast majority of us who are content to work for a salary and never start a business — can enjoy bigger and tastier pieces of the pie. They may not be Steve Jobs, and they may be driven by personal greed, but they are heroes who benefit society all the same.

Having discussed the role of capitalism as the powerful engine of mankind's material progress, a sobering dose of reality is in order. Above all, we should note that capitalism is no panacea or

[1] The 2016 Hollywood movie *Joy* vividly chronicles how difficult it is for everyday capitalists — the inventor of an innovative mop — to succeed. The struggle of the main character to succeed against all odds is truly inspiring and heroic. The movie describes the importance of innovation in capitalist success, even for everyday capitalists. It also illustrates the potential for large firms to misuse patents to obstruct startups although in the movie the patent misuser was a two-bit con artist based in Texas.

magic bullet for mankind's myriad challenges. In fact, critics of capitalism argue that capitalism is part of the problem rather than part of the solution. One does not have to be a rabid anti-capitalist to see that the same capitalism which has given us so much material abundance is also the source of many problems. Even the most ardent advocates of capitalism would admit as much. The fundamental reason is that greed or self-interest can be a good thing or a bad thing. The same greed that drives entrepreneurs to invent the personal computer, mobile phone, CNN (Cable News Network), Facebook, and Ryanair drives man to exploit fellow man, breeds gaping inequality, and wrecks the environment.

Furthermore, it is sometimes difficult to draw the boundary between good capitalism and bad capitalism. For example, Southwest Airlines, Ryanair, AirAsia and other low-cost airlines make air travel, an exclusive privilege of the rich and the famous just a few decades ago, accessible to the masses. The founding of Southwest in Texas in 1967 kicked off an air travel revolution by sharply bringing down air fares. The revolution spread from the US to Europe and eventually to Asia and all parts of the world. The low fares of the budget carriers directly lowered the cost of air travel and, just as importantly, they had a knock-on impact on the existing full-service carriers. The Ryanairs and Easyjets limit the ticket price the British Airways and Air Frances can charge. While it would be far-fetched to say that air travel is a basic human right like food and shelter, ordinary people are no less entitled to visit loved ones, experience different countries, and see the world than their richer fellow citizens. The explosive growth of air passenger traffic confirms the immense demand for air travel among ordinary people. In the absence of budget airlines, much of that demand would have gone unmet.

> **"**
>
> One does not have to be a rabid anti-capitalist to see that the same capitalism which has given us so much material abundance is also the source of many problems. Even the most ardent advocates of capitalism would admit as much. The fundamental reason is that greed or self-interest can be a good thing or a bad thing.
>
> **"**

While more people can experience the joy of flying thanks to budget airlines — AirAsia's advertising slogan is "Now Everybody Can Fly" — the explosive growth of air travel they help foster comes at a huge environmental cost. In particular, air travel is an increasingly significant source of carbon emissions and contributor to global warming. Three round trips between Chicago and Frankfurt produce 10.4 tons of carbon dioxide per passenger. The corresponding figure for Philadelphia and San Francisco is 6 tons, and 2 tons for Detroit and New Orleans. By ways of comparison, in one year, the average US household's electricity consumption emits 6.6 tons, the average medium-sized car in the US emits 3.5 tons, and the average US commute emits 1.9 tons. Air travel currently accounts for only about 5% of global carbon emissions, but the rapid growth of air travel suggests that that share will grow over time.[2] The pioneers of low-cost carriers — Rollin King and Herb Kelleher (Southwest Airlines), Christopher Ryan, Liam Lonergan, and Tony Ryan (Ryanair), Tony Fernandes (AirAsia) — are at once heroes of mass travel and villains of global warming.

Upon closer thought, however, it is not capitalism per se but the technology of air travel that contributes to global warming.[3] Aircrafts burn a lot of kerosene fuel and emit a lot of carbon dioxide per passenger. Emissions from aircrafts are more persistent and damaging than emissions from cars or other ground-level sources. But the environmental harm from air travel is not limited to emissions alone. Vapor trails and ozone production, and a number of other factors specific to high altitudes, contribute at least as much as carbon dioxide to global warming, and possibly much more. In addition, the processing of aviation fuel and the

[2] All figures are from *The New York Times* Sunday Review, Elisabeth Rosenthal, "Your biggest carbon sin may be air travel," 26 January 2013.

[3] "Air travel to contribute more to global warming," Third World Network, by Someshwar Singh, http://www.twnside. org.sg/title/air-cn.htm; "The surprisingly complex truth about planes and climate change," The Guardian, by Duncan Clark, 9 September 2010, http://www. theguardian.com/environment/blog/2010/ sep/09/carbon-emissions-planes-shipping "Air travel and climate change," David Suzuki Foundation, http://www. davidsuzuki.org/issues/climate-change/ science/climate-change-basics/air-travel- and-climate-change/

manufacture of aircraft emit additional carbon dioxide. Therefore, the key to reducing the environmental damage from air travel does not lie in stifling capitalism or capitalist inventions such as budget airlines, or curtailing the masses' demand for air travel. Rather, it lies in promoting technological progress that reduces carbon dioxide emissions, ozone production, and other environmental by-products of air travel. Moreover, technological progress is most likely to come from an innovative, risk-taking, profit-seeking private sector company, not the government.

"

Therefore, the key to reducing the environmental damage from air travel does not lie in stifling capitalism or capitalist inventions such as budget airlines, or curtailing the masses' demand for air travel. Rather, it lies in promoting technological progress.

"

THE TWO FACES OF CAPITALISM, ADIDAS, AND RANA PLAZA DISASTER

The two-sided Janusian face of capitalism can be seen everywhere. Multinational clothing and footwear companies like Gap, H&M, Old Navy, Uniqlo, Zara, Adidas, Nike, and Puma typically outsource their production to developing countries, in search of ample pool of low-wage workers and lax labor standards. From the profit perspective, such outsourcing makes perfect sense since clothing and footwear are labor-intensive. The central importance of labor costs in the industry explains how Bangladesh, one of world's poorest — ranked 164th out of 189 countries in 2013[1] — and most densely populated countries, with a population of over 150 million, managed to become one of the world's biggest apparel exporters, despite having a weak infrastructure and an otherwise embryonic manufacturing sector. In 2012, Bangladesh was home to 5,600 garment factories, and the world's second largest garment manufacturer, behind only China. Labor costs, and labor costs alone, explain why those factories are based there.

But there is a dark side to the clothing and footwear success of Bangladesh. Low pay and poor working conditions make clothes and footwear cheap for consumers in rich countries,

[1] World Bank's World Development Indicators, accessed 8 August 2014.

and boost the profits and share prices of multinational companies. However, the same low pay and poor working conditions create misery and even lethal danger for workers. This dark side came to global spotlight when Rana Plaza, an eight-story commercial building that housed a number of garment factories just outside Dhaka, the capital city and largest city of Bangladesh, collapsed on 24 April 2013.[2] The disaster, one of the worst factory accidents in history, killed more than 1,100 people and injured another 2,500. The upper four levels of the building had been built without a permit, and the building had been designed for offices rather than factories and heavy machinery, amidst concerns from architects. Furthermore, cracks appeared on Rana Plaza on the day before the collapse, and the office and shop tenants evacuated the building. Yet factory owners declared the building safe and ordered their workers to report for work. The disaster highlights the corporate world's blatant disregard for workers' safety and, more generally, workers' welfare in its relentless pursuit of profit.

Yet export-oriented garment industry is a vital engine of growth for the Bangladeshi economy as a whole. In 2013, the industry produced and exported almost US$20 billion, much of it to the West under contracts to well-known clothing brands, accounting for one eighth of GDP (gross domestic product) and almost 80% of total exports. It is by far the country's largest source of foreign exchange and a key driver of industrialization. Just as importantly, the industry provides around 4 million jobs, 90% of them held by women. The meager wages earned by young female workers may seem like a pittance in the West, but they are a potent source of female empowerment. The likely lot of their friends who remain in the poor, conservative Muslim villages of rural Bangladesh is to get married off

[2]"Despite low pay, poor work conditions, garment factories empowering millions of Bangladeshi women," International Business Times, by Palash Ghosh, 25 March 2014, http://www.ibtimes.com/despite-low-pay-poor-work-conditions-garment-factories-empowering-millions-bangladeshi-women-1563419

and bear children by their mid to late teens. The wages they make enable the workers to help support their families back home, and to enjoy a degree of independence and freedom which can only be imagined in the villages.

The Rana Plaza disaster has also brought about some concrete reforms in the Bangladeshi garment industry. Predictably, there has been a great deal of outrage among consumers in the West about the substandard working conditions which came to light as a result of the disaster. Such outrage has forced the Western multinationals to commit themselves to improving the safety standards, pay, and other working conditions at the local factories to which they outsource the production of their clothes and footwear. The minimum wage of garment workers jumped from around US$40 to more than US$70. New legislation passed in the summer of 2013 allows workers to form trade unions without the consent of factory owners. As a result, the number of registered trade unions shot up from three to 120. Many of the garment factories are being upgraded, and the monitoring of safety conditions has improved. While there is still a long way to go, Rana Plaza has been a catalyst for positive change. Above all, Rana Plaza has forced Western brands to become more responsible for the behavior of their Bangladeshi contractors to whom they outsource their production, rather than implausibly claim they have no idea what is going on behind factory doors.

> "
> Predictably, there have been strident calls among some in the West for drastic sanctions against the garment factories in Bangladesh, including outright closures. Fortunately, cooler heads have prevailed and the garment industry continues to thrive. For all its flaws, Bangladesh is a better place with the industry than without it.
> "

Predictably, there have been strident calls among some in the West for drastic sanctions against the garment factories in Bangladesh, including outright closures. Fortunately, cooler heads have prevailed and the garment industry continues to thrive. For all its flaws, Bangladesh is a better place with the industry than without it. Ultimately, the demand for the industry comes from the consumers of rich countries for cheaper clothing and footwear. Broadly speaking, it is a win-win situation — Western consumers get more affordable clothes and Bangladeshi workers get much-needed jobs. The fundamental solution is not to throttle the Bangladeshi garment industry but to enlighten Western consumers about the working conditions of its workers. While some hardened consumers might not care at all about the safety of workers in a distant land, most do care and do not mind paying a little more for safer, more humane lives for those workers. Social media such as YouTube have exponentially increased the speed at which bad publicity travels and spreads. This imposes a sanction on firms that misbehave — for example, outsourcing to unscrupulous contractors like those who ran factories at Rana Plaza — and unleashes powerful competitive pressures that encourage good behavior.

"

The fundamental solution is not to throttle the Bangladeshi garment industry but to enlighten Western consumers about the working conditions of its workers.

"

GOVERNMENT AS POLICEMAN OF CAPITALIST GREED, AND MAN-MADE DISASTER IN KOREA'S BEVERLY HILLS

16

It might seem that there is an obvious solution to the problem of corporate greed and misbehavior which, when taken to the extreme, results in human tragedies like Rana Plaza. That solution is government regulation. In both rich and poor countries, various labor laws, rules and regulations protect basic worker rights, enhance workers' job security, and improve their terms of employment. They are designed to protect workers from exploitation by employers, and to guarantee them a minimum level of acceptable working conditions and safety standards. For example, many countries have minimum wages to help ensure a minimum living standard for workers. Minimum wages vary greatly across countries, from less than US$0.30 in India to a little more than US$2 in Brazil to US$7.25 in the US.[1] The large gaps are not surprising in light of large international differences in living standards and living costs. Another example comes from occupational health and safety, which refers to the safety, health, and welfare of workers. Many countries have legislation which mandates employers to create a safe workplace for their workers, and government agencies which are responsible for enforcing such legislation.

[1] "List of minimum wages by country," Wikipedia, http://en.wikipedia.org/wiki/List_of_minimum_wages_by_country

In the context of Rana Plaza disaster, the most relevant government regulation is the building code, which sets forth minimum standards for the design and construction of buildings and other structures. The central purpose of building codes is to protect the health, safety, and welfare of future occupants by helping to ensure that the buildings are structurally strong. In addition to structural integrity, the codes touch upon mechanical integrity — e.g. light and water supply — as well as avenues for entry and exit, fire prevention and control, and energy efficiency. For example, smoke detectors, fire sprinklers, and fire escapes help minimize the loss of human life during fire outbreaks. The codes become law when they are formally enacted by a government and specify a minimum level of resistance against natural disasters such as earthquakes. Just as labor standards limit the ability of greedy and unscrupulous employers to take advantage of their workers, building codes limit the ability of greedy and unscrupulous building owners to compromise safety for profit. Both illustrate the need for government to rein in the excesses of capitalist greed.

Such greed-fueled excesses are by no means confined to low-income countries such as Bangladesh. In fact, prior to Rana Plaza, the worst structural collapse of a building in modern history took place in the heart of Gangnam, the posh Seoul district — the Beverly Hills of Korea — parodied by the singer Psy in his 2012 megahit Gangnam Style, which unleashed a global craze for a horse-riding dance and became the most watched YouTube video ever. To get back to the somber realities of the accident, on 29 June 1995, the Sampoong Department Store collapsed, killing 502 people and injuring another 937.[2] While the architectural cause of the collapse was structural overload, its fundamental underlying cause was unbridled

[2]"Sampoong Department Store Collapse," http://en.wikipedia.org/wiki/Sampoong_Department_Store_collapse

human greed and a shocking lack of concern for the safety of shoppers and tenants.

For starters, the building was originally designed as a four-story residential apartment, but the owner changed it to a department store during its construction. This change in building plan involved installing escalators at the expense of a number of support columns. When the original contractor balked at the plan out of safety concerns, the builder simply fired them and used his own construction company. Subsequently, the owner decided to add a fifth floor that would house eight restaurants. When the construction firm tasked with the extension informed the owner that the structure cannot support an additional floor, the owner hired another firm. Furthermore, the installation of the building's air conditioning unit on the roof created a load which exceeded the building's design limit by four times. Compounding the aforementioned problems, substandard concrete and a flawed construction technique were used. In short, in light of the litany of structural flaws, it was a miracle that Sampoong stood for as long as it did — five years.

Even though big cracks began to appear on the ceiling of the fifth floor in April, the store owner and management did not take any meaningful action. Scandalously, even though the number of cracks jumped sharply on the morning of 29 June, the day of the disaster, the management did not shut down the building or issue evacuation orders. The loss of revenues apparently mattered more than the potential loss of human life. All too predictably, the department store executives themselves left the building well before the collapse. The natural question to ask is — where were the government regulators who are supposed to enforce regulations that ensure the safety and soundness of buildings?

"

Scandalously, even though the number of cracks jumped sharply on the morning of 29 June, the day of the disaster, the management did not shut down the building or issue evacuation orders. The loss of revenues apparently mattered more than the potential loss of human life.

"

Indeed much of the titanic public outrage which erupted after the collapse was directed at the Korean government, in addition to the primary culprits — the Sampoong conglomerate group and its owners. While it would be too much to ask any government to detect all construction safety risks, surely, the government of a rich country like Korea must have the capability to detect and prevent a disaster of Sampoong's magnitude. After all, it was not just one or two misdeeds, but a criminal Mount Everest of misdeeds that caused the department store to collapse.

"

While it would be too much to ask any government to detect all construction safety risks, surely, the government of a rich country like Korea must have the capability to detect and prevent a disaster of Sampoong's magnitude.

"

73

GOVERNMENT AS CORRUPT POLICEMAN, JAPANESE DESCENT FROM HEAVEN, AND SWISS BANK ACCOUNTS

17

Perhaps not altogether surprisingly, a number of city officials who were in charge of overseeing the construction of the Sampoong Department Store building, were found to have received bribes for looking the other way when the owners made illegal changes that eventually brought down the structure. Those officials were jailed, along with Sampoong executives and construction company officers. In an ideal world, omniscient and benevolent government bureaucrats with a deep sense of public service strictly enforce building codes that prevent Rana Plazas and Sampoong Department Stores from being built in the first place. However, in the real world, in the world in which we live, bureaucrats are often neither omniscient nor benevolent, and the only deep sense many have is an uncanny, almost canine, sixth sense for sniffing opportunities to line their pockets with bribes from those they are supposed to regulate.

To be sure, and to be fair, there are plenty of honest and competent bureaucrats who serve the general public effectively and efficiently. For every drug enforcement agent who takes money from drug lords, there is a dedicated beat cop who puts his life on the line every day to keep our

> **"** However, in the real world, in the world in which we live, bureaucrats are often neither omniscient nor benevolent, and the only deep sense many have is an uncanny, almost canine, sixth sense for sniffing opportunities to line their pockets with bribes from those they are supposed to regulate. **"**

streets safe. There is even the odd government worker who works in the government for lower pay rather than in the better-paying private sector out of a genuine sense of public service. But in countries all over the world, rich and poor alike, a common popular refrain is "why can't the government be more like the private sector?" The implicit comparison is between the workers of the two sectors. Government reform which improves competence and honesty of government workers will help the government become a more effective policeman of capitalist greed. The Singaporean government model of small yet well-paid civil service, with draconian punishment for corruption, is one potential blueprint for reform. That model is certainly a big improvement over most governments, which serve as an employer of last resort for hordes of mediocre talent who have few alternative job opportunities.

As the Rana and Sampoong disasters show, the effectiveness of government regulation in tackling capitalist greed depends on government competence and honesty. A corrupt, incompetent government with limited institutional capacity can only do much in combating exploitative capitalism. Among other things, such a government will not have enough well-qualified officials to, say, inspect the structural integrity of buildings or safety of working conditions. In addition, those officials will be all too eager to overlook structural defects or workplace dangers in exchange for envelopes from developers and factory owners. Government competence and honesty are in short supply in developing countries, which limits the effectiveness of the government in policing capitalist greed. Again, government reform is essential for improving the policeman's effectiveness.

But even in advanced countries, incompetence and corruption are substantial problems among government bureaucrats in charge of regulating

> **"**
>
> Government reform which improves competence and honesty of government workers will help the government become a more effective policeman of capitalist greed.
>
> **"**

the private sector. There are often unhealthily cozy links between government bureaucrats and the private sector. In Japan, for example, there is a long tradition of senior bureaucrats landing cushy, well-paid jobs at firms they used to supervise. The practice, known as *amakudari* or "descent from heaven", creates a conflict of interest — i.e. bureaucrats keeping an eye out for post-retirement job opportunities — which impedes effective implementation of regulations. If the company and industry these bureaucrats are regulating is the main source of their post-retirement income, they are unlikely to investigate or crack down on whatever violations committed.

In short, government regulation is the most powerful solution for reining in the excesses of capitalism but it is at best an imperfect solution. In developing countries, institutionally weak governments often lack the competence and integrity to enforce regulations. But even in advanced economies, there are structural problems that hinder effective regulation. Public sector pay lags behind private sector pay, and this creates potent temptations for corruption. While taking bribes is the only way for government officials to provide enough for their families in many developing countries, there is no shortage of tainted officials in richer countries, although the prevalence of corruption is much lower. In both rich and poor countries, the nickel-and-dime type of corruption — e.g. overlooking traffic violations for US$8 — matters. But what matters more is the much bigger type that involves huge dollars and senior politicians or officials — e.g. millions of dollars into Swiss bank accounts in exchange for multi-billion-dollar jet fighter deals.

> **"**
>
> In short, government regulation is the most powerful solution for reining in the excesses of capitalism but it is at best an imperfect solution. In developing countries, institutionally weak governments often lack the competence and integrity to enforce regulations.
>
> **"**

REGULATORY CAPTURE, FUKUSHIMA NUCLEAR DISASTER, AND OVERPRICED ELECTRICITY IN PHILIPPINES

18

The phenomenon of the government regulator being unduly influenced by the companies and industries it is supposed to regulate is known as regulatory capture. That is, instead of serving the public interest, the regulator is captured by the interest group and serves that interest group's vested interests rather than the public interest. For example, if the government agency in charge of public health is captured by the tobacco industry, the rules and regulations against smoking in public will be weaker than warranted by the risks that secondhand smoke poses for non-smokers. There are plenty of real-world examples of regulatory capture.[1]

For example, in the US, there are concerns that the Environmental Protection Agency (EPA) has given a free environmental pass to energy companies for fracking, the technological process of extracting natural gas from shale rocks trapped deep within the earth by fracturing the rocks with high-pressure fluids. A 2005 legislative clause known as the Haliburton loophole banned the EPA from regulating fracking despite environmental risks. While the shale gas revolution unleashed by fracking has boosted US energy output and benefited the US economy,

[1] "Regulatory capture," http://en.wikipedia.org/wiki/Regulatory_capture

there are legitimate environmental concerns, ranging from groundwater contamination to air quality risks.

Other US examples include lack of proper regulatory enforcement by the Federal Aviation Administration (FAA) and the Federal Communications Commission (FCC). For example, a US Department of Transportation report found that in 2006 and 2007 FAA managers allowed Southwest Airlines to fly 46 aircraft that did not undergo safety inspections. An investigation by the US House of Representatives committee in charge of air transportation found a systematic pattern of regulatory failure, which permitted 117 aircraft to be commercially flown, even though they were not in compliance with FAA safety regulations. Unhealthy coziness between commercial airlines and the authorities that were supposed to regulate airlines seriously jeopardized passenger safety, and only good fortune prevented a major catastrophe.

Since 2008, there have been some legislative efforts to dilute the coziness, including the imposition of a two-year waiting period for FAA inspectors and supervisors before they can work for commercial airlines. The FCC is also subject to similar types of criticisms. For example, Peter Schuck of Yale Law School argues that the FCC, which has the power to selectively grant lucrative communications licenses to television and radio stations, may have been captured by media conglomerates. For example, an FCC commissioner joined Comcast just four months after approving a controversial merger between Comcast and NBCUniversal.

There are also plenty of examples of regulatory capture outside the US. In Japan, as noted earlier, senior bureaucrats from regulatory agencies often land cushy, well-paid jobs in

"

Unhealthy coziness between commercial airlines and the authorities that were supposed to regulate airlines seriously jeopardized passenger safety, and only good fortune prevented a major catastrophe.

"

companies they used to supervise. With this kind of incentive structure, it would be surprising if the regulators serve the public interest rather than the interest groups they are supposed to regulate. For example, despite safety concerns, Japan's Nuclear and Industrial Safety Agency (NISA) approved a 10-year extension for the oldest reactor at the Fukushima Daiichi nuclear power plant just one month before a massive earthquake and tsunami struck on 11 March 2011, contributing to one of the biggest nuclear disasters in history. More generally, critics allege that close ties between NISA and the nuclear industry led to a culture of weak oversight of an industry with potentially large safety risks. Whatever one's views about nuclear power and their pros and cons, all sides agree that public safety is a top priority for nuclear power. The undue influence of industry on regulators in such a sensitive sector shows just how far and deep the disease of regulatory capture runs in Japan.

While regulatory capture is a serious problem in advanced countries, which have relatively strong and honest governments, the problem is much worse in developing countries, which suffer from weaker and even more corrupt governments. The electricity market of the Philippines is a classic example of how regulatory capture holds back a developing country's industrialization and progress. The Philippines has one of Asia's most expensive electricity rates, higher than even Japan's, astonishingly for a country that has largely missed out on the East Asian miracle and remains one of the region's poorest countries.[2] In fact, the two — high electricity rates and poor economic performance — are related. Lack of reliable and affordable electricity has stymied the emergence of a dynamic manufacturing sector found in many other Asian countries, from Korea to China to Malaysia.

[2]"Philippines electricity crisis: How regulatory capture undermines emerging markets," Huffington Post, by Richard Javad Heydarian, 22 February 2014, http://www.huffingtonpost.com/richard-javad-heydarian/philippines-electricity-crisis_b_4490680.html

Erratic, overpriced power supply not only hurts consumers, but also factories and companies and the entire economy.

The root of the problem lies in the privatization process of the Filipino electricity industry. When the government walked away from the electricity business and sold it to the private sector — a process known as privatization — there were widespread hopes of more, better and cheaper power. Those hopes were quickly dashed when the industry — lock, stock and barrel — was handed over to politically well-connected oligarchs with little interest in the nation's development or public welfare, and a vested interest in stuffing their own wallets. The outsized profits raked in by the oligarchs are good news for the oligarchs themselves and the politicians in their pockets, but bad news for everybody else. The very purpose of privatization, which is to produce more and better goods by replacing the government, which is notoriously lousy at producing things, with the generally more efficient private sector, is subverted when the government is too weak and corrupt to effectively regulate the private sector.

"

The very purpose of privatization, which is to produce more and better goods by replacing the government, which is notoriously lousy at producing things, with the generally more efficient private sector, is subverted when the government is too weak and corrupt to effectively regulate the private sector.

"

RUSSIA'S CATASTROPHIC PRIVATIZATION, THAKSIN SHINAWATRA, AND SILVIO BERLUSCONI

19

While egregious, the Philippines electricity industry is far from alone in how privatization gone wrong can be as bad as, if not worse than, the government's production of goods and services. Examples abound around the world, especially in developing countries but also in advanced countries, of privatization harming the public interest rather than promoting it. Perhaps the most notorious example of socially harmful privatization comes from post-Soviet Russia. In the early to mid-1990s, after the breakup of the Soviet Union and fall of communism, the Russian government embarked upon a massive program of transferring strategic state-owned assets in the industrial, energy, and financial sectors — e.g. oil fields, pipelines, and refineries — to the private sector. Given the impending collapse of the centrally planned socialist economy, it was desirable and even necessary to privatize as much of the economy as quickly as possible. Even so, most of the assets fell into the hands of a small group of politically well-connected oligarchs who have done little to improve their companies or serve the public interest with their new assets. The largely negative perception of

> **"**
> Perhaps the most notorious example of socially harmful privatization comes from post-Soviet Russia.... Most of the assets fell into the hands of a small group of politically well-connected oligarchs who have done little to improve their companies or serve the public interest with their new assets.
> **"**

privatization among Russian citizens suggests that overall it has been a failure.

Upon closer thought, regulatory capture is the natural outcome of the relationship between the government and the private sector in a capitalist economy. The extent of the problem is more severe in developing countries, where weak governments are ripe for picking by the private sector. Actually, the private sector too is underdeveloped, in some cases embryonic, in those countries, and many leaders of the private sector rise to the top not because they are talented entrepreneurs who create a lot of new value by producing superior products, but because they enjoy close ties with the political elite. Most reasonable people would agree that a captain of industry who owes his success to political connections and a captain of industry who owes his success to bold entrepreneurship, creative innovation, and visionary leadership are as different as day and night. There is very little doubt as to which of the two captains of industry — Mr. President's Son or Mr. Steve Jobs — is better for the economy and society.

In fact, some leading businessmen hail from the political elite and some leading politicians hail from the business elite, and the boundaries between the two are blurred. Thailand's former Prime Minister Thaksin Shinawatra, whose populist policies created a seemingly permanent political stalemate between Thailand's rural poor and urban middle class, was a telecom tycoon and one of the country's wealthiest men. He is just one example of the pervasive influence of the private sector on government in developing countries — albeit an extreme example of the government literally captured by the private sector. In developing countries, there are also countless examples of politicians enriching

"

Upon closer thought, regulatory capture is the natural outcome of the relationship between the government and the private sector in a capitalist economy. The extent of the problem is more severe in developing countries, where weak governments are ripe for picking by the private sector.

"

themselves by abusing the powers of their office and becoming wealthy businessmen. Business pervades politics, and politics pervades business.

The widespread practice of using public office for personal gain knows no borders and cuts across the entire political spectrum. For example, it is alleged that President Nestor Kirchner of Argentina and his wife and successor President Cristina Kirchner — well known for leftist, populist, anti-business policies that have seriously damaged the economy[1] — made a small fortune from the development of a new resort complex in the far south of the country. There is nothing wrong with making a fortune, except that the ways in obtaining profits were dubious such as preferential access to large plots of land in prime locations at very low prices. In the Third World, it is often all but impossible to know where politics ends and business begins, or vice versa. It goes without saying that the blurring of the boundaries between politics and business weakens the central role of the government as an honest broker and referee of the never-ending competition between companies and industries in a capitalist economy.

The incestuous relationship between politics and business in which politicians and businessmen scratch each other's back, with businessmen paying off politicians and politicians protecting the interests of their benefactors, is more pronounced in the developing countries, but it is also very much in evidence in the advanced economies. Silvio Berlusconi, a media tycoon and billionaire, served intermittently as the Italian prime minister for a total of nine years between 1994 and 2011. Embarrassingly for Italian democracy, Berlusconi has been a frequent criminal defendant and was even convicted of tax fraud in 2013. The lengthy litany of criminal allegations against him include

[1] Fortunately for Argentina, in December 2015 Cristina Kirchner was succeeded by the centrist Mauricio Macri, who has promised to pursue more sensible economic policies. It remains to be seen whether he can undo the economic havoc wrought by the husband and wife tag team of Nestor and Cristina, all the more so since he was mentioned in the Panama Papers scandal (see http://www.bbc.com/news/world-latin-america-35991155). But unlike his two predecessors, at least he is not playing Robin Hood with money his government does not have, running the economy into the ground in the process. That is good news for all Argentines, especially the poor. Unfortunately for Argentina, while the economy was clearly improving, it proved too difficult for the Macri government to clean up the huge mess created by his populist predecessors in a short period of time. As a result, Argentina suffered yet another currency crisis in May 2018 — the currency plunged by more than 20% against the US dollar — and the country turned to the International Monetary Fund (IMF) for assistance.

abuse of office, extortion, child sexual abuse, money laundering, and embezzlement, to name just a few. In fact, he allegedly told confidantes that the main reason he entered politics was to avoid imprisonment![2] In Italy, for many criminal offenses, high political office grants immunity from prosecution.

[2] http://en.wikipedia.org/wiki/Silvio_Berlusconi

K STREET LOBBYISTS, RICHARD GEPHARDT, AND DONALD TRUMP

20

More staid and mature democracies like America are not exempt from unhealthy coziness between business and politics. It is not for nothing that billions of dollars are sloshing around inside the beltway encircling Washington, D.C.[1] Money buys political influence, and political influence helps your business. The hordes of lobbyists running around Washington, D.C. are part of a multi-billion dollar industry in which special interest groups try to buy influence from politicians and the government. For example, large oil multinationals will seek to weaken regulations that restrict their ability to drill for oil in environmentally fragile regions such as northern Alaska above the Arctic Circle. While oil exploration creates a lot of jobs in the short run and strengthens America's energy independence in the long run, the environmental costs of drilling for oil in such regions are potentially large. At a minimum, environmental issues should be a key factor in the government's decision

Of course, environmental lobby groups concerned about the environmental impact of such drilling will seek to strengthen those regulations. But the odds clearly favor Big Oil companies such as Shell, BP, and ExxonMobil, which rank among the

[1] http://sunlightfoundation.com/blog/2013/11/25/how-much-lobbying-is-there-in-washington-its-double-what-you-think/

biggest companies in the entire corporate world, with their bulging war chests of lobbying dollars, over non-profit, non-government environmental organizations such as Greenpeace. While we are not big fans of Greenpeace, its blind dogmatic opposition to nuclear energy and other issues, or some of its publicity-seeking antics, it is definitely at a huge disadvantage vis-à-vis its corporate adversaries in terms of lobbying resources. Money talks in Washington, D.C. and it talks loud and clear. Moreover, in terms of financial resources, between Greenpeace and Big Oil, it is simply no contest.

Not surprisingly, many top beltway lobbyists are former members of Congress. One well-known example is Richard Gephardt, who served in the US House of Representatives for 28 years, 14 years as the leader of the Democrats, and ran unsuccessfully for the presidency in 1988 and 2004. After leaving Congress in 2005, he joined a lobbying firm as a senior counsel and shortly after founded his own successful lobbying firm, the Gephardt Government Affairs Group. His client list reads like a Who's Who of blue chip firms in the corporate world, including Goldman Sachs, Visa, and Boeing. The firm's revenues shot up tenfold to more than US$6 million by 2010.

What makes Gephardt's success as a corporate lobbyist all the more ironic is that as a congressman, he represented a working-class district of St. Louis and consistently championed populist, anti-business, pro-union views. Whatever one makes of his turnabout, one cannot but empathize with the financial temptations of a post-congressional career on K Street, the heart of Washington's lobbying industry. Even a former junior member of the US Congress can expect to take home US$1 million. This explains why so many former senators and

> **"**
>
> Not surprisingly, many top beltway lobbyists are former members of Congress. One well-known example is Richard Gephardt, who served in the US House of Representatives for 28 years, 14 years as the leader of the Democrats, and ran unsuccessfully for the presidency in 1988 and 2004.
>
> **"**

congressmen head straight to K Street when they retire, rather than back home to California, Nebraska, or Texas.[2]

In a capitalist economy money talks and everybody listens, including politicians and government officials. It is said that power corrupts but in a capitalist economy, it is more precisely money that corrupts. In developing countries, bureaucrats often have to augment their meager salaries with bribes just to achieve a reasonable standard of living. "Bribery" can sometimes take more subtle and indirect forms, especially in rich countries such as Japan and South Korea, where senior civil servants tend to view plum post-retirement jobs in firms that they use to regulate as a prerogative of their position. Insurance regulators may snag well-paying positions with little work at large insurance corporations in Tokyo and Seoul. It was also mentioned earlier that retiring US congressmen and senators face an irresistible material temptation to work for the same corporate interests that they used to regulate. This blunts their incentive in carrying out their task of effectively regulating the companies and industries.

Politics is a costly business in both democracies and dictatorships. Running for political office takes a lot of money, which most politicians do not have, unless they are a Donald Trump. The combination of the high cost of politics and lack of personal funds leaves politicians financially dependent on political donations from special interest groups. Just to make their name known to the voters takes a lot of expensive air time on television, radio, and other mass media. Ironically, billionaire politicians may be the cleanest politicians, least beholden to special interest groups, even though there is a risk that they will hijack the government to further

[2] "The trouble with that revolving door," New York Times, by Thomas B. Edsall, 18 December 2011, http://campaignstops. blogs.nytimes.com/2011/12/18/the-trouble-with-that-revolving-door/?_php=true&_type=blogs&_r=0; https://www.techdirt. com/articles/20130819/00581624225/50-retiring-senators-now-become-lobbyists-up-3-few-decades-ago.shtml

their own business interests. Therefore, Trump's assertion that being rich qualifies him for the US presidency because he cannot be bought is not entirely groundless, even though some of his campaign pledges, such as banning all Muslims from entering America or building a great wall between America and Mexico (to be paid for by Mexico), border on the insane.

Contrary to popular belief, running a dictatorship does not come cheap, even though dictators do not have to run for office. This is because dictators have to buy off political support with money — bullets, tear gas, and clubs help but their effectiveness is limited — and that money usually comes from wealthy businessmen. It is naïve to think that authoritarian governments can rely on sticks alone to rule their countries. They need carrots and sticks, and carrots cost a lot of money. For sure, a sizable share of the ill-gotten wealth enriches the dictator, his kin, and his friends, but much of it is used as political funds to buy political support. In a capitalist economy, money lubricates the wheels of politics, in democracies and dictatorships alike, which is why the government is a far from perfect policeman for reining in the excesses of capitalism.

“

Therefore, Trump's assertion that being rich qualifies him for the US presidency because he cannot be bought is not entirely groundless.

”

BLOWN CALLS IN SPORTS, CAPITALIST COMPETITION, GOVERNMENT AS REFEREE, DEMOCRATIC CAPITALISM VERSUS ELITE CAPITALISM, AND MERIT CAPITALISM VERSUS HEREDITARY CAPITALISM

21

The raw, muscular, dynamic capitalism of entrepreneurs and firms competing vigorously with each other to capture consumer dollars is, in essence, a contest. The quality of any contest depends critically on the rules of the game as well as the accuracy and impartiality with which the rules are enforced. A good game needs a good referee. Sports fans around the world vividly remember the moments when their favorite team was cheated of a victory by an incompetent or biased referee's mistake. Like when a perfectly legitimate goal by your center forward is inexplicably ruled offside, or when the opposing team's dive-prone striker is awarded a dubious game-deciding penalty kick in the 93rd minute, or your best defender is red-carded and thrown out of a game for a robust but 100% legal tackle. Or, like when your powerful forward is called for a charge on an obvious block late in the fourth quarter in a tight playoff game, or the ball is awarded to the other team when it went off their fingertips in the same situation. Or, like when your cornerback's excellent pass coverage is rewarded with a bogus pass interference call.

Most sports fans conveniently forget the moments when their team benefits from a similar

> **"**
>
> The raw, muscular, dynamic capitalism of entrepreneurs and firms competing vigorously with each other to capture consumer dollars is, in essence, a contest. The quality of any contest depends critically on the rules of the game as well as the accuracy and impartiality with which the rules are enforced. A good game needs a good referee.
>
> **"**

89

blown call. More importantly, the magnitudes of the referee mistakes described above are due to neither incompetence nor bias, but human error. Referees are not computers or robots but human beings, and human beings make honest mistakes. While we feel aggrieved and even outraged at the injustice suffered by our teams, most sports fans would concede that the "good" calls and "bad" calls cancel each other out over time. In other words, by and large, we are reasonably confident that victory or defeat is decided by how the teams (or individual players in the case of golf, tennis or other individual sports) perform against each other, rather than by the calls that referees make or fail to make. What would make us lose all confidence that the better team wins are blatant game changers such as forcing Lionel Messi to play with a bowling ball tied to his foot, forcing LeBron James to play with his hands tied behind his back, or forcing Usain Bolt to start 20 meters behind others in a 100-meter sprint. When the game is so blatantly rigged, there is no chance that the better team will prevail.

Yet by far the biggest attraction of capitalism is that the best man wins. Popular support for capitalism is deeply rooted in the notion that capitalism is a fair system which rewards superior companies that deliver high quality at low cost and punishes inferior companies that produce lousy, overpriced junk. Under capitalism, entrepreneurs and firms compete vigorously with each other to create value and capture consumer hearts and dollar. But this can only happen if the market environment is free and competitive. If the market is blatantly rigged so that some firms have an unfair advantage over others, then it is unlikely that the firm which produces the best product at the lowest cost — i.e. the firm which creates the most value — will win. The case for and legitimacy of capitalism

"

Yet by far the biggest attraction of capitalism is that the best man wins. Popular support for capitalism is deeply rooted in the notion that capitalism is a fair system which rewards superior companies that deliver high quality at low cost and punishes inferior companies that produce lousy, overpriced junk.

"

ultimately rest on fair competition, and that case and legitimacy are seriously compromised when competition is rigged so that some players have a big head start on others.

Therefore, the overriding, paramount, central role of the government in the capitalist game is that of a strong, impartial referee who sets forth the rules of the game and enforces those rules. Just as a good referee of a sports match ensures that the best team or the best player wins, a good government ensures that the best entrepreneurs and companies survive and thrive. The government must create a level playing field where anybody with a good idea and the drive to turn that good idea into reality has a good shot at entrepreneurial success. The government contributes to the success of the private sector and the market economy in many ways, from building infrastructure such as roads and ports to providing public education to maintaining law and order. But its biggest contribution is to be an honest, fair and effective referee of the never-ending competition among entrepreneurs and companies. If the government does this well, competition will be vigorous, and the economy will prosper and thrive.

Critically, the legitimacy of capitalism and popular support for capitalism are rooted in the belief that capitalism is a fair and equitable economic system in which the best man wins, the best company conquers the market, and anybody with drive, talent and creativity can aspire to become another Steve Jobs. An apt name for this kind of capitalism is democratic capitalism or people's capitalism or merit capitalism, in the sense that everybody has a realistic chance to compete and win. Democratic capitalism is the only kind of capitalism that is sustainable and durable. Its legitimacy and broad popular support make it robust and resilient to shocks.

> **Critically, the legitimacy of capitalism and popular support for capitalism are rooted in the belief that capitalism is a fair and equitable economic system in which the best man wins, the best company conquers the market, and anybody with drive, talent and creativity can aspire to become another Steve Jobs. An apt name for this kind of capitalism is democratic capitalism or people's capitalism or merit capitalism, in the sense that everybody has a realistic chance to compete and win.**

91

A core element of democratic capitalism is upward social mobility, or the ability of bright children of coalminers or small farmers or factory workers to become bankers or CEOs (chief executive officers) or successful entrepreneurs. It is the belief that you can move up in the world with hard work that encourages individuals to work hard and perform well. Democratic capitalism is capitalism at its ideal best. It is an economic system under which individuals and companies win or lose based on what they do, not who they are or who they know.

However, the reality of capitalism often differs, and differs vastly, from its ideal state. Imagine the referee of a sports event, say a soccer or basketball game, taking part in the event as a player! In this scenario, it is difficult to expect objectivity and impartiality from the referee. To put it mildly, there is a serious conflict of interest between the referee's role and the player's role. The referee's job is to ensure that the better team wins, while the player's job is to help *his* team wins. However, in the capitalist reality, this — the referee being an active contestant — is exactly what happens all too often. Across the world, in all continents and in both rich and poor countries, the government is involved in producing a wide range of goods and services, like electricity and telecom services, food and consumer goods, as well as oil and other natural resources. When the government gets into the business of producing things, it often restricts competition and becomes a monopolist, inflicting big losses on the economy as a whole. Since the government has the power to regulate the private sector, it can regulate away private sector competition by prohibiting the entry of private sector firms into the market.

Government monopolies are clearly a major problem. But what is even more harmful for

> **"**
> A core element of democratic capitalism is upward social mobility, or the ability of bright children of coalminers or small farmers or factory workers to become bankers or CEOs (chief executive officers) or successful entrepreneurs.... However, the reality of capitalism often differs, and differs vastly, from its ideal state.
> **"**

the future of capitalism is the steady erosion of democratic capitalism or merit capitalism and its replacement by elite capitalism or hereditary capitalism. The steady erosion is driven by the cancer at the heart of today's capitalism — wide and worsening income inequality between the rich and the poor. The contrast between the two types of capitalism is stark, to say the least. Under democratic capitalism, your wealth is due to your contribution to the economy, for example by inventing a socially useful new product or technology. That is, your wealth is based on merit. Under the other, less benign kind of capitalism, the children of self-perpetuating elites inherit their wealth from their parents, who are rich, politically powerful, or both. You are rich because your parents are rich. You do not earn your wealth, you inherit it. Inequality and elite capitalism are the scourges of modern-day capitalism, as are government monopolies.

"

But what is even more harmful for the future of capitalism is the steady erosion of democratic capitalism or merit capitalism and its replacement by elite capitalism or hereditary capitalism. The steady erosion is driven by the cancer at the heart of today's capitalism — wide and worsening income inequality between the rich and the poor.

"

TELECOMS, AT&T, AND NATURAL MONOPOLY

22

Telecom is a classic example of an industry which was dominated for decades by government monopolies. Other public utilities such as electricity, gas, and water supply are also traditional domains of government monopolies. In country after country after country, telephony started out as a government-owned monopoly before liberalization opened up the industry to private sector competition. A more competitive market, in turn, tends to bring about lower prices and better service. To be fair, there is an underlying economic argument, of sorts, for government production of telecoms and other public utilities. The natural monopoly argument, according to which one firm can produce certain goods at lower average cost than two or more firms, implies that monopoly is natural and desirable. A natural monopoly can occur if, for example, an industry requires very large capital investments such as on telephone lines. Building a second telephone line would be duplicative and costly.

That is the theory. In practice, the end of a natural monopoly — for example, AT&T, which dominated the US telephone local service and long-distance service market, as well as telephone equipment market, for decades until

> **"**
> In country after country after country, telephony started out as a government-owned monopoly before liberalization opened up the industry to private sector competition. A more competitive market, in turn, tends to bring about lower prices and better service.
> **"**

its break-up in 1982 — often brings down prices and improves quality. The price of long-distance telephone services fell sharply when AT&T was broken up, due to a surge of competition in the market with the entry of new competitors such as MCI and Sprint.[1] Telecom liberalization similarly fostered competition and lowered prices in many other countries, with large benefits for consumers and the entire economy.

In Singapore, long distance call rates plummeted since the entry of StarHub and M1 into a telecom market monopolized by SingTel until the mid-1990s. In many countries, especially in developing countries with weak tax collection systems, governments are loath to relinquish their monopoly of telecoms and other public utilities since they are important revenue sources. However, while such a focus on maximizing government revenues is understandable, it entails big losses for the economy as a whole. For example, extensive telecom liberalization that lowered prices and expanded access contributed greatly to the advanced state of information technology (IT) in Korea, which tops the world in broadband wireless penetration rate. In fact, in 2012, the penetration rate surpassed 100% in Korea, where mobile technology and staying connected are part and parcel of daily living for everybody.[2]

More generally, the natural monopoly argument suffers from a fatal flaw. The argument is usually brought to life to justify government's production of goods and services. Since the government acts in the public interest, who better to produce a good or a service for which one provider is better than many providers? Even if one accepts the technical aspects of the natural monopoly argument — e.g. it is duplicative and wasteful to build a costly second network, be it electricity grid, telephone line, or gas or water

[1] "Breakup of the Bell System," http://en.wikipedia.org/wiki/Breakup_of_the_Bell_System

[2] "South Korea hits 100% mark in wireless broadband," http://www.cnet.com/news/south-korea-hits-100-mark-in-wireless-broadband/

pipeline — the argument does not answer the central question of who should be the natural monopolist. This is hardly surprising since the main purpose of the natural monopoly argument is to justify the government's monopoly, or the monopoly of a private sector firm with tight links to the government.[3]

The argument is couched in the language of public interest — i.e. lower costs and prices — but in fact, it serves the interests of the government and its crony firms. Whether a monopoly is natural or unnatural is ultimately for the market, rather than the government, to decide. If monopoly is indeed the natural or desirable outcome in a market or industry, then the monopolist should be the firm that delivers the best product at the lowest cost. If the government does a strong job of refereeing the market, then there is a good chance that the monopolist *will* indeed be the best firm — the firm that delivers the best product at lowest price.

[3]"The myth of natural monopoly," Mises Daily, by Thomas J. DiLoreonzo, 13 May 2011, http://mises.org/daily/5266/

PRIVATIZATION, RUSSIAN BILLIONAIRES, AND CARLOS SLIM

23

Some in the low-tax, small-government crowd believe that the less regulation, the better for private enterprise, entrepreneurship, and overall economic performance. Yet nothing could be further from the truth. What is required for a good soccer match or a good basketball game is not an absence of referee, but a good referee with a solid knowledge of the rules, along with a willingness and ability to enforce the rules fairly and decisively. There is a presumption among some right-wingers that privatization will automatically lead to improved efficiency, lower prices, and other economic gains. But in the absence of a sound regulatory framework, neither consumers nor economy at large benefits from the transfer of ownership from the government to the private sector. For example, when India privatized its airports, the result was a sharp *increase* in landing fees, which had a detrimental impact on air traffic. In this case, the result of privatization is simply the replacement of a bad public monopoly with an even worse private monopoly.

By the same token, the wave of privatization which swept Russia has not made the privatized industries and firms more efficient or productive.

> "Some in the low-tax, small-government crowd believe that the less regulation, the better for private enterprise, entrepreneurship, and overall economic performance. Yet nothing could be further from the truth. What is required for a good soccer match or a good basketball game is not an absence of referee, but a good referee with a solid knowledge of the rules, along with a willingness and ability to enforce the rules fairly and decisively."

In view of Russia's short history of capitalism in post-Soviet era, the country's surprisingly long list of multi-billionaires — Alisher Usmanov, Mikhail Fridman, and Roman Abramovich, the owner of Chelsea football club in London — may be many different things, but they are no Steve Jobs or Bill Gates or Jeff Bezos. Russian billionaires are not testaments to the vibrancy of Russia's so-called capitalism, but to its hollowness and weakness. Russia remains an economically stagnant petrostate with little other than oil and gas to offer the rest of the world, a Saudi Arabia of the North. In Russia, the lack of effective regulation has given rise to a peculiar type of capitalism in which corrupt politicians and government officials collaborate with powerful businessmen to strip the country bare of its abundant natural resources.

The two elite cliques gain hugely from this type of crony capitalism, which produces precious little benefits for long-suffering ordinary Russian citizens.[1] The highly publicized case of oil oligarch Mikhail Khodorosky, who lost much of his fortune and was jailed for eight years until December 2013 after publicly criticizing the government for corruption, shows that politics and business are inextricably linked with each other in Russia. Russian oligarchs rise and fall on the strength of their ties to the government, rather than their ability to produce better and cheaper products. This explains the weakness and fragility of the Russian economy. Economic lethargy, in turn, helps to explain Russia's aggressive and nationalistic foreign policy, most evident in its military adventures in neighboring Ukraine and distant Syria. Nationalistic military adventure is a tried and tested option for shoring up the political support of a disgruntled citizenry in the face of economic stagnation and lack of economic opportunities.

[1] Not surprisingly, Russia came out top of the world in *The Economist*'s 2016 crony capitalism index. http://www.economist.com/news/international/21698239-across-world-politically-connected-tycoons-are-feeling-squeeze-party-winds

Likewise, lack of effective regulation and weak legal system enabled América Móvil, Mexico's private sector telecom giant, to dominate both the fixed line and wireless markets for years. In 2012, Telmex, América Móvil's landline arm, held a 80% share of Mexico's landline market while Telcel, its wireless arm, held a 70% share of the country's wireless market. It is a measure of América Móvil's market dominance that its owner, Carlos Slim, is widely believed to be the richest man in the world, with a staggering net worth of more than US$70 billion. The huge profits from the telecom monopoly channeling to Slim's vast personal wealth inflict huge social costs. What is good for Telmex and Telcel may be very good for Slim, but it is definitely not good for Mexico or the Mexican economy.

The predictable result of unregulated monopoly, which restricts competition from abroad as well as home, has been some of the highest rates for both landline and wireless services in the world, inflicting heavy losses on Mexican consumers and businesses. A January 2012 report from the OECD (Organisation for Economic Co-operation and Development) estimated that the high rates cost Mexican telecom industry US$192.2 billion in lost revenue between 2005 and 2009, or close to 2% of GDP (gross domestic product) per year.[2] The report correctly points out that the massive cost to the Mexican economy underlines the fundamental importance of rules and regulation that ensure open and fair competition, are enforced by a strong regulator, and deliver good quality services at a low price. It is worth repeating that what makes capitalism work well is not "no regulation", but "good regulation". Good regulation refers to the quality of regulation, not the quantity of regulation. Fortunately for Mexico, and unfortunately for Slim, in July

[2]"Talk is not cheap: Carlos Slim's telecom monopoly costing Mexican economy billions," International Business Times, 2 April 2013, http://www.ibtimes.com/talk-not-cheap-carlos-slims-telecom-monopoly-costing-mexican-economy-billions-1166039

2014, the Mexican government implemented significant reforms geared toward breaking up the Slim monopolies and introducing greater competition into the telecom market.[3] Mexican consumers and Mexican companies, and the Mexican economy as a whole, will reap big benefits. Count on it.

[3] "Mexico's president signs telecoms reform rules into law," Reuters, 14 July 2014, http://www.reuters.com/article/us-mexico-reforms-idUSKBN0FJ2DU20140714

HENRY FORD, JOSEPH SCHUMPETER'S CREATIVE DESTRUCTION, AND THE POWER OF PATENTS

24

It is almost impossible to overstate the central role of competition in economic growth and the material progress of mankind. In particular, competition drives entrepreneurs to constantly innovate and to produce new and better products and technologies to capture the hearts and dollars of consumers. The bewildering variety of goods and services we observe in a successful capitalist economy is testament to the power of competition. Conversely, the drab uniformity and bareness of a Moscow supermarket in the Cold War days resulted from the utter lack of competition. Under capitalism, the central role of the government is to referee the competition between private sector firms, so that the best firms win and deliver the best value for consumers. Competition is basically a dynamic — over time — concept rather than a static — at a single point in time — concept. Unlike a football match, which ends after 90 minutes, or an NBA (National Basketball Association) basketball game, which ends after four quarters, the game of competition never stops.

In other words, it is much more accurate to view competition as a dynamic process that evolves over time, as opposed to a state of affairs at a single point in time. More precisely, the game

> " It is almost impossible to overstate the central role of competition in economic growth and the material progress of mankind. In particular, competition drives entrepreneurs to constantly innovate and to produce new and better products and technologies to capture the hearts and dollars of consumers. The bewildering variety of goods and services we observe in a successful capitalist economy is testament to the power of competition. "

of competition yields its biggest benefits for mankind *over time* — through new and better products and technologies which emerge *over time* when firms compete vigorously with each other to win the affection of their customers as well as their cash-stuffed pockets. Sound and effective regulatory environment that creates a level playing field for all firms is the gateway to unlocking the vast potential of dynamic competition. Free market advocates who unconditionally call for as little regulation as possible are wrongheaded. To be sure, too much regulation squeezes the life out of entrepreneurship and can hold back entire economies — witness pre-1991 India. But there is clearly a need for regulation to make capitalism work, just as there is a need for referees in football matches. What matters for the quality of competition is the quality of regulation, just as the quality of refereeing matters for the quality of a football match. Good regulation has many ingredients, but strong protection of intellectual property rights is a core ingredient.

Companies compete with each other in many different ways. One important mode of competition, familiar to most consumers, is price competition. The intensity of price competition depends heavily on the structure of the market. If there is only one seller in a market — or a monopolist, meaning one seller in Greek and Latin — then he will charge what the market will bear, or as high a price as possible. That is why monopoly is good for the producer, but bad for the consumers. The entry of new firms tends to reduce the price since each firm will now lower its price to try to increase its sales and market share. For example, the entry of a new airline into a route monopolized by one airline typically results in a sharp fall in air fare. Good for consumers, bad for the monopolist airline. This explains why firms and industries

"

Free market advocates who unconditionally call for as little regulation as possible are wrongheaded. To be sure, too much regulation squeezes the life out of entrepreneurship and can hold back entire economies — witness pre-1991 India. But there is clearly a need for regulation to make capitalism work, just as there is a need for referees in football matches.

"

around the world lobby their governments to erect high tariffs to protect them from "unfair" foreign competition. The constant clamoring of American companies for protection from "unfair" Chinese imports is a classic example. But what is unfair to American companies is cheap and therefore good for American consumers. In fact, cheap Chinese imports increase the purchasing power of American consumers and improve their living standards.

While price competition thus delivers substantial economic benefits, other types of competition deliver even larger gains. Not all competition is created equal, and one type of competition — competing on the basis of innovation — towers above the rest. The benefits from new products and technologies often dwarf benefits from price competition. Suppose that in 1910, before Henry Ford came up with ways to mass produce the automobile — the Ford Model T — horse carts were the dominant mode of transportation. Suppose further that the market for horse carts is intensely competitive, with horse cart companies vigorously undercutting each other's prices to gain larger market shares. Yet the benefits of the Model T so far outweigh the those of price competition in the horse cart market that price competition among horse cart companies becomes irrelevant. In fact, even if Ford were initially a monopolist, society would gain far more from a monopolistic automobile market than a competitive horse cart market.

Indeed it is precisely the prospects of juicy monopoly profits that encourage Henry Ford, Steve Jobs, Elon Musk, and millions of other entrepreneurs throughout human history to invest their time and effort in producing new, better products in the first place. Entrepreneurial capitalists compete, and compete furiously, with each other to produce new products and

> **"**
> Indeed it is precisely the prospects of juicy monopoly profits that encourage Henry Ford, Steve Jobs, Elon Musk, and millions of other entrepreneurs throughout human history to invest their time and effort in producing new, better products in the first place.
> **"**

103

services that provide greater satisfaction for consumers. Without this kind of competition, we may still be relying on horse carts for transportation, enjoying low prices as a result of fierce competition among horse cart companies! The social benefits of competition based on new products, services, technologies, business models, and ideas are often incomparably larger than the social benefits of price competition. The replacement of black and white televisions by color televisions, the replacement of fixed-line telephones by mobile phones, the replacement of desktop computers by laptops, and the list goes on and on. Even far less revolutionary, more mundane inventions and innovations are part of what the visionary Austrian economist Joseph Schumpeter called the process of creative destruction, which propels human progress.

Understanding Schumpeter's seminal concept of creative destruction is helpful for understanding our notion of entrepreneurial capitalism. Capitalism driven by innovative, profit-seeking, risk-taking entrepreneurs is epitomized by Steve Jobs, Steven Wozniak, and their buddies dabbling in and experimenting with different ideas in a suburban California garage, creating a whole new product, a whole new industry, and a whole new world. According to Schumpeter, the kind of completion that matters is not price competition, nor competition based on marketing or minor quality improvements, but "… the competition from the new commodity, the new technology, the new source of supply, the new type of organization (the largest-scale unit of control for instance) — competition which commands a decisive cost or quality advantage and which strikes not at the margins of the profits and the outputs of the existing firms but at their foundations and their very lives. This kind of competition is so much more effective than the other as a bombardment is in comparison with forcing a door, and so much more important that it becomes a matter of comparative indifference whether competition in the ordinary sense functions more or less promptly."

The Schumpeterian kind of competition, the kind of competition that matters the most in the real world, requires strong intellectual property right protection by the government. Patents in particular encourage entrepreneurs to invest their time and energy in creating new and better products and services. They also confer a legal monopoly on the inventor of a new product or a new production technique for a limited period of time — e.g. 20 years for US patents. Since the inventor is protected by law from competition, he is able to charge what the market will bear. The high monopoly price inflicts losses on consumers and society as a whole, and the entry of new firms will lower prices, expand output, and improve social welfare. This is true but without the incentive of monopoly profits, Henry Ford would not have spent his time and energy trying to mass produce automobiles in the first place. There is clearly a tradeoff between the mass production of automobiles, which delivers huge social benefits, and social losses due to the high prices and low output of automobiles under the patent-created monopoly. This explains why the duration of patents is limited.

Patents and more broadly, protection of intellectual property rights, highlight the vital role of the government in promoting and refereeing competition among private sector entrepreneurs and companies. Sound and effective government regulation raises the quality of competition, which results in more and better goods and services, and contributes to economic dynamism and growth. In short, good regulation is vital for healthy competition, and

> **"**
> The Schumpeterian kind of competition, the kind of competition that matters the most in the real world, requires strong intellectual property right protection by the government. Patents in particular encourage entrepreneurs to invest their time and energy in creating new and better products and services.
> **"**

healthy competition is vital for entrepreneurship and economic progress. In some sense, competition and monopoly are two sides of the same coin. Not all monopoly but healthy monopoly which results from producing a better product or service that brings happiness to consumers. After all, in a capitalist market economy, firms compete with each other to gain the largest possible market share, to become a monopolist. According to Harold Demsetz, a prominent economist who developed the concept of socially beneficial monopoly based on consumer satisfaction, it makes all the difference in the world whether a firm becomes a monopolist because it is owned by the dictator's nephew or because it produces cheaper, better products. Good government regulation ensures that the right kind of monopoly (and competition) prevails.

> **❝**
>
> According to Harold Demsetz, a prominent economist who developed the concept of socially beneficial monopoly based on consumer satisfaction, it makes all the difference in the world whether a firm becomes a monopolist because it is owned by the dictator's nephew or because it produces cheaper, better products. Good government regulation ensures that the right kind of monopoly (and competition) prevails.
>
> **❞**

OVERREGULATION, THE FINAL STRAW FOR ASPIRING ENTREPRENEURS

25

S ound and effective regulation is absolutely indispensable for creating a level playing field for firms to compete vigorously with each other on the basis of price, quality, and technology. Yet, as is always the case, too much of a good thing can be bad thing, a very bad thing indeed. Here the anti-government crowd has a much stronger case against the government. Anybody who has ever started his own business knows fully well that overregulation and excessive red tape are major hurdles to doing business. There are so many other things one has to do to start a business besides filling out forms, applying for licenses, and handling other administrative matters. Obtaining a bank loan, finding reliable suppliers, hiring good workers, identifying a suitable store location, and the list goes on and on.

But of the myriad challenges any would-be entrepreneur faces, the most demoralizing and deflating must surely be the following — a gum chewing, cartoon dawdling, thumb twiddling bureaucrat who blurts out "I am not in charge of this" after you waited in a queue for three hours, and sends you back to another bureaucrat with similarly too much time on his hands, the same guy who sent you over to the gum chewer in

> **"**
>
> Sound and effective regulation is absolutely indispensable for creating a level playing field for firms to compete vigorously with each other on the basis of price, quality, and technology. Yet, as is always the case, too much of a good thing can be bad thing, a very bad thing indeed.
>
> **"**

the first place. The only reason that you want to meet the bureaucrat in the first place is to seek his help in filling out a mindbogglingly complex form, the whole purpose of which is pointless at best and anti-business obstructionism at worst. This is the kind of overregulation that stifles millions of entrepreneurs and would-be entrepreneurs around the world every day.

Becoming a successful entrepreneur is tough enough without the aggravation of some overbearing, self-important, bribe-seeking bureaucrat breathing down your neck. Overregulation is the deadly poison that nips entrepreneurship in the bud. In fact, the common reaction of the would-be entrepreneur — after a long day of working hard to make a living — to the nosy, overeager bureaucrat with plenty of time on his hands and looking for something to do is a natural and perfectly understandable "I do NOT need this shit." Actually, the reaction would have been much stronger and the language unprintable here. It is hard not to feel for the entrepreneur and share his rage.

Crucially, many of the world's poorest countries tend to have some of the world's worst red tape and bureaucracy. This is a grave phenomenon as these are the countries that can least afford a stifling bureaucracy that saps the life out of the private sector. The World Bank has constructed an ease of starting business index, which measures how easy, or difficult, it is for would-be entrepreneurs to start their own business. The index compares different countries and is based on (1) number of necessary procedures — e.g. paperwork to complete, license requirements, and so forth, (2) number of days it takes to start a business, (3) financial cost of the administrative procedures associated with starting a business, and (4) minimum capital requirements. Out of 189 countries ranked by the World Bank in

"

Becoming a successful entrepreneur is tough enough without the aggravation of some overbearing, self-important, bribe-seeking bureaucrat breathing down your neck. Overregulation is the deadly poison that nips entrepreneurship in the bud.... Crucially, many of the world's poorest countries tend to have some of the world's worst red tape and bureaucracy. This is a grave phenomenon as these are the countries that can least afford a stifling bureaucracy that saps the life out of the private sector.

"

2013, the five worst performers are Equatorial Guinea, Democratic Republic of Congo, Haiti, Eritrea, and Myanmar. Conversely, the five top rankers are New Zealand, Canada, Singapore, Australia, and Hong Kong SAR (China). There are some developing countries that perform well — Armenia, Georgia, and Rwanda — and are in the top ten, but in general, poorer countries do worse than richer ones.

The excessive red tape and bloated bureaucracy that throttle those who want to start their own business in the poorer countries are all the more unfortunate because would-be entrepreneurs in those countries face a wide array of other challenges. As daunting as the red tape and bureaucracy are, it is only the tip of the iceberg for would-be entrepreneurs in developing countries. The World Bank has constructed a broader index, the ease of doing business index, which measures how easy, or difficult, it is to do business in a particular country, and uses the index to rank countries. The ease of doing business index is an average of ten different sub-indices. In addition to the ease of starting business index, the nine other indices pertain to: (1) dealing with construction permits, (2) getting electricity, (3) registering property, (4) getting credit, (5) protecting investors, (6) paying taxes, (7) trading across borders, (8) enforcing contracts, and (9) resolving insolvency. In 2013, the bottom-five countries, out of 189 countries, are Republic of Congo, South Sudan, Libya, Central African Republic, and Chad, all low-income countries with the exception of oil-rich Libya. At the top end are Singapore, Hong Kong SAR (China), New Zealand, United States, and Denmark.

The aforementioned indices are subjective to some extent, but they unambiguously point to a fact of life — it is not easy to be an entrepreneur in a poor country. This fact of life, in turn, helps to

"

The excessive red tape and bloated bureaucracy that throttle those who want to start their own business in the poorer countries are all the more unfortunate because would-be entrepreneurs in those countries face a wide array of other challenges. As daunting as the red tape and bureaucracy are, it is only the tip of the iceberg for would-be entrepreneurs in developing countries.

"

explain why the poor country is poor. Furthermore, while the index is fairly comprehensive, there are countless other factors that influence the business environment besides the ease of doing business index and the ten sub-indices that make up the index. For example, poor physical infrastructure for transportation — inadequate roads, bridges, railways, ports, and airports — combine with regulatory bottlenecks — e.g. cumbersome customs clearance procedures which keep goods stuck in ports seemingly forever — to sharply raise the cost of moving goods and the overall cost of doing business. Another example is the lack of workers with the right skills and expertise. The weak education systems of poor countries fail to equip workers with the practical skills, especially technical and professional know-how, they need to be useful and valuable at the marketplace. Finding enough good workers is a perennial headache of employers in those countries.

In short, being an entrepreneur in a developing country is a heroic enterprise requiring Herculean courage, ingenuity and patience, even without the aggravation of some self-important, meddling, bribe-seeking bureaucrat breathing down one's neck. Developing countries desperately need a vibrant private sector to generate the economic growth they need to raise general living standards and lift citizens out of poverty leading to more dignified, humane and productive lives. No country has ever grown rich by growing the government. Furthermore, unlike, say, building up a good highway network, cutting back overregulation and an expanded bureaucracy is relatively costless and can be done in a short period of time. It is a criminal tragedy that so many developing countries shoot themselves in the foot by building up a mountain of pointless regulations and army of bureaucrats that snuff the life of their embryonic private sectors.

"

In short, being an entrepreneur in a developing country is a heroic enterprise requiring Herculean courage, ingenuity and patience, even without the aggravation of some self-important, meddling, bribe-seeking bureaucrat breathing down one's neck.... No country has ever grown rich by growing the government.... It is a criminal tragedy that so many developing countries shoot themselves in the foot by building up a mountain of pointless regulations and army of bureaucrats that snuff the life of their embryonic private sectors.

"

ARAB BUREAUCRACY, RIDHA YAHYAOUI, AND ISLAMIC STATE

26

Due to lack of jobs and economic opportunities, which, in turn, is a result of an absence of a dynamic, self-sustaining, job- and wealth-creating private sector, the government becomes, in effect, the employer of last resort. Bloated public sectors bulging with redundant bureaucrats with too much time on their hands inevitably spells trouble for the private sector. Did you ever wonder why getting your passport stamped at the airport immigration counter seems to take a longer time the poorer the country? The explanation is simple: the redundant bureaucrat feels dispassionate about his job and perhaps looks for a bribe on the side. Harassing the private sector to justify their self-worth is a favorite pastime of these bureaucrats. The all too predictable outcome is a growing horde of bureaucrats and mountain of regulations squeezing the life out of a sick and declining private sector which, in turn, strengthens the role of the government as the employer of last resort. In countries blessed with natural wealth — e.g. Saudi Arabia and the other petrostates of the Middle East — government jobs are essentially a costly form of welfare benefits. In less fortunate countries, the proliferation of regulations is typically

"
Bloated public sectors bulging with redundant bureaucrats with too much time on their hands inevitably spells trouble for the private sector.... Harassing the private sector to justify their self-worth is a favorite pastime of these bureaucrats. The all too predictable outcome is a growing horde of bureaucrats and mountain of regulations squeezing the life out of a sick and declining private sector which, in turn, strengthens the role of the government as the employer of last resort.
"

accompanied by pervasive bribe-seeking and bribe-taking.

As noted earlier, an often overlooked but critical driver behind the rise of jihadist Islamic radicalism is the economic stagnation of the Arab world and the broader Islamic world. While 21st-century jihadist Islamic radicalism is a complex, multidimensional phenomenon with a wide range of social, cultural, and religious root causes, economics is clearly a key factor. Millions of unemployed and underemployed young men with raging hormones and nothing useful to do provide hordes of eager and ready recruits for al Qaeda, the Islamic State, and other jihadist outfits with their slick propaganda websites peddling visions of a purposeful life defending Islam and an enticing afterlife of beautiful virgins. Come to think of it, even without slick propaganda websites, those same young men would be itching to get out of their meaningless and hopeless lives. Anything, including suicide bombing, would be better than the empty lives that countless young Arab men lead as a result of the sclerotic economies of their countries.

Moreover, a big reason that Arab economies are sclerotic is the millions of bureaucrats running around, strangling the very life out of the would-be entrepreneurs of their countries, from Syria and Iraq to Algeria and Tunisia. The reason that there are so many bureaucrats is that the government is the only source of jobs, especially for college graduates. Some young Arabs are literally dying to work for the government, as the tragedy faced by Ridha Yahyaoui in January 2016 attests.[1] If the only jobs on offer are government jobs, well, that is a powerful testament to the utter lack of economic opportunity. The Arab world is the perfect example of the vicious cycle of ever-expanding government bureaucracy

[1] Like Mohamed Bouazizi, 28-year-old Ridha Yahyaoui hailed from Tunisia, the birthplace of Arab Spring movement. After being turned down for a government job, he climbed a utility pole in the town of Kasserine and threatened suicide. He was electrocuted when he touched the wires. According to the World Bank, in 2015 half of the Tunisian university graduates were still unemployed at 35. As in much of the Arab world, the lack of a dynamic private sector means that the government is the employer of last resort. The government's relentless expansion takes a toll on its efficiency. For example, Tunisian Chemical Group, a state-owned company, suffered a two-thirds drop in output when it tripled its head count between 2010 and 2012. http://www.economist.com/news/middle-east-and-africa/21689616-unemployment-undermining-tunisias-transition-dying-work-government

and ever-slowing economic growth. As the government bureaucracy expands, too many bureaucrats with plenty of time on their hands invent and create yet more useless, pointless, and nonsensical regulations, which they impose on the hapless private sector. Those regulations, which are added to a layer of redundant rules, further discourage and demoralize entrepreneurs and private enterprises. It is a vicious cycle indeed!

The result is that yet more life is squeezed out of the private sector, which creates jobs and wealth, and the broader economy. The resulting economic stagnation leads to lack of jobs and economic opportunities, rendering the government the employer of last resort. As the government hires yet more workers, especially restless college graduates, the bureaucracy expands even further, and imposes yet more useless, pointless, and nonsensical regulations, further strangling the private sector, and so forth and so forth. Bureaucracy and private enterprise, the lifeblood of a dynamic successful economy, simply do not go well together, never have, never will. What is surprising about the Arab Spring is that it took so long for the long-suffering Arab populace to erupt against their bureaucrat oppressors.

Horror stories abound about the Arab world's bureaucratic nightmare.[2] Starting a business in Egypt requires getting permits from as many as 78 different government agencies! It is no wonder that the economy of Egypt, the most populous country in the Arab world, has been stuck in first gear for decades. No country ever got rich by making it almost impossible for entrepreneurs to start a business. In some parts of the oil-rich Persian Gulf region, which includes Saudi Arabia and Kuwait, the government employs as much as half of all working citizens. More generally,

[2] http://www.economist.com/news/middle-east-and-africa/21678243-regions-countries-desperately-need-reform-their-public-sectors-aiwa-yes

according to the World Bank, government bureaucracies employ more workers relative to the total workforce in the Arab world than in any other parts of the world. No country ever got rich by having so many paper-pushing bureaucrats and so few workers in the much more productive private sector, which actually produces something of economic value.

Not only are Arab bureaucrats good at stymieing their country's private sectors with piles of bad regulations, they also fail to provide the public services they are supposed to deliver. The Arab Spring was rooted in popular demand for democracy as well as better public services. In many parts of the Arab world, the government fails to perform even the most basic public services such as rubbish collection, an outrage which provoked widespread public protests in Lebanon in 2015. More broadly, the quality of education, health care, and other key public services remains abysmal. This is not surprising since many public sector workers do not work at all, and some do not even bother to show up. Nor are there any incentives for bureaucrats to work hard since slackers are not fired and those who excel are not rewarded. While these kinds of problems plague governments all over the world, they are especially pronounced in the Arab world.

The rise of jihadist Islamic radicalism has shaken the world to its foundations, and is now widely viewed as one of the greatest global security threats. Al Qaeda's horrific, game-changing terrorist attacks on the US on 11 September 2001, epitomized by the kamikaze-style destruction of the World Trade Center twin towers in New York City, was only the opening salvo in a wave of increasingly bolder attacks. The most recent examples include the bombing of Russia's Metrojet airliner on 31 October 2015,

"
Not only are Arab bureaucrats good at stymieing their country's private sectors with piles of bad regulations, they also fail to provide the public services they are supposed to deliver. The Arab Spring was rooted in popular demand for democracy as well as better public services.
"

the Paris massacres on 13 November 2015, the attacks in San Bernardino, California, on 2 December 2015, the assault on Brussels on 22 March 2016, mass shooting at a nightclub in Orlando, Florida, on 12 June 2016, the suicide bombings at Istanbul's main airport on 28 June 2016, and the Bastille Day truck attack in Nice, France, on 14 July 2016.[3] The terrorist incidents are increasing in frequency and brazenness, with no end in sight.

All of the recent attacks were perpetrated or inspired by the Islamic State, whose atrocities make al Qaeda look like a cuddly teddy bear by comparison. The rise of the Islamic State is partly the consequence of a simmering sectarian conflict between the majority Sunnis and minority Shias within Islam, and there are other complex non-economic factors as well. But to a large extent, the rise of Islamist fanaticism reflects the dismal failure of the Arab world to make meaningful progress on the economic front, a failure that has provided al Qaeda, Islamic State, and the like with millions of potential recruits. To repeat, blowing oneself up and murdering others in the process may not seem like such a bad option for unemployed young men with raging hormones leading barren, hollow lives, loitering around some run-down street corner in the Middle East or Europe.

[3] In addition to such headline-grabbing attacks outside the Middle East, Islamist terrorists are perpetrating countless atrocities in Afghanistan, Iraq, Pakistan, Syria, and other countries within or near the region. For example, two suicide bombers struck a peaceful protest in Kabul, Afghanistan, on 23 July 2016, and claimed at least 80 lives.

INGENIOUS NIGERIAN ENTREPRENEURS, DODD-FRANK, AND OBAMACARE

27

Many foreigners express a deep sense of wonderment and admiration at the ingenuity, resourcefulness, and creativity of entrepreneurs who succeed against all odds in countries that impose prohibitive barriers against private enterprise. A classic example of such a country is Nigeria, one of the world's top producers and exporters of crude oil. The West African country managed to squander hundreds of billions of its immense oil wealth over several decades through continuous misrule. While Nigeria is hardly alone in suffering from uninterrupted bad governance, the massive scale of incompetence and corruption — wholesale theft is the most accurate description — is mindboggling. Nigeria has to import most of its gasoline despite being a large oil exporter, due to lack of refining capacity. Most damningly, ordinary Nigerians have enjoyed almost no benefit from their country's huge oil wealth, all of which has been captured by a small clique of top government officials and their cronies.[1]

Predictably, Nigeria has developed a heavy economic dependence on oil and does not have much of a non-oil economy. On paper, the non-oil sector accounts for over 80% of the

[1] "Petroleum industry in Nigeria," http://en.wikipedia.org/wiki/Petroleum_industry_in_Nigeria

economy, but it produces very little that can be sold to the rest of the world. As a result, oil accounts for well over 90% of all exports, 90% of all foreign exchange earnings, and 90% of all federal government revenues. Nigeria imports the bulk of the food and manufacturing goods it needs — its agriculture and manufacturing sectors are equally inefficient and unproductive. The root cause of Nigeria's stagnant non-oil economy is the lack of a vibrant private sector that can produce goods and services desired by Nigerians, let alone foreigners. In addition to woeful infrastructure — e.g. frequent power breakouts and potholed roads, Nigerian entrepreneurs chafe under the weight of voluminous red tape and hordes of bribe-seeking petty officials who are too low down the pecking order to get their hands on the big prize of oil revenues.

The admiration and respect of foreigners, especially foreign journalists, at the ingenuity, resourcefulness and creativity of Nigerian entrepreneurs who manage to survive against formidable odds is understandable.[2] Heroic is the adjective that comes to mind. Unfortunately, the vast majority of ordinary Nigerians have gained nothing from their country's huge oil bonanza. Just imagine how much better off Nigeria would be if the country had half-decent governments that provided basic infrastructure such as roads and electricity, and basic services such as education and health care. Or, if it failed to provide basic infrastructure and services, then at least the Nigerian government can make life much easier for entrepreneurs by easing the red tape and bureaucracy that are throttling their business activities. The entrepreneurial ingenuity of Nigerian entrepreneurs in a bleak and daunting business environment is no cause for celebration. To the contrary, it should be cause for anger and outrage. Under even

[2] "Africa's testing ground," http://www.economist.com/news/business/21613341-make-it-big-africa-business-must-succeed-nigeria-continents-largest-market-no

half-decent governments, such resourceful entrepreneurship would have made Nigeria an incomparably richer country and ordinary Nigerians would have led far more decent, humane, fulfilling lives.

The scourge of overregulation which snuffs the life out of a rudimentary private sector is especially toxic for developing countries. Without the nurturing and growth of a thriving private sector in these developing countries, there is a dearth of business activities that are needed to power economic growth and job creation which would lift up general living standards and reduce poverty. Unfortunately, the scourge is by no means confined to developing countries. It infects advanced economies, including even America, the country most widely viewed as the strongest bastion of private enterprise in the world. One classic example is the Dodd–Frank Wall Street Reform and Consumer Protection Act of 2010, which came into effect after the Global Financial Crisis. Its aim and scope were entirely sensible and desirable — to prevent another financial meltdown by encouraging banks to become more transparent and preventing them from taking too much risk. But the problem with Dodd–Frank is that it is mind-numbingly long and complex.[3] It is 848 pages and counting, since many clarifications are still pending. Some of those clarifications are hundreds of pages long. Not surprisingly, almost nobody has ever actually read Dodd–Frank, and the very few who have cannot understand it. This is not regulation, it is insanity.

Dodd–Frank is part of a much broader trend toward an ever-growing mountain of regulations that suffocate American businesses. The two major political parties are equally guilty in the relentless expansion of regulations. A favorite area of regulation for Republicans is national

[3] "Over-regulated America," The Economist, 18 February 2012, http://www.economist.com/node/21547789

security. While perfectly understandable in the aftermath of the 9/11 terrorist attacks, the related broader trend of hostility toward foreigners, especially immigrants, is harming America's long-term growth prospects. A huge comparative advantage of America is its enduring allure for talented entrepreneurial foreigners from all corners of the world. Blanket immigration restrictions, whatever the impact on national security, keep out those economy-growing, job- and wealth-creating foreigners. Barring talented foreigners who bring much-needed skills and entrepreneurial drive is an unintended consequence of the Republicans' obsession with national security, with dire effects for the American economy.

The Democrats, for their part, create new regulations in an endless quest to expand the welfare state. A classic example is the Obama administration's contentious health care reform of 2010, better known as Obamacare. As with safeguarding national security, the intentions are sensible and desirable — to extend health care insurance coverage to millions of uninsured, predominantly poor Americans. However, Obamacare is staggering in its complexity and becoming even more complex. One hour of patient treatment is said to create at least 30 minutes of paperwork, and often much longer than that. On 3 July 2014 alone, the Obama administration added 1,296 pages of new regulations to Obamacare.[4] Just imagine how much better the US health care system would be if doctors and nurses spent their time looking after patients rather than filling out form after form after form. No wonder American is saddled with a worst-of-all-worlds health care system — ballooning costs without the benefit of better quality.

In sum, while a sound and effective regulatory framework is absolutely vital for creating a level

[4] "ObamaCare: Death by paperwork," 9 July 2014, http://nypost.com/2014/07/09/obamacare-death-by-paperwork/

playing field for all companies, crucially including the new firms that are often responsible for breakthrough technologies and products, overregulation can indeed break the spirit of even the most bold and enterprising entrepreneurs. Yes, it is a cliché to say that reducing excessive red tape can promote competition and growth. But like a lot of clichés, it happens to be absolutely true. Any entrepreneur in any country has a horrendous story or two about pulling out his hair due to sheer desperation at having to deal with some incomprehensibly complex and ultimately pointless regulation. It is tough enough to be an entrepreneur even without this kind of aggravation. Red tape is the straw that breaks the camel's back for many entrepreneurs. It is a measure of the toxic impact of too much regulation on entrepreneurship that small American businesses complain more about overregulation than taxes.[5]

[5] "Red tape blues," The Economist, 5 July 2014, http://www.economist.com/news/united-states/21606293-small-businesses-fret-less-about-taxes-over-regulation-red-tape-blues

MARKET FAILURE, GLOBAL WARMING, AND CARBON TAX

28

Even the most fervent proponents of the market or, equivalently, the most ardent opponents of government intervention in the economy, would accept that there is a legitimate economic role for the government. In particular, we have seen that the role of the government as a fair and effective referee of competition between private sector firms is critical to even the most laissez-faire market economy. A fair and effective referee helps to ensure that the best firm — in other words, the firm that delivers the best value for consumers — wins the game of competition. The level playing field drives forward the dynamic competition that propels entrepreneurs to create new and better products and technologies, and relentlessly lifts living standards and human well-being. We cannot overemphasize the critical importance of the government's referee role, but it is by no means the government's only role in a market economy.

While capitalism and the free market are one of mankind's greatest inventions, they are far from perfect. Human greed can be a force for good — the greed that drives entrepreneurs and firms to invent and innovate, in the hopes of hitting a commercial home run — as well as a force

> **"** In particular, we have seen that the role of the government as a fair and effective referee of competition between private sector firms is critical to even the most laissez-faire market economy.... While capitalism and the free market are one of mankind's greatest inventions, they are far from perfect. **"**

121

for evil — it can literally kill. Unfettered market forces can often lead to socially undesirable, sometimes downright horrifying outcomes. Reckless disregard for the safety of workers caused the Rana Plaza disaster in Bangladesh. Equally blatant disregard for the safety of shoppers resulted in the equally horrendous Sampoong Department Store disaster in South Korea. Gallingly, the owners of the Bangladeshi clothing factories and department store had ample time to evacuate their buildings, but they deliberately failed to do so to make a few extra bucks. In effect, hundreds of lives were sacrificed at the altar of greed. It goes without saying that in the absence of a strong government that effectively curtails the excesses of capitalist greed, the world would have many more Ranas and Sampoongs. Reining in capitalism gone wild is a core function of the government in a market economy.

Market failure is the general term used by economists to refer to the free market producing bad outcomes. That is, although the market generally produces good outcomes — e.g. the astronomical gap in living standards between capitalist South Korea and socialist North Korea — it sometimes fails to do so. Perhaps the most significant example of market failure is environmental destruction and climate change. In a world of no environmental regulations or taxes, firms and industries would pollute as much as they want since they face zero consequences. Although pollution imposes large costs on society — as anybody who has suffered the smog of Cairo, Los Angeles, Beijing, New Delhi, Mexico City, or hundreds of other cities will readily attest — the firm will not take those costs into account in their production decisions because those costs are borne by somebody else, not the firm. The gap between the firm's total costs and internal costs

> **"**
>
> Market failure is the general term used by economists to refer to the free market producing bad outcomes. That is, although the market generally produces good outcomes — e.g. the astronomical gap in living standards between capitalist South Korea and socialist North Korea — it sometimes fails to do so. Perhaps the most significant example of market failure is environmental destruction and climate change.
>
> **"**

is external costs. Unless the society's problem becomes the firm's own problem — that is, unless the external costs are internalized — the firm will choose a dirtier but commercially more profitable production method.

Government intervention can narrow the gap between internal costs and external costs. In terms of environmental protection, environmental regulations and taxes impose costs on polluting firms, and thus encourages them to reduce the amount of pollution they produce. Regulations often set a quantitative limit — for example, in the European Union the maximum of carbon dioxide a new automobile can currently produce is 130 grams per kilometer. Carbon tax, perhaps the best known environmental tax, is a tax on the carbon content of fossil fuels, which generate greenhouse gas emissions when they burn. Whether government intervenes through environmental regulations or taxes, firms incur higher costs, which is why the private sector tends to be hostile to such regulations or taxes. In spite of fierce private sector resistance, or precisely because of fierce private sector resistance, the government must alter the incentives that companies face, so they behave in ways that are less destructive to the environment.

Especially so since global warming and climate change point to a gloomy future in which environmental degradation will seriously jeopardize humanity's quality of life and productive capacity. There is a great deal of scientific debate about the exact impact of climate change but most reasonable people would agree that it is one of the greatest challenges confronting mankind in the 21st century. One does not have to be a whale-saving Greenpeace militant to see the large and growing body of evidence that we are heading

"

In spite of fierce private sector resistance, or precisely because of fierce private sector resistance, the government must alter the incentives that companies face, so they behave in ways that are less destructive to the environment.

"

toward substantial and irreversible environmental change. The evidence includes, among others, rising global temperature, melting Arctic icecap, and declining biodiversity. The environmental big picture is crystal clear — the writing is on the wall unless we drastically change the way we produce and consume goods and services.

To downplay global warming and assert that it is not a serious problem is irresponsible denial, like burying one's head in the sand. It is utterly irresponsible because what is at stake is the future of our children. Advocating less costly and more efficient solutions is fine, as are more benign views about the extent of the environmental problem. But it is unacceptable lunacy to call for business as usual in the face of mounting evidence of global environmental destruction. On the other hand, when it comes to irresponsible behavior, the other extreme — i.e. environmental radicals — can more than stand their own ground. Listening to these extreme environmentalists, sometimes you can help but wonder whether they are calling for a return to Stone Age. For example, nuclear power does have safety — e.g. Fukushima — and other issues, but the radicals' blind opposition to a relatively clean source of energy smacks of unthinking, dogmatic criticism for the sake of criticism. What is sorely lacking in the environmental debate is an intelligent, dispassionate, and evidence-based exchange of views that can lead us to concrete, actionable solutions. The future of mankind demands nothing less.

❝

To downplay global warming and assert that it is not a serious problem is irresponsible denial, like burying one's head in the sand.... What is sorely lacking in the environmental debate is an intelligent, dispassionate, and evidence-based exchange of views that can lead us to concrete, actionable solutions. The future of mankind demands nothing less.

❞

SAVING AMAZON RAINFORESTS AND WORLD ENVIRONMENT ORGANIZATION

29

One example of a smart solution to environmental problems is Singapore's electronic road pricing (ERP) system. The system is only partly aimed at environmental protection since its primary objective is to ease traffic jams in the super-rich Asian city-state. The risk of traffic congestion in Singapore, as in other cities around the world, peaks in the morning, when workers move from the suburbs (or outer parts of the city) to their downtown offices, and in the evening when workers go home. At the same time, emissions from cars cause greater damage to air quality when they are clustered together, for example during rush hour. Singapore's ERP system charges motorists for entering the downtown during peak hours. As its name suggests, the system relies on electronic sensors which automatically deduct a peak hour charge from a motor vehicle whenever it enters the restricted zone. The system is ingenious because it precisely targets the problem — too many cars in downtown during peak hours.

Effective environmental protection need not be high tech. Without the use of any state-of-the-art technology, Brazil has turned from a global leader in environmental destruction to a global leader in environmental protection. More

> **"**
> Effective environmental protection need not be high tech. Without the use of any state-of-the-art technology, Brazil has turned from a global leader in environmental destruction to a global leader in environmental protection.
> **"**

125

precisely, during the last 10 years, the Brazilian government has succeeded in reducing the deforestation of the Amazon rainforest by 70%, from 19,500 square kilometers to 5,800 square kilometers per year. This matters not only for Brazil but for the world because much of the Amazon rainforest, by far the largest in the world, lies in Brazil. By absorbing carbon dioxide and converting it into oxygen, the Amazon rainforest produces more than 20% of the world's supply of oxygen. For this reason, it is called the lungs of the world. Brazil's success in curbing the rape of the Amazon is believed to have prevented the release of 3.2 billion tons of carbon dioxide into the atmosphere, a staggering amount equal to the annual emission of the entire European Union in 2013.

There was no single magic bullet in Brazil's stunning success in slowing down the momentum of deforestation. The success is stunning because not so long ago farmers and cattle ranchers were cutting down trees at a pace which fueled widespread worries about the extinction of the huge rainforest. A gradual, evolutionary three-stage process, rather than a single big shock, was responsible for saving — fingers crossed — the Amazon. Bans, better governance in Amazonian areas, and consumer pressure on companies all contributed. The process started in the mid-1990s. During the first stage, the government tried to enforce bans and restrictions, with limited success.

During the second stage, the focus lay in strengthening policing, by increasing the number of enforcement officers, to give more teeth to the bans and restrictions. The centerpiece of the third stage was to encourage local governments to clamp down on deforestation by imposing financial penalties on the worst performers — i.e. counties with the highest rates of deforestation.

"

... during the last 10 years, the Brazilian government has succeeded in reducing the deforestation of the Amazon rainforest by 70%, from 19,500 square kilometers to 5,800 square kilometers per year.... There was no single magic bullet in Brazil's stunning success in slowing down the momentum of deforestation.

"

Greenpeace-led consumer boycotts against products from deforested Amazonian areas also helped. The Brazilian government's efforts to save the Amazon involved a lot of trial and error, and took a long time to bear fruit, but they paid off because they were underpinned by strong political will and commitment.

Tackling global warming and climate change requires political will and commitment of an altogether greater magnitude because it requires governments of all countries in the world to cooperate. Tackling climate change is a classic example of the free rider problem. Climate change is caused by the emissions of all countries, which means that all countries should cut down on their emissions. In other words, climate change is a global problem requiring a global solution. Yet because cutting down emissions is expensive — more precisely, tough environmental regulations impose big costs on firms, which have to invest in environment-protecting equipment and technology — countries want their counterparts to cut down their emissions while doing precious little to cut down their own emissions. That is, all countries want to free ride on the green investments of other countries, with the predictable result that very few countries undertake meaningful green investments.

What is urgently needed is meaningful and high-level international dialogue and cooperation among the countries of the world. Sadly, let alone dialogue and cooperation, there has been a great deal of acrimonious finger-pointing and recriminations among countries. Precisely because all countries contribute to global warming, it is natural for countries to minimize their role in global warming and thus their role in fighting global warming, and pass the buck to other countries. For example, developing

"

What is urgently needed is meaningful and high-level international dialogue and cooperation among the countries of the world. Sadly, let alone dialogue and cooperation, there has been a great deal of acrimonious finger-pointing and recriminations among countries.

"

countries such as China and India highlight the enormous amount of pollution caused by advanced countries such as US and Western Europe in the past. On the other hand, the latter point to the environmental damage currently wrought by the former as they industrialize. Given the urgency of making progress against global warming, this kind of bickering is all the more unfortunate. It is also very expensive because it wastes precious time — time that could and should be spent searching for solutions.

Perhaps a good point of departure to come to grips with global warming and environmental damage is to set up a World Environment Organization (WEO). Just as the World Bank was tasked with ending global poverty, the WTO (World Trade Organization) was tasked with facilitating global trade, and the IMF (International Monetary Fund) was tasked with safeguarding global financial stability, the WEO would be tasked with protecting the global environment. True, there are ample reasons to doubt the effectiveness of such an international body. After all, even long-established outfits such as the IMF, World Bank, and WTO attract plenty of criticism for their many shortcomings. For example, global trade liberalization — the domain of the WTO — has moved at a glacial pace in recent years although the lack of progress is due to irreconcilable self-interest of its member states — i.e. all countries want to export more and import less, especially since global growth has slowed down since the Global Financial Crisis.

But if there is one challenge that should unite all of mankind, it is the stop the wanton destruction of the global environment. As such, at a minimum, an international organization devoted to environmental issues will provide a permanent forum for discussing and exploring

"

Perhaps a good point of departure to come to grips with global warming and environmental damage is to set up a World Environment Organization (WEO). Just as the World Bank was tasked with ending global poverty, the WTO (World Trade Organization) was tasked with facilitating global trade, and the IMF (International Monetary Fund) was tasked with safeguarding global financial stability, the WEO would be tasked with protecting the global environment.

"

concrete, specific solutions to what is arguably mankind's biggest 21st century challenge. Skeptics may very well doubt the value of yet another international bureaucracy, but the mere existence of such a body would crystalize mankind's resolve to leave behind a livable planet for our children. Upon closer thought, it is nothing short of scandalous that there is no global body that deals with global warming and climate change on a permanent basis. We can debate about the need for and costs of yet another international bureaucracy but at the end of the day, the large potential benefits probably outweigh the costs in this case.

"

Upon closer thought, it is nothing short of scandalous that there is no global body that deals with global warming and climate change on a permanent basis.

"

BIG MAC, NATIONAL DEFENSE, AND THE CASE FOR PUBLIC EDUCATION

30

Market failure such as environmental destruction provides a clear-cut rationale for government intervention in a market economy. The market generally works, but not always, and in those cases government intervention can produce a better outcome. One shudders to think of what a satellite photo of the Amazon rainforest would look like today in the absence of the Brazilian government's forceful and effective measures to slow down deforestation. One particular form of market failure is that the market fails to produce or produce too little of certain goods that improve society's well-being. Such goods are called public goods, which refer to goods consumed by all members of the general public, as opposed to private goods which are consumed by individuals for their own private enjoyment. My consumption of a private good — e.g. a Big Mac [although the health conscious might view the iconic burger as a bad rather than a good] — directly reduces your consumption. On the other hand, my consumption of a public good does not reduce your consumption.

The classical example of a pure public good is national defense. A country's military protects all its citizens from the threat of invasion by foreign

"

One particular form of market failure is that the market fails to produce or produce too little of certain goods that improve society's well-being. Such goods are called public goods, which refer to goods consumed by all members of the general public, as opposed to private goods which are consumed by individuals for their own private enjoyment.

"

countries, regardless of whether they pay for it or not. There is a good reason why the government rather than the private sector provides national defense around the world. The private sector cannot compel citizens to pay for national defense, but the government can. It has the power of taxation, which obliges companies and households to pay taxes to finance the provision of public goods, such as national defense, that benefit everybody. Because we can enjoy national defense regardless of whether we pay or not, we have an incentive to let others pay for it and then freeride on their payment. Since this is true for every company and household, the predictable end result is that too little national defense will be provided, hurting everybody. The government's power of taxation solves this problem since it forces everybody to contribute to a good that benefits everybody.

Another good example of a public good is basic research and development (R&D). R&D is a vital economic activity since it is the foundation of invention and innovation, which leads to new products and technologies. There is an important distinction between basic research, which can enhance human knowledge but may not be directly applicable to the real world, versus applied research, which is more practical study that seeks to directly solve real-world problems. Example of basic research is advancing the frontiers of mathematics or physics theory. Examples of applied research include a self-driving car or a laptop with greater computing capacity. Private firms are more likely to pursue applied research, which results in profitable products and technologies. Furthermore, the social benefits of basic research — i.e. benefits to society as a whole — are much larger than its private benefits.[1] Yet the two types of research are closely intertwined because basic research is often the cornerstone of applied research.[2]

[1] This means that private firms that engage in basic R&D incur costs producing knowledge that will benefit all firms, including its competitors, which weakens their incentives to pursue basic R&D in the first place.

[2] For example, US government research funded by tax payers, some of it linked to national defense, played an indispensable role in the development of the internet. Of course, the private sector dominated subsequent commercial internet-based innovations such as search engines and social media.

Lack of profitability explains why most basic R&D is done by the government rather than the private sector, which concentrates on applied R&D.[3]

While the production of public goods such as national defense and basic R&D provides a compelling rationale for government intervention in a market economy, the boundary between public and private good is usually not so clear cut. There are only few examples of pure public goods, and most public goods are impure public goods which combine elements of both public good and private good. Take education for example. In most countries, the government provides education up to high school, and in some countries, it even provides university education. Yet it is not immediately obvious why this is the case. After all, I benefit from my own education, in the form of more knowledge and higher salaries. But of course children cannot pay for their own education since they are going to school — and hence do not work and make money.

So in the absence of free public education, children with poor parents would be deprived of the opportunity to get an education. Even the most hardcore laissez-faire, free market economist would agree that an education system in which only children blessed with better-off parents can go to school will inflict huge social and economic costs. For one, it will rob the society and economy of the talents and skills of youngsters who came out on the wrong end in the parental lottery. Furthermore, such a system will further entrench the transmission of poverty, as well as wealth, from generation to generation since education is one of the most important determinants of success in life. There is no inherent tradeoff between efficiency and equity here. A fairer society does not have to

[3] Nevertheless private companies undertake some basic research. Furthermore, in many countries, the private sector invests more in overall R&D than the government. In China, private sector R&D is four times larger than government R&D and in America, the ratio is 2.5. "From zero to not much more," The Economist, 4 June 2016.

settle for a smaller pie. In fact, the size of the pie will be bigger, and possibly much bigger, in a society where anybody with talent and drive, and not just the children of millionaires, can aspire to become the next Andrew Carnegie or Steve Jobs. A fairer society has a much larger pool of potential Andrew Carnegies or Steve Jobses, which will give rise to much greater scope for wealth and job creation.

There are thus some compelling arguments for why the government tends to be a dominant player in the education business. The arguments are much stronger for primary and secondary education since a society in which everybody at least knows their ABCs and 123s functions better than a society with large pockets of illiteracy and innumeracy. Hence a primary and secondary education benefits not only the student, but also society at large. On the other hand, a university education largely benefits the student, in the form of better job prospects and higher wage relative to a high school graduate. Therefore, there is no compelling rationale for the government to provide free university education, for the same reason that there is no compelling rationale for the government to provide automobiles.

The case for public universities is even weaker in advanced countries with well-developed financial systems. In those countries, students can and do borrow from banks and other financial institutions to finance their university education. The case for public universities is somewhat stronger in developing countries with underdeveloped financial systems where bright but disadvantaged students face much greater difficulties in financing their education. The failure of such students to go to universities not only imposes costs on the students themselves but also on society at large. Their unfulfilled

"

There are thus some compelling arguments for why the government tends to be a dominant player in the education business. The arguments are much stronger for primary and secondary education.

"

potential robs society of doctors, engineers, pilots, accountants, architects, and a whole range of other valuable skills. When an untalented kid blessed with rich parents takes the place of a talented kid stuck with poor parents at the medical school, the country gets a bad doctor instead of a good one. The consequent loss of skills is all the more damaging for developing countries which often suffer from a gaping shortage of skills.

"

When an untalented kid blessed with rich parents takes the place of a talented kid stuck with poor parents at the medical school, the country gets a bad doctor instead of a good one.

"

THE MYTH OF FREE HEALTH CARE

31

ealth care is another activity in which governments around the world are involved, to varying degrees. In some countries, the government is in the business of providing health care, and in some other countries, the government does not provide health care but provides health insurance. It is not obvious why the government should be in the health care business or health insurance business. After all, when I consult a doctor, receive treatment and medicine, or undergo a heart bypass surgery, I am the one who benefits and the only one who benefits. In that sense, the health care business is no different from the automobile business or the perfume business or the laptop business. One argument for government intervention in health care is that a society where everybody is healthy benefits all members of society, for example by preventing an epidemic of contagious diseases. Therefore, the government should provide health care to all, or so the argument goes. It is a lame argument.

A somewhat more convincing argument for government intervention rests on the notion that good health is a basic human right. Why should a poor person be deprived of access to basic medical services simply because he cannot pay

> "
> In some countries, the government is in the business of providing health care, and in some other countries, the government does not provide health care but provides health insurance. It is not obvious why the government should be in the health care business or health insurance business.
> "

135

for it? Equivalently, why should access to medical services be the exclusive preserve of the rich, powerful, and famous? But upon closer inspection, this superficially appealing argument suffers from a gaping logical hole that severely dents its credibility. The analogy comes from food. Surely, food is as much a basic human right as good health, if not even more so. Yet the government is not in the food business, at least not in most of the world. One might also argue that housing is a basic human right since everybody needs a roof over their heads. Yet the government is not in the housing business. Health care is essentially a service like any other service, not that much different from haircuts or beauty salons.

Instead of the government providing food for everybody, it is left for the individual in most countries to decide how much to eat and what to eat. Yes, there are government programs for the poor in both rich countries — e.g. food stamps in the US — and developing countries — e.g. subsidies for basic foods such as bread and rice in these countries. But the extent of government intervention in food is far less than in health care. There is an obvious explanation for this asymmetry. The middle class, which is the most active and influential group of voters, can easily afford food but the same is not true for health care. This is why subsidized food is not the political hot potato that subsidized health care is. The political dominance of the middle class also explains why the government subsidizes university education in many countries. What the middle class wants, the middle class usually gets, at least in a democracy.

Health care is costly, which explains why discussions about the appropriate role of the government in health care provoke such raw emotions, as evident in the heated debate over Obamacare. Universal health care, or even the much more limited objective of universal health

"

Health care is costly, which explains why discussions about the appropriate role of the government in health care provoke such raw emotions, as evident in the heated debate over Obamacare.

"

care insurance, requires a large amount of income redistribution from the rich to the poor. The tough truth about health care, which is widely viewed as a basic human right, is that, at the end of the day, somebody has to pay for it. Government's provision of health care and health care insurance may seem like free goods but that is purely an illusion. There is nothing free about free public health care, just as there is nothing free about free public education. Taxes are required to finance the government's provision of health care and the rich tend to pay the bulk of taxes in most economies. In addition to the burden of mindboggling paperwork that Obamacare imposes on businesses, especially small enterprises, it arouses such passionate opposition from its detractors because it is widely seen as the hardworking and fit having to pay for the medical bills of the lazy and unfit, as explained as follows.

The strongest case against publicly provided health care is that health is ultimately an individual's own responsibility. To a large extent, we can determine the state of our own health by what we eat, how much exercise we do, and how we live. Of course, there are other factors at play, in particular our good luck or bad luck in the genetic lottery. But nevertheless, it is ludicrous to suggest that our lifestyle, which is our and our choice alone, does not affect how healthy we are. Therefore, why should I pay for the obesity of an undisciplined glutton, or the lung cancer of a lifetime smoker, or the damaged liver of an alcoholic, or the psychological problems of a drug addict, or the toothache of a sweet-loving person? Any more than I should pay for the car accident of a reckless driver, or the unemployment of a lazy good-for-nothing bum, or the bankruptcy of an impulsive stock market speculator? If others pay for my undesirable behavior, that makes me more likely to engage in undesirable behavior in the first place.

> **"**
>
> The strongest case against publicly provided health care is that health is ultimately an individual's own responsibility. To a large extent, we can determine the state of our own health by what we eat, how much exercise we do, and how we live.
>
> **"**

BEST USE OF TAX PAYERS' MONEY 2, LIMITED GOVERNMENT BUDGETS, AND BOLSA FAMILIA

32

However, there are compelling grounds for government support for education and health care. In fact, as explained earlier, public education and health care are the best uses of tax payers' money since they promote equality of opportunity — i.e. level the playing field for the poor. They reduce the income gap between the rich and the poor, *and* promote economic growth. This explains why governments around the world support and, in some cases, provide education and health care. But it is important to remember that the government too has finite resources, just like households or companies. After all, the amount of taxes paid by tax payers is finite. What this means is that the government has to make some tough choices when it comes to spending tax payers' money, even on education and health care, the best use of tax payer's money.

In the case of education, the case for government intervention is much stronger for primary and secondary schools than it is for universities. A primary and secondary education is required to function as a useful member of a modern society — for example, most jobs require at least a secondary education to be an effective worker — and thus not impose a

> **"**
>
> ... public education and health care are the best uses of tax payers' money since they promote equality of opportunity — i.e. level the playing field for the poor. They reduce the income gap between the rich and the poor, *and* promote economic growth.... But it is important to remember that the government too has finite resources, just like households or companies.
>
> **"**

burden on the rest of society — e.g. chronically unemployed or career criminal. Similarly, the case for government intervention is strongest for basic public health care for the poor. For example, at relatively low cost, basic maternity significantly improves the chances of mother and baby surviving a new birth, and inoculation programs against contagious diseases like chicken pox and malaria protect public health. More generally, since better education and health care help the poor compete with the rich, it makes sense to target the poor in public support for education and health care. That is, there is a stronger case for helping the poor.

There are, however, unintended negative consequences from the government's involvement in the education and health care industries. In particular, government subsidies for health care and education, which are supposed to keep down the cost of these areas, often have the perverse effect of doing exactly the opposite. The costs of health care and education, in particular university education, have risen sharply across the world, both in absolute dollar amounts and in relative terms as share of GDP (gross domestic product). The worldwide escalation of health care and university costs is rooted in many causes — for example, the relentless advance of ever more sophisticated (and expensive) medical technology, and fierce competition among universities to attract students (e.g. the building of fancier facilities) which contributes to higher tuition fees.

It has to be noted that explosive growth of demand is also a major driver of higher costs. Demand growth, in turn, is partly driven by government subsidies that reduce the cost of education and health care. When students pay only part of the cost of attending university or when patients pay only part of the cost of going

> **There are, however, unintended negative consequences from the government's involvement in the education and health care industries. In particular, government subsidies for health care and education, which are supposed to keep down the cost of these areas, often have the perverse effect of doing exactly the opposite.**

139

to hospital, too many students go to universities and too many patients visit doctors. Even if the higher demand does not directly lead to higher prices, it can lead to too much demand and hence long queues — e.g. a year's wait or more for a simple medical procedure. There is clearly a potential for a vicious cycle of higher subsidies feeding higher prices, which result in yet more subsidies and yet higher prices. In principle, public support for education and health care is sensible and desirable. In practice, in light of government's limited budget, that support will be limited and best spent on programs that help the poor become healthier and better educated.

Two successful government programs that improved the education and health care of the poor without breaking the government's budget are Brazil's Bolsa Familia and Mexico's Oportunidades. Both are examples of ingenious programs known as conditional cash transfers or CCC, which give poor families a cash allowance or transfer in exchange for fulfilling certain conditions, and hence the term CCC. The condition usually pertains to education or health care. For example, the family can get the cash only if they get regular medical check-ups at clinics, vaccinate their children against major diseases, or send their children to schools. CCC can thus help to mitigate poverty in the short run and enable the poor, especially impoverished children, to become more productive workers in the long run. The balance of evidence indicates that well-run CCC such as Bolsa Familia and Oportunidades can make a substantial dent in poverty rates *and* improve education and health among the poor at relatively little cost to the government.

Overall, there is a compelling case for government support for education and health care, but it is by no means an unlimited case.

We all look to the government to support us with our ever-mounting school and hospital bills, but the government too has a finite budget. Therefore, the government should concentrate its limited resources on a selective basis on areas where the case for a government role is the strongest. In education, it is best to let the government focus on primary and secondary education, and to allow a great role for the private sector in university education. In health care, it is best for the government to significantly scale back its involvement and concentrate its smaller resources on providing basic health care, especially for the poor. But scaling back public education and health care will be politically difficult, not least because both are popular among voters, especially middle-class voters who tend to decide election outcomes.

"

Therefore, the government should concentrate its limited resources on a selective basis on areas where the case for a government role is the strongest.

"

$1-A-WEEK PRIVATE SCHOOLS, MATHARE SLUM IN KENYA, AND PABLO ESCOBAR

33

One especially potent reason for the government to limit its involvement in health care and especially education is quality. Many well-to-do parents in high- and middle-income countries have been sending their children to private schools for years. They do so despite paying the taxes that finance the public schools. The reason is simple — the often-abysmal quality of public education. Since education is such an important determinant of success in life, parents are absolutely rational in giving their children the best possible education, if they can afford it. More often than not, avoiding public schools is not merely a matter of avoiding second best; instead it is avoiding the unacceptable, abysmal worst. In some public schools, there are even legitimate concerns about the safety of their children, let alone how much they learn. Sending those children to private schools is not just a matter of giving them a better education; it can be a matter of keeping them safe and alive.

Surprisingly, the demand for private schools is not limited to middle-class parents and students fed up with lousy public schools. In fact, private schools are booming in poor countries with

> **"**
>
> Many well-to-do parents in high- and middle-income countries have been sending their children to private schools for years. They do so despite paying the taxes that finance the public schools. The reason is simple — the often-abysmal quality of public education.
>
> **"**

weak governments that fail to provide even the most basic services such as education. Take, for example, Mathare, a slum of half a million people in Nairobi, the main city of Kenya in Africa. Mathare, Nairobi had just four public schools in August 2015, but no fewer than 120 private schools.[1] And, Mathare is not alone. The pattern of the private sector providing education when the government fails to do so is repeated across Africa, Middle East and South Asia. Most private schools in poor countries are single operators that charge the students a few dollars a month, but chains are now emerging. Bill Gates and Mark Zuckerberg are investors in one such chain, Bridge International Academies. You might think that governments would at least have the decency to welcome private schools which fill the void created by their own incompetence and corruption. But you would be wrong. The response of poor-country governments to private schools has ranged from indifference to hostility. Scandalous.

The example of successful private schools in poor countries which suffer from large-scale government failure illustrates an important point. Governments can support basic services such as health care and education without actually producing those services. Government can fund the production of services but leave their production to the private sector. If the government is terrible at providing health care, education, or other basic services, as is often the case, especially in developing countries but also in advanced countries, it is better for the government to give money to poor households and offer them the choice of a number of private sector providers. This is the basic idea behind the school voucher program in the US. In the case of Kenya and other developing countries, private schools entail a number of tangible

[1] http://www.economist.com/news/leaders/21660113-private-schools-are-booming-poor-countries-governments-should-either-help-them-or-get-out

benefits. They bring in private capital, often offer better value for money for the students than public schools, and tend to be more innovative.

What is even more galling than the rock-bottom quality of education at many public schools across the world is the strident opposition of the public-school establishment to any efforts to improve it. Teachers' unions fight tooth and nail against any efforts to give students more choice — for example, the school voucher system — and make their performance more accountable — for example, firing the teachers with perennially poor teaching evaluations. The vigorous resistance is good for teachers' job security, but bad for the children's education. Of course, it would be grossly unfair to blame the abysmal performance of many public schools entirely on teachers and the educational establishment. A massive contributor to the massive failure of public education in the US and elsewhere is massive parental indifference. If your parents don't care whether you go to your classes or not, it is hard to see why others, including your teachers, could or should care about what you do with your life.

Poor quality of services provided by the government is by no means limited to education. In many countries, the cost of medical care is superficially cheap because it is heavily subsidized by the government. The low cost is superficial for a couple of reasons. First, citizens pay the taxes that finance the subsidies. When the government of a generous European welfare state provides free health care to its pampered citizens, there is nothing free about that health care, which is financed by high taxes hoisted on those same pampered citizens. Second, and more seriously, the superficially low cost comes at the cost of lower quality. More specifically, too much demand at the

> **"**
>
> What is even more galling than the rock-bottom quality of education at many public schools across the world is the strident opposition of the public-school establishment to any efforts to improve it. Teachers' unions fight tooth and nail against any efforts to give students more choice — for example, the school voucher system — and make their performance more accountable — for example, firing the teachers with perennially poor teaching evaluations.
>
> **"**

low price results in shortage — i.e. too many patients chasing after too few doctors. Horror stories abound about long queues and hence prolonged waiting periods for relatively simple procedures, sometimes even resulting in deaths. Crucially, when the government foots most of the medical bill, patients are encouraged to consume excessive medical care — for example, undergoing procedures or surgeries which they would not undergo if they had to pay a larger share of the cost.

The failure of the government to provide services of acceptable quality extends to other spheres as well. In many developing countries, the wealthy hire private security to protect their life and property in light of the incompetence and venality of the police. There is simply no trust in their ability or integrity. In fact, poorly paid officers are often crooks themselves, albeit usually low-ranking employees of big-time career criminals. In many drug-infested countries of Latin America, so many police officers are in the payroll of the drug lords that the US Drug Enforcement Administration (DEA) often works with the local army instead in its pointless anti-drug offensives. Given the meager pay of the police officers and the huge amount of cash that the drug lords have, it is difficult to blame the cops for taking the bribes. Indeed in some drug-infested countries, the entire law and order system is rotten to the core, and it is impossible to distinguish cops from crooks.

Needless to say, many military officers are also on the drug lords' payroll although the degree of infestation tends to be lower. Busting a cartel or two may be good for publicity purposes, especially for showing that the government is doing something about the drug problem, but it is pointless as the flow of drugs will not stop until the voracious US demand for drugs dries

> **"**
> The failure of the government to provide services of acceptable quality extends to other spheres as well. In many developing countries, the wealthy hire private security to protect their life and property in light of the incompetence and venality of the police.
> **"**

up. Seemingly infinite demand in the US and hence guaranteed high profits mean that for every drug lord who is gunned down or goes to jail, there are hundreds, if not thousands, who are willing to die to take his place. Without any serious efforts to tackle demand, the US-led war on drugs is doomed to fail. One school of thought calls for liberalizing the illegal drug industry, since the illegal nature of the industry and hence high risk account for its rich profits. By liberalizing cocaine, heroin, marijuana, and other drugs, their price would drop, the industry would not be so profitable, and there will be fewer Pablo Escobars, or so the argument goes. While this argument has some merits, it fails to consider the increase in demand due to lower price, and hence many more drug-crazed school bus drivers ferrying our children.

"

Without any serious efforts to tackle demand, the US-led war on drugs is doomed to fail. One school of thought calls for liberalizing the illegal drug industry, since the illegal nature of the industry and hence high risk account for its rich profits.

"

FAILED STATES, GENOCIDAL GOVERNMENTS, BOKO HARAM, AND BASHAR ASSAD

34

Yet the government's production of goods and services is not limited to goods and services for which there are at least some plausible economic grounds for a government role. Governments around the world produce a bewildering variety of goods and services, many, if not most, of which leave us scratching our heads and wondering why the government, rather than the private sector, is producing them. As pointed out earlier, the case for government intervention is greatest for pure public goods such as national defense or police forces. Even here the government sometimes fails miserably — notice the initial failure of the Iraqi armed forces to protect its own citizens from the advent of the jihadist group IS (Islamic State) which took over large swathes of Iraq, including the second largest city of Mosul, before they recovered to defeat IS and reassert control over lost territory. Perhaps the best definition of a failed state is a state that fails to provide even the most basic services, such as a minimum level of protection from violence.

By that reasonable definition, many countries of the world are failed states, far more than just the well-known cases such as Afghanistan, Libya and Somalia. Not many observers view

> "
> **Governments around the world produce a bewildering variety of goods and services, many, if not most, of which leave us scratching our heads and wondering why the government, rather than the private sector, is producing them.**
> "

147

corrupt, inefficient, oil-rich Nigeria — Africa's largest economy — as a failed state, although far fewer view it as a successful state. Yet if the glaring failure of Nigerian armed forces to protect Nigerian citizens from a ragtag jihadist militia calling itself the Boko Haram is not an example of a failed state, I do not know what is. The earlier example of the Kenyan government providing just four public schools for 500,000 people also represents abysmal failure of the state. The virtual capture of Mexico's law enforcement authorities and other parts of the Mexican government by the drug cartels, as well as the senseless, gruesome drug-related violence that terrorizes and paralyzes large swathes of the country illustrate another example of utter government failure, in a country that is much richer and more developed than Nigeria.

Predictably, citizens form their own armed forces to protect their lives and properties when the government fails to do so. This is what Kurds in the northern Syrian city of Kobane have done — their efforts to fend off and eventually beat back the IS made global news headlines almost daily. Even worse, governments sometimes become the source of violence, let alone protect citizens from violence. While the Syrian government run by Bashar Assad was conspicuously missing from Kobane, it is very much in action in other parts of the country, bombing, shooting, mutilating, raping, and even gassing its own citizens. History is replete with episodes of the government using its armed forces to slaughter its own citizens, women and children included, and today's Syria is by no means alone in that regard.

Some of the worst government-perpetrated mass murders of civilians in the 20th century include Joseph Stalin's forced famine in the Ukraine in the early 1930s, Mao Zedong's Great Leap Forward economic and social campaign of the late 1950s

"

Yet if the glaring failure of Nigerian armed forces to protect Nigerian citizens from a ragtag jihadist militia calling itself the Boko Haram is not an example of a failed state, I do not know what is. The earlier example of the Kenyan government providing just four public schools for 500,000 people also represents abysmal failure of the state.

"

and early 1960s, the Nazi Holocaust unleashed upon Europe's Jews, the Ottoman mass slaughter of its Armenian inhabitants, the Cambodian genocide perpetrated by Pol Pot's lunatic fringe regime, the genocidal ethnic cleansing in Rwanda in 1994, the Bosnian genocide of the early 1990s, and the genocide in the Darfur region of Sudan. In terms of sheer numbers, the worst was the Great Leap Forward, an ill-advised campaign to turn private farms into collective farms and industrialize the Chinese countryside as quickly as possible, that killed between 18 and 45 million, a staggering number. Regardless of the numbers killed, all government-sponsored acts of violence — and the above list is far from exhaustive — are repulsive, morally wrong, and unforgivable.

Another contemporary example of a bloodthirsty government butchering its own citizens comes from Syria's next door neighbor, Iraq. While Saddam Hussein's Iraq is today viewed as some kind of paradise in light of the quagmire that it has become since the US military intervention, it should be remembered that the dictator was no teddy bear. Just one grisly example of his government's tendency to attack its own citizens is the Halabja chemical attacks, perpetrated by Saddam's forces against their ethnic Kurdish fellow citizens in March 1988. The attack left as many as 5,000 people dead and remains the worst chemical attack on civilians in history. Another disgusting example is the penchant of Uday Hussein, Saddam's son, to randomly pick any woman he fancied, even a newlywed bride, and rape and kill her. Whatever one's view of the US military intervention in Iraq — and there are plenty of reasons why it was a terrible mistake — it is highly unlikely that Iraq would be a better place now if the US had never intervened. Criticizing the war is fine, but glorifying Saddam's Iraq, as many anti-war critics tend to do, is ignorant, unconscionable, and inexcusable nonsense.

> **"**
> Regardless of the numbers killed, all government-sponsored acts of violence — and the above list is far from exhaustive — are repulsive, morally wrong, and unforgivable.
> **"**

FAILING AIRLINES, STRIKING PILOTS, AND BLOATED STATE COMPANY PAYROLLS

Going back to the issue of government production, the tentacles of government production often extend to a wide range of goods and services well beyond those for which there is any remotely plausible justification for government production. For example, until quite recently, many governments around the world, including those in rich countries, owned and ran the telecoms and airlines industries of their countries. Many still do. Yet it is not obvious, even remotely, why the government should be in the business of flying passengers and cargo or in the business of connecting people via mobile or fixed line telephone services. It is no accident that government-owned airlines, the French national flag carrier Air France to name just one, make losses year after year after year, yet they keep on flying. In September 2014, when the airline was barely emerging from almost a decade of losses, Air France pilots went on a two-week strike, forcing the cancelation of 8,500 flights and disrupting the travel plans of more than 1 million passengers, and costing the airline more than US$400 million.[1] More recently, in May 2018, the airline's chief executive resigned in response to the trade union's impossible wage demands which

[1] http://www.nytimes.com/2014/10/09/business/international/air-france-puts-cost-of-pilots-strike-at-more-than-400-million.html?_r=0

made the airline unmanageable.[2] What keeps unprofitable, inefficient state-owned airlines flying in the face of seemingly endless losses are government bailouts financed by tax payers.

More fundamentally, and ironically, it is precisely the promise of such bailouts — that is, implicit guarantees by the government to come to the rescue when the company faces bankruptcy — that makes the bailouts necessary in the first place. Faced with mounting losses, a private sector company would make some big changes to improve the bottom line. In the case of airlines, this would involve shutting down marginal, unprofitable routes with too few passengers. More fundamentally, a tried and tested private sector response to poor corporate performance is to cut a bloated workforce — too many pilots, flight attendants, and ground staff — as well as excessive wages and benefits — too many pilots, flight attendants, and ground staff earning wages and benefits that outpace the growth of their productivity. Wages outpacing productivity — the amount of airline services produced by a worker — obviously spells trouble for the airline. If the unsustainable trend continues, the airline will be unable to pay its workers, let alone invest in new aircraft and other equipment it needs to compete with other airlines.

While a bloated workforce earning excessive wages and benefits is certainly not the only cause of poor corporate performance, it tends to be a hallmark of government-owned or government-linked companies such as Air France. In stark contrast to private sector companies who must answer to their shareholders, government companies are answerable only to the government, and that is the crux of the problem. Shareholders constantly demand superior performance from

[2] https://www.economist.com/gulliver/2018/05/10/air-france-klm-is-being-brought-to-its-knees-by-its-unions

the management, and management teams that do not deliver good results are sacked. The relentless pressure faced by corporate management from their shareholders does not leave much room for slack, and it certainly does not leave any room for chronic losses and a bloated, overpaid workforce.

The government, on the other hand, is not accountable to anybody but itself. Unlike private sector companies, which try to maximize profits, the primary objective of government companies is usually not profit. Instead, it is usually some vague and ill-defined public interest. For example, a presumed need for a national flag carrier motivated the establishment of government-owned airlines in many countries. Yet it is not clear why each country needs a national flag carrier and, even if that were the case, why that national flag carrier needs to be run by the government. An equally puzzling argument for why the government needs to be in the airline business — an argument that is especially relevant for large countries — is to provide air services to remote areas. It is not clear why you would need an entire full-service airline to do this, when a few light aircraft can do the job.

The lack of a clear profit motive means that there is no compelling incentive for an unprofitable government-owned company to lay off workers even when a bloated, overpaid workforce is a big reason that the company is losing money. It also means that the kind of radical corporate surgery which is required to revive an ailing company is out of the question for a government company because it is much more difficult to fire pampered government company workers than to sack private company workers. The reason it is difficult to fire government company workers is that it is a political issue. The workers of

"

The lack of a clear profit motive means that there is no compelling incentive for an unprofitable government-owned company to lay off workers even when a bloated, overpaid workforce is a big reason that the company is losing money.

"

government companies are, in effect, public sector workers, not that much different from government officials, school teachers, and policemen.

Moreover, public sector workers typically enjoy a much higher level of job security than their counterparts in the private sector. The risk of being laid off is much higher for, say, a Delta Airlines pilot, than it is for, say, an Air France pilot. Firing government workers or the workers of government-owned companies is politically costly for politicians, which is why politicians of all stripes hesitate to fire them. It also explains why it is politically difficult, if not impossible, to shrink a bloated public sector and why the relative size of the government — measured by the ratio of government spending to GDP (gross domestic product) — has grown in many countries, both rich and poor, across the world. Government spending and public sector employment is like toothpaste — once it comes out, it is awfully tough to put it back in. The huge political cost of firing public sector workers makes it almost impossible. In principle, this is a good reason to be careful about expanding public sector employment in the first place. But, in practice, jobs mean votes.

Furthermore, in many economically stagnant developing countries like those in the Middle East, public sector is the *only* source of jobs — employer of last resort — especially for college graduates, and a major form of political patronage. The civil servants of such bloated public sectors, with too much time on their hands and too little work to do, spend much of their ample time devising additional rules and regulations, which further snuff the life out of their lifeless private sectors. And, where there are pointless, irksome rules and regulations, there are hordes of petty bureaucrats with open

"

Firing government workers or the workers of government-owned companies is politically costly for politicians, which is why politicians of all stripes hesitate to fire them. It also explains why it is politically difficult, if not impossible, to shrink a bloated public sector.

"

153

palms to be greased. There is an obvious vicious cycle here. A bloated, unproductive public sector with too many nose-picking bureaucrats strangles the progress of the private sector with overregulation and bribery demands. The stunted private sector, in turn, generates too few jobs, which, in turn, further bloats the public sector since the government is the employer of last resort. This is also a fairly accurate description of pre-crisis Greece, where tourism and the government were the only two growth industries. A bloated public sector workforce enjoying bloated pay and benefits is not, most definitely not, a recipe for economic vitality and dynamism.

Just as it is politically difficult, if not impossible, to cut back a bloated public sector, it is equally difficult to get the government out of an industry — for example, the airline industry — once it gets into it. This explains why privatization, or selling a government-owned company to the private sector, is at best a fraught, painful process. The reason is simple — the workers of that government-owned airline will fight tooth and nail to prevent the privatization of their airline since they know that privatization means job losses and pay cuts. Most governments are unwilling and unable to face the political costs of privatization, and the airline remains in government hands. Therefore, even if there is no remotely plausible basis for government's production of a particular good, once it starts producing that good, it will continue to do so, no matter how inefficient and unprofitable it is. Government production is like toothpaste, impossible to put back once it comes out. Only a great deal of political courage will stop the madness.

> **"**
>
> Therefore, even if there is no remotely plausible basis for government's production of a particular good, once it starts producing that good, it will continue to do so, no matter how inefficient and unprofitable it is. Government production is like toothpaste, impossible to put back once it comes out. Only a great deal of political courage will stop the madness.
>
> **"**

FIRING GOVERNMENT WORKERS

Unlike the private sector, where hiring and firing workers ultimately depends on their productivity — i.e. how much they contribute to the company's profits — public sector employment often depends on political considerations. More specifically, political leaders, whose top priority is to maximize votes rather than profits, are reluctant to fire workers because doing so creates a political backlash and costs votes. What is more, in many countries around the world, not only in poor countries but even in many rich countries, a job in the public sector is a prevalent form of political patronage, doled out as gifts in exchange for political support. Horror stories abound — dead people collecting government salaries or pensions, infants and children doing the same, so-called government workers — so-called because they do not do any work whatsoever — drawing salaries for two jobs while not even bothering to show up at either, and so forth. The amount of wasted, misused and stolen tax payers' money is often staggering.

The point of all this is not that all government workers are all lazy, unproductive, and discourteous slackers. Plenty of them fit that bill — yes, we all experienced the rude, gum-chewing,

> "Horror stories abound — dead people collecting government salaries or pensions, infants and children doing the same, so-called government workers — so-called because they do not do any work whatsoever — drawing salaries for two jobs while not even bothering to show up at either, and so forth. The amount of wasted, misused and stolen tax payers' money is often staggering."

155

gossiping-on-the-phone, eye-rolling low-level government bureaucrat telling you "you are in the wrong line" 45 minutes after you were told exactly the same thing by another rude, gum-chewing, gossiping-on-the-phone, eye-rolling low-level government bureaucrat. Or, an immigration officer at the airport in some miserable Third World country who derives perverse pleasure from taking 20 minutes to stamp a single passport, endlessly asking stupid, irrelevant, prying questions, as if entering the God-forsaken dump is some kind of a God-given privilege. This is more than a matter of irritation as it imposes some serious costs, such as missed connecting flights. Of course, some immigration officers at the airports of rich countries can be equally rude, incompetent and exasperating, especially toward visitors from developing countries.

To be fair, there are plenty of private sector workers who are equally lazy, unproductive, and discourteous. Many of them have their jobs only because their father or uncle or brother or sister or friend is the CEO (chief executive officer). Furthermore, there are plenty of honest, hardworking, intelligent, capable, and dedicated government workers who do their jobs very well. In fact, we are only too grateful when a street cop saves us from a violent thug who is about to empty us of our wallets or inflict some serious damage to our bodies or both, or when courageous firefighters jump into hellish fire to save an infant, or when soldiers fight terrorists in distant lands to protect our national security. So clearly, the public sector does not have a monopoly on lazy, rude, and incompetent workers, nor does the private sector have a monopoly on hardworking, courteous, and competent workers. Moreover, both sectors have their share of capable, dedicated and industrious workers who go out of their way to serve their clients.

"

To be fair, there are plenty of private sector workers who are equally lazy, unproductive, and discourteous. Many of them have their jobs only because their father or uncle or brother or sister or friend is the CEO (chief executive officer). Furthermore, there are plenty of honest, hardworking, intelligent, capable, and dedicated government workers who do their jobs very well.

"

But where the public sector and private sector differ, and this is a huge difference, is that it is much harder to lay off poor performers in the public sector than in the private sector. Firing workers, including CEOs and managers, is always an unpleasant and harsh exercise, especially for the fired workers themselves, but it is absolutely necessary for the health of companies and the broader economy. It is precisely the threat of being laid off is what keeps workers on their toes and induces them to give at least a minimum level of effort and performance. It is exactly the same threat that gives incentives to CEOs and managers to manage their companies well. Letting redundant workers go from declining industries and companies frees them up for thriving industries and companies which face shortages of workers. Of course, the redeployment of workers is not seamless, and often requires the workers to acquire new skills through training and retraining. Nevertheless, flexible movement of labor in response to the rise and fall of firms and industries is the lifeblood of a dynamic economy.

Furthermore, the economy is in a constant state of flux due to the process of Schumpeterian creative destruction in which existing products and technologies are made obsolete by new and better products and technologies. In a dynamic successful economy new, innovative companies and industries constantly challenge and replace old, stagnant ones. Workers and other resources flow relatively smoothly from dying economic activities to emerging ones in such an economy. If labor laws and regulations make it difficult for employers to fire workers, they will not hire too many workers in the first place, except temporary and part-time workers. Therefore, overly restrictive labor laws and regulations are not only bad for employers; somewhat paradoxically, they are bad for

"

Firing workers, including CEOs and managers, is always an unpleasant and harsh exercise, especially for the fired workers themselves, but it is absolutely necessary for the health of companies and the broader economy.... Letting redundant workers go from declining industries and companies frees them up for thriving industries and companies which face shortages of workers.

"

workers too. They undermine economic activity, and they hurt employment.

This is why flexible labor markets are critical for economic dynamism and entrepreneurial capitalism. Such markets are also good for workers because they generate more jobs over time, even though it will not seem like that for the horse cart builder who had just been laid off due to the automobile or the library cataloguer who was made redundant by Google. But the economy is much bigger and there are more jobs in a world of automobiles and Google than in a world of horse carts and library catalogues. Imagine that you are paid the same salary regardless of how hard you work or how well you do your job. In such a world, you have absolutely no reason to work hard or do your job well. Yet public sector workers — blue collar, white collar, and management — work precisely in that kind of a world. Furthermore, militant trade unions often protect the interests of public sector workers who enjoy a degree of job security that their private sector counterparts can only dream of. The influence of coddled public workers is especially pernicious in the education industry.

ff

This is why flexible labor markets are critical for economic dynamism and entrepreneurial capitalism.... Furthermore, militant trade unions often protect the interests of public sector workers who enjoy a degree of job security that their private sector counterparts can only dream of. The influence of coddled public workers is especially pernicious in the education industry.

jj

TOXIC PUBLIC SCHOOLS, TOXIC TEACHERS' UNIONS, AND THEIR HARMFUL IMPACT ON INEQUALITY

37

The consequences are predictably toxic, especially for students, in both advanced countries such as the US and developing countries such as Mexico. In both groups of countries, public school teachers are the single biggest obstacle to education reform. Good teachers who can effectively communicate knowledge to their students are indispensable for good schools. Top-class computer labs, science labs, gyms, and other facilities all help make learning more enjoyable, but they are simply no substitute for knowledgeable, dedicated teachers who want to teach and who are good at teaching. Online teaching, videoconferencing, and other remote teaching platforms have come a long way but they will never be the same as in-person classroom teaching. Yet ironically teachers stand in the way of better schools and a better education. In the US, for example, politically powerful public school teachers oppose education reforms tooth and nail in order to protect their narrow self-interest.

More specifically, they vociferously oppose the widely touted proposal of giving school vouchers to parents so they can choose the best school for their children. The idea behind school choice

" In both advanced and developing countries, public school teachers are the single biggest obstacle to education reform.... In the US, for example, politically powerful public school teachers oppose education reforms tooth and nail in order to protect their narrow self-interest. **"**

is to force schools to compete with each so that good schools and good teachers will be rewarded, and bad school and bad teachers will be weeded out. Good for the students but bad for the teachers, which is why teachers fight school choice as if their lives depended on it. Selfish self-interest also explains why teachers are stridently opposed to proposals to limit tenure — or the privilege of working for life — to teachers who can actually teach. It also explains their tooth and nail opposition to merit pay — or paying more to better teachers. The unsurprising end result is a race to the bottom or dumbing down of the US public education system. No wonder that upper middle-class US parents, and even many middle-class US parents scramble to send their children to private schools. In fact, given the abysmal overall quality of public education, sending children to private schools has become a twisted kind of litmus test for whether parents love their children. So better off parents give public schools a miss despite the fact that they pay the bulk of the taxes that finance those schools.

Again, to be fair, there are plenty of dedicated and hardworking public school teachers who excel in the classroom and genuinely care about their students. Most of us who went to public schools remember a teacher or two who made a lasting positive difference in our lives. But surely, if public school teachers spent more time preparing for their classes and less time defending their narrow-vested self-interests, the quality of public education would improve greatly. Although the quality of public education is bad enough in the US, it is often much worse and outright abysmal in developing countries like Mexico. Not surprisingly, the crux of the problem is militant teachers' unions who fight tooth and nail for their pay and benefits, but do not show anywhere near the same level of passion or

"

But surely, if public school teachers spent more time preparing for their classes and less time defending their narrow-vested self-interests, the quality of public education would improve greatly. Although the quality of public education is bad enough in the US, it is often much worse and outright abysmal in developing countries like Mexico.

"

enthusiasm for teaching their students. Their violent strikes, which often paralyze entire cities, deter the Mexican government from embarking on any meaningful reform.

In fact, education reform is a central pillar of Mexican President Enrique Peña Nieto's strategy to improve the competitiveness of the Mexican economy. Mexican teachers currently enjoy a plethora of benefits and more than 500 days of pay for 200 days of school.[1] The reform plan includes sensible but hardly earthshattering measures such as exposing teachers to independent evaluation and sacking teachers who fail to show up for three consecutive days without any valid reason. Unfortunately for Mexican students, the reform has predictably provoked a maelstrom of violent protests from the teachers' unions,[2] and the Mexican government is having second thoughts about reform. Equally predictably, and unfortunately for the Mexican economy, Mexican students do very poorly in basic reading, writing, and math tests compared to students in other countries. For example, less than 20% of Mexican students performed adequately in 2012, compared to more than 75% in South Korea. Bad teachers and bad education is a big reason why Mexico and the rest of Latin America, in contrast to South Korea and other East Asian tigers, remain mired in the middle-income trap, despite the huge advantage of proximity to the US market.

In short, teachers' trade unions have a bad reputation in both the advanced and developing countries, and with good reason. Somewhat ironically, they are often bedrocks of support for left-leaning political parties. In the US, for example, teachers' unions are a reliable source of votes and political support for the Democrats. Ironical because left-wing political parties are, in principle at least, devoted to improving the lot of

[1] "Flunking the test," The Economist, 7 March 2015, http://www.economist.com/news/americas/21645748-failing-schools-pose-big-challenge-president-enrique-penietos-vision-modernising

[2] "A battle to feed young minds," The Economist, 9 July 2016.

the poor and reducing the income gap between the rich and the poor. But the selfish actions of teachers' unions, which are geared toward protecting teacher interests at the expense of student interests, make inequality worse rather than better by widening the education gap between rich children and poor children. Public education is the most powerful tool for the poor to catch up with the rich, but the narrow self-interest of public school teachers worsens the quality of public education and hence the effectiveness of the equity-promoting tool.

Education is the single most important means of social and economic mobility, moving up in the world. Unlike rich children, poor children do not have the option of escaping dismal public schools by going to private schools. It is scandalous that the selfishness of lousy teachers whose main objective is not to teach, but to protect their jobs, hobbles the life prospects of poor children. It is even more scandalous that supposedly pro-poor leftist political parties help those teachers whose selfishness strangles the ability of the poor to improve their life chances. If they truly care about the poor, they should be at the very forefront of public education reform. Instead, in the US and other countries, the support for school vouchers that poor parents can use to send their children to private schools and other education reform comes largely from conservative or right-wing political parties. But education reform is not a right-wing or left-wing issue. All political parties should stand strongly united behind education reform.

"

Education is the single most important means of social and economic mobility, moving up in the world. Unlike rich children, poor children do not have the option of escaping dismal public schools by going to private schools. It is scandalous that the selfishness of lousy teachers whose main objective is not to teach, but to protect their jobs, hobbles the life prospects of poor children.

"

LAZY UNCARING PARENTS, FINLAND'S WORLD-CLASS EDUCATION SYSTEM, AND TEACH FOR AMERICA

38

Public education matters greatly not only for equity — i.e. the income gap between the haves and have-nots, or how fairly the pie is divided up among the citizens of a country — but also for economic growth — i.e. how fast the size of the pie grows over time. The larger the pie, the more there is to be divided up between all citizens. Imagine two countries which are identical in every respect except the skill and knowledge level of their workers. For example, suppose in one country, all workers know their ABCs and 123s while only half the workers do in the other country. Needless to say, the country where all workers are literate and numerate will be far richer than the country where only half the workers are. More generally, human capital — i.e. the skills and knowledge of the workforce — matters at least as much as, and probably more, much more than, physical capital — i.e. factories, machines, and roads — in determining a country's living standards. For example, Germany and Japan were reduced to rubble at the end of the Second World War, but were able to rebuild their economies quickly due to high levels of human capital. The biggest contribution of the government to any economy, rich or poor, is to provide high-quality public education.

> **"**
> ... Germany and Japan were reduced to rubble at the end of the Second World War, but were able to rebuild their economies quickly due to high levels of human capital. The biggest contribution of the government to any economy, rich or poor, is to provide high-quality public education.
> **"**

163

Finally, there are a couple of critical points about education that we should never lose sight of. First, parents who care about their children and parents who actively contribute to the education of their children are vital to the education process. Too many parents these days are too busy to learn about, or even interested in learning about, the lives and dreams of their own children. Yet parents sharing their experiences and knowledge with their children, or just communicating with their children, can be as valuable to their growth and development as what they learn in the classroom. This explains why children from broken homes or otherwise unstable families tend to do worse with their lives than children from stable families with two parents. In the US, for example, one big reason that black American children tend to lag white American children in school and later in life is the fragility of the black family. While black underperformance has a number of social and economic causes, including deeply ingrained racism, especially evident among some police officers, any solution to closing the gap between black and white Americans must involve strengthening the fabric of the black family. That, much more than the tired practice of blaming anything and everything on racism and oppression, will empower black America. Before blaming children gone wrong on bad teachers and bad schools alone, parents should take a good look at the mirror and ask themselves what kind of a job they are doing as parents.

Second, at the end of the day, the quality of schools and education system is determined by the quality of teachers rather than the quality of the buildings and other hardware. Teachers who know their subjects well, and who can communicate their knowledge to their students — this is the one indispensable ingredient of a good school and a good education system. No

"

... parents who care about their children and parents who actively contribute to the education of their children are vital to the education process. Too many parents these days are too busy to learn about, or even interested in learning about, the lives and dreams of their own children.... At the end of the day, the quality of schools and education system is determined by the quality of teachers rather than the quality of the buildings and other hardware.

"

amount of advanced lab equipment, state-of-the-art computers, or space age gym facilities can make up for lazy, incompetent and uncaring teachers who do not know their stuff and, the little they know, they cannot properly teach their students. But the truth is that in most countries, teaching at the primary and secondary levels is not a well-respected, well regarded, or well-paid profession. Such widespread disrespect for teaching is epitomized by the dictum "Those who can, do, and those who can't, teach." In this kind of environment, it is unrealistic to expect the teaching profession to attract the best and the brightest.

Finland is one of the few countries where teaching is a well-respected profession which attracts well-qualified, highly motivated people, and is looked up upon by the whole population. This goes a long way toward explaining why Finnish students consistently perform near the top of PISA (Programme for International Student Assessment) tests, a set of standardized tests which allows for international comparison of student performance in core subjects such as mathematics and sciences. Related to this, Finland also consistently performs well in international comparisons of invention and innovation. While Nokia may have come and gone, there are plenty of creative and innovative Finnish firms that have offset the decline of the Finnish telecom equipment maker that once dominated global hand phone markets and accounted for more than 20% of Finland's GDP (gross domestic product). But Finland is very much the rare exception rather than the rule.

While selfish public school teachers and their trade unions are indeed bad news for students, economic growth, and equity, there is a more fundamental problem — that of attracting capable, motivated, energetic young people

"

Finland is one of the few countries where teaching is a well-respected profession which attracts well-qualified, highly motivated people, and is looked up upon by the whole population. This goes a long way toward explaining why Finnish students consistently perform near the top of PISA (Programme for International Student Assessment) tests.

"

to the teaching profession, and retaining their interest in the job. The dearth of high-quality teachers helps to explain why private tutors with a good reputation do well financially. In South Korea, for example, where intensely college entrance exams determine one's life chances, and a few points can mean the difference between getting into a top-tier university versus getting into a middle-of-the-pack university, cram school teachers who deliver top scores for their students easily make a not-so-small fortune. This state of affairs clearly tilts the field in favor of well-off students.

Innovative initiatives such as Teach for America or Teach for China can help improve the quality of teaching. The two programs and similar programs in other countries place recent graduates from top universities as teachers at schools in low-income, disadvantaged communities. But much more fundamentally, what is required is an overall societal environment which values learning and knowledge. In other words, what is required is a society which accords teachers a measure of respect and recognition, and a society where teachers feel they are doing something socially worthwhile, even if they will never make more than a tiny fraction of what an investment banker at Goldman Sachs or J.P. Morgan will make. Even if the monetary rewards of teaching are relatively small, teachers will teach better in a society that values teaching and appreciates the sacrifices and contributions that teachers make.

"

But much more fundamentally, what is required is an overall societal environment which values learning and knowledge. In other words, what is required is a society which accords teachers a measure of respect and recognition, and a society where teachers feel they are doing something socially worthwhile, even if they will never make more than a tiny fraction of what an investment banker at Goldman Sachs or J.P. Morgan will make.

"

IRON CURTAIN, GOVERNMENT PRODUCTION OF GOODS AND SERVICES, AND THE EAST ASIAN MIRACLE

39

Our discussion so far suggests that the private sector is inherently better at producing goods and services than the government. Common sense alone tells us that entrepreneurs motivated by the desire to make money are better at producing goods and services than bureaucrats who face no such compelling incentives. With a few exceptions such as national defense, this is generally true. While Ronald Reagan and his hawkish national defense policy are widely credited as having ended the Cold War, the West's victory was due to its vastly superior economic system. It was the night-and-day contrast in material well-being between the two sides of the Iron Curtain, not tanks and fighter jets, which brought about the downfall of the Berlin Wall, the Soviet Union, and communism. Once the masses on the wrong side of the Iron Curtain saw how the masses on the other side lived, it was curtains for the Iron Curtain. Capitalism is such a patently superior system for producing goods and services and delivering higher living standards than socialism that it needs no repetition here.

Even a visitor from outer space would have immediately noticed the difference in the quantity, quality and variety of groceries sold

> " Common sense alone tells us that entrepreneurs motivated by the desire to make money are better at producing goods and services than bureaucrats who face no such compelling incentives.... Once the masses on the wrong side of the Iron Curtain saw how the masses on the other side lived, it was curtains for the Iron Curtain. "

at a supermarket in West Germany versus East Germany, or South Korea versus North Korea. The sheer bankruptcy of socialism as an economic system was evident not only in shortages of goods, but perhaps even more in the mind-numbing drabness, shabbiness, and monotony of whatever gets produced. At a fundamental level, the clear-cut superiority of capitalism over socialism underlines the superiority of the private sector over the government in producing goods and services. After all, communism, the logical conclusion of socialism, is an economic system in which the government owns all companies, factories, farms, and other productive facilities, whereas under capitalism most of those facilities are privately owned by individuals.

While communism is, for all intents and purposes, dead and buried, and survives in only a few holdouts such as Cuba and North Korea, government production of goods and services is alive and kicking in both advanced and developing countries. In the advanced countries, the government produces a large share of GDP (gross domestic product), or all goods and services produced by an economy in a given year. According to the 2014 Index of Economic Freedom by the Heritage Foundation and the Wall Street Journal, government spending accounted for a whopping 56.1% of GDP in France, 45.4% of GDP in Germany, 42% of GDP in Japan, 48.5% in United Kingdom, and 41.6% of GDP in the US. Furthermore, there has been a secular increase in the share of government in GDP across the rich world. To some extent, the increase reflects a well-known stylized fact — as a country grows richer, its citizens tend to demand more and better public services — e.g. education. More fundamentally, the growing share is a consequence of the prevalence of government-led income redistribution programs

> **"**
> While communism is, for all intents and purposes, dead and buried, and survives in only a few holdouts such as Cuba and North Korea, government production of goods and services is alive and kicking in both advanced and developing countries.... Furthermore, there has been a secular increase in the share of government in GDP across the rich world.
> **"**

in the rich countries, which typically accord a higher priority to equity than in poorer countries, where rapid growth remains the overriding priority.

The economic role of the state in developing countries is based on a somewhat different rationale. It is based partly on society's demand for a less unequal society, as it is in the rich countries, but there is a powerful additional cause — the lack of a well-developed private sector. As explained earlier and as evident in countless examples from the real world, the private sector, which is motivated by the profit motive, is patently better at producing goods and services than the government, which is motivated by political factors such as job security for public employees. But if there is no private sector to begin with, or only an embryonic private sector, then there is greater scope for state involvement in the economy. In contrast to advanced countries, which boast large, vibrant, well-established private sectors with gigantic companies like Apple, Siemens and Toyota, developing countries often suffer from small, stunted, anemic private sectors that lack any dynamism. In this sense, the rationale for government production is stronger in developing countries such as China than in advanced countries such as America. In short, where there is no private sector to speak of, the government has to step in and fill the void.

In fact, developing countries, especially in East Asia, experienced remarkable economic growth and success after the government intervened heavily in the economy during the early stages of their economic development. Postwar Japan was a pioneer of industrial policy, which refers to the government's identifying promising industries and firms, and promoting the growth of the targeted industries and firms through

"

The economic role of the state in developing countries is based on a somewhat different rationale. It is based partly on society's demand for a less unequal society, as it is in the rich countries, but there is a powerful additional cause — the lack of a well-developed private sector.

"

more and cheaper loans, stronger protection from imports, subsidies and tax exemptions, and other state assistance. The sustained rapid growth of first Japan, followed by South Korea, Taiwan, Hong Kong and Singapore, and then Malaysia, Thailand and Indonesia — a region-wide phenomenon dubbed the East Asian Miracle by the World Bank in 1993 — is often touted as evidence that industrial policy succeeds, especially by economists and policymakers who favor heavy government intervention in the economy.

“

... the East Asian Miracle is often touted as evidence that industrial policy succeeds, especially by economists and policymakers who favor heavy government intervention in the economy.

”

INDUSTRIAL POLICY, PARK CHUNG-HEE, AND LEE KUAN YEW

40

However, industrial policy was just one component of a package of sound policies — for example, balanced government budgets, large infrastructure investments, and heavy investments in education and human capital — that the East Asian countries pursued. It is the entire package of growth-friendly policies that fostered growth rather than just industrial policy. Indeed the empirical evidence on the impact of industrial policy on East Asia's economic performance is mixed at best, with some studies finding a beneficial effect, others a harmful effect, and yet others no effect. The lack of firm evidence in favor of industrial policy is hardly surprising. In fact, even in the absence of any sophisticated analysis by economists, it is clear that industrial policy is nonsense. Common sense alone suggests that industrial policy makes no sense. More precisely, there is a gaping hole in the basic logic of industrial policy — i.e. risk-averse government bureaucrats, rather than risk-taking, profit-seeking businessmen, determining which industries to invest in. In fact, the hole is so gaping that it would stump even the most ardent supporters of industrial policy. This fatal logical flaw casts serious doubt on whether even the

" Common sense alone suggests that industrial policy makes no sense. More precisely, there is a gaping hole in the basic logic of industrial policy — i.e. risk-averse government bureaucrats, rather than risk-taking, profit-seeking businessmen, determining which industries to invest in. "

very concept of industrial policy is meaningful or sensible.

More specifically, government bureaucrats, even clever and dedicated ones, may be competent in several areas, but predicting which firms and industries would flourish — i.e. picking winners — is clearly not one of them. Entrepreneurship is not part of their risk-averse, small-minded DNA. Otherwise, they would leave government and set up businesses that grow fast and make a fortune. If government bureaucrats are such geniuses at spotting business opportunities, pray tell me why aren't they out in the real world making big bucks, instead of sitting in their cozy government office? Because those bureaucrats want other people to become rich off their brilliant business acumen? The notion that government bureaucrats are more civic minded and hence less susceptible to material temptation than the rest of us is utter hogwash. The colossal amounts of bribes that government officials around the world rake in suggest that they are no different than the rest of us when it comes to love of money. The big difference between entrepreneurs and corrupt bureaucrats is that corrupt bureaucrats want to make money without taking any risk. The huge bribes they extort amount to a big tax on risk-taking by entrepreneurs. The predictable result is less risk-taking, less entrepreneurship, and slower economic growth.

This is not to belittle the role of a strong, competent, and relatively honest government administration, which is absolutely pivotal for a poor country to escape poverty. Far from it! In fact, strong administration is probably the one indispensable ingredient of economic growth and development. No poor country has achieved sustainable economic progress without good government. For example, competent, visionary,

> **"**
>
> Entrepreneurship is not part of their risk-averse, small-minded DNA. Otherwise, they would leave government and set up businesses that grow fast and make a fortune. If government bureaucrats are such geniuses at spotting business opportunities, pray tell me why aren't they out in the real world making big bucks, instead of sitting in their cozy government office?
>
> **"**

and relatively honest bureaucracy goes a long way toward explaining how South Korea rose from the ashes of the Korean War, one of the poorest countries in the world, to become an economic powerhouse. On the other hand, incompetent, bumbling, and rotten-to-the-core bureaucracy explains why much of the Third World remains mired in economic stagnation, high unemployment, and a general sense of despair and hopelessness. In other words, bad government often prevents far too many developing countries from making meaningful economic progress.

The South Korean government played a vital role in laying the foundation of the Korean miracle because the country's bureaucrats, for the most part, pursued sound, sensible, and farsighted policies — for example, investing heavily in roads, ports, power plants, telecoms, and other infrastructure as well as education that make all firms and industries more productive — which provided a conducive environment for a dynamic private sector to emerge and thrive. In short, the bureaucrats in Seoul created an environment which allowed for the emergence of world-class companies such as Samsung Electronics or Hyundai Motor Company. However, bureaucrats did not build, nor are they capable of building, such companies. That is the job of bold, big-dreaming, risk-taking, profit-seeking, game-changing entrepreneurs like Lee Byung-chul and Chung Ju-yung, founders of Samsung and Hyundai, respectively. The role of the government is to pave the way for a vibrant and productive private sector, NOT to replace it.

Unfortunately, Korea is the exception rather than the rule. The number of developing economies that made the jump from the Third World to First World — i.e. from the minor leagues to the major leagues — can be counted with the

> **"**
> In short, the bureaucrats in Seoul created an environment which allowed for the emergence of world-class companies such as Samsung Electronics or Hyundai Motor Company. However, bureaucrats did not build, nor are they capable of building, such companies. That is the job of bold, big-dreaming, risk-taking, profit-seeking, game-changing entrepreneurs like Lee Byung-chul and Chung Ju-yung, founders of Samsung and Hyundai, respectively.
> **"**

fingers of two hands, or even just one hand. The well-known ones include Taiwan, Hong Kong, and Singapore. For the majority of the Third World that did not make the leap, their failure was due to their lazy, corrupt, incompetent bureaucrats squeezing the life out of the private sector and economic growth. Argentina, to name just one, has suffered through a century of populism, corruption, and mismanagement. Not surprisingly, the country, which is blessed with abundant natural resources as well as a well-educated workforce, has steadily slid down the global wealth rankings. It is hard to believe that this country was one of the richest in the world a century ago. South Korea and Argentina are both powerful reminders of the importance of having a good government for economic progress. Equivalently, they are also powerful testaments to the enormous economic damage that bad government can inflict.

Strong, visionary political leadership that offers a coherent strategy for economic growth and development often goes hand in hand with a competent, honest, effective bureaucracy which implements that strategy. South Korea had its President Park Chung-hee, a former general who laid the foundation for South Korea's economic miracle. A series of ineffective governments between the end of the Korean War in 1953 and the early 1960s meant that South Korea remained one of the world's poorest countries. Those governments were democratically elected, but did precious little to foster economic growth or improve the lives of the man on the street. Democracy is a good thing in and of itself, but it is neither a necessary or sufficient condition for economic growth and development. A quick look at the two Asian giants illustrates this important point. India is a vibrant Western-style multiparty democracy, while China is clearly not. Yet authoritarian

"

Strong, visionary political leadership that offers a coherent strategy for economic growth and development often goes hand in hand with a competent, honest, effective bureaucracy which implements that strategy. South Korea had its President Park Chung-hee, a former general who laid the foundation for South Korea's economic miracle.

"

China has outperformed democratic India for decades and has become the world's second largest economy while India, despite strong growth in recent years, is still struggling to fulfill its enormous potential. In short, China has done a much better job of lifting general living standards and reducing poverty.

Turning back to South Korea, one cannot overemphasize the role of transformational political leadership in turning the dirt-poor country to the world's greatest economic success stories. With a single-minded and dogged belief, faith, and conviction, President Park, an army general who took power in a coup d'état in 1961, set the country on the way to the Miracle on the Han River, the broad-shouldered waterway that cuts the gleaming, skyscraper jungle capital city of Seoul in half. Many of the public investments that he launched — for example, a 325-kilometer expressway connecting the capital Seoul to Busan, the main port and the second largest city — were ridiculed as white elephants or waste of public money during his rule, but they seem all too sensible, not remotely visionary, just plain sensible, in retrospect. Nevertheless, it was visionary back then when the first shovel broke the ground of the expressway for the very first time.

Economic success stories in the Third World are few and far between but South Korea is not alone. Like Park Chung-hee's South Korea, they often embody the combination of strong, visionary political leadership and competent, honest bureaucracy. A good example is Lee Kuan Yew's Singapore. Lee, who passed away in March 2015, transformed Singapore from a small tropical swamp island into one of the world's richest countries in a single generation through visionary leadership. Singapore welcomed foreign

> **"**
>
> Economic success stories in the Third World are few and far between but South Korea is not alone. Like Park Chung-hee's South Korea, they often embody the combination of strong, visionary political leadership and competent, honest bureaucracy. A good example is Lee Kuan Yew's Singapore.
>
> **"**

investors with open arms back in the 1960s when doing so was out of fashion. At that time, developing countries, which had just gained independence from often oppressive and exploitative Western colonial powers, stridently opposed foreign investors. As a result of Lee's foresight, Singapore remains, to this day, one of the favorite destinations of world-class multinational companies. The economic benefits to Singapore, rapid growth and low unemployment to name just two, have been enormous.

An equally visionary masterstroke of Lee was to adopt English as the official national language of the multiracial city-state. In addition to fostering racial harmony among the Chinese, Malays, and Indians, the policy gave Singapore a decisive advantage as an investment destination for large Western companies. Lee also pioneered Singapore's zero tolerance approach toward corruption. While government officials found guilty of corruption face severe consequences, they are among the best paid public employees in the world. The basic concept behind the Singaporean civil service model is to recruit the best and brightest, and pay them well to keep them honest. There is much to be said for the Singaporean model of a small, elite civil service, compared to many developing countries, where the civil service serves as an employer of last resort for hordes of underpaid, mediocre bureaucrats, whose dull lazy eyes light up only when they sniff an opportunity to harass the private sector and extract bribes. Actually, this also describes plenty of bureaucrats in advanced countries, although the scope for bribes is much more limited due to much stronger laws and institutions, and hence a higher risk of getting caught and going to jail.

❝

There is much to be said for the Singaporean model of a small, elite civil service, compared to many developing countries, where the civil service serves as an employer of last resort for hordes of underpaid, mediocre bureaucrats, whose dull lazy eyes light up only when they sniff an opportunity to harass the private sector and extract bribes.

❞

RECEP ERDOĞAN, AND THE RWANDAN GENOCIDE

A more recent example of visionary leadership teaming up with an effective civil service to transform a country comes from Turkey, where Recep Tayyip Erdoğan served as the prime minister from 2003 to 2014 and is currently serving as president since 2014. Through forceful leadership and sound economic policies, Erdoğan has fostered entrepreneurial dynamism, catalyzed rapid economic growth, and catapulted the country into the global limelight after a long period of decline. Turkey, the proud heir to the Ottoman Empire, one of the most powerful empires in human history, is finally beginning to fulfill its potential and becoming a force to be reckoned with. The Turkish renaissance is perhaps best epitomized by the emergence of Turkish Airline as Europe's top airline. Closely related to that, Istanbul's Ataturk airport has emerged as a global air hub, one of the best-connected airports in the world with flights to all corners of the world. It is true that a sharp slowdown of growth[1] since the global crisis, growing authoritarianism, festering Kurdish insurgency,[2] and a coup attempt[3] is taking some shine off the Turkish miracle but nevertheless, in the broader scheme of themes, Erdoğan made Turkey relevant again.

[1] In May 2018, the Turkish lira depreciated sharply, due to Turkey's high inflation, large trade deficit, and other weak fundamentals. The Turkish government further eroded market confidence by appearing to interfere with the central bank's policymaking and suggesting that monetary policy tightening will make inflation worse. The notion that higher interest rates will raise inflation rates is, to put it mildly, intuitively implausible and running against conventional economic wisdom. http://www.economist.com/news/special-report/21689874-turkey-performing-well-below-its-potential-erdoganomics

[2] http://www.economist.com/news/special-report/21689879-what-does-it-mean-proud-be-turk

[3] In July 2016, rogue, anti-Erdoğan elements of the Turkish armed forces sought to oust Erdoğan and take over the government. The coup was swiftly crushed by the mainstream military and popular resistance. In the aftermath of the military coup attempt, the Erdoğan government arrested 6,000 soldiers and fired thousands of policemen, prosecutors, judges, academics, teachers, and civil servants. The purge appears to be a deep and wide suppression of all opponents of the government. See, for example, "Erdogan's revenge," The Economist, 23 July 2016.

Since Erdoğan took power in 2003 as the prime minister — since August 2014 he is serving as the president, but he still looms behind the scenes as the country's most powerful political leader — Turkey has been transformed from a sulking has-been to a confident, aspirational regional power.[4] Before the advent of Erdoğan, Turkey had little to sell to the rest of the world other than workers. Labor exports were epitomized by thousands of young men who migrated to West Germany during the economic miracle of the 1960s and 1970s to work in factories and mines as *Gastarbeiter* or guest workers. Those workers and their descendants number almost 3 million today. Under Erdoğan, Turkey has become the undisputed economic powerhouse in its part of the world, which straddles the Middle East and southeastern Europe. Turkey is now Europe's largest producer of television sets and automobiles, and a major exporter of high-quality consumer goods. It even exports high-precision machines to Germany. In 2015, Turkey was the world's eighth largest food producer and sixth most popular tourist destination in the world.[5] Turkish firms have also become a major force in the global construction industry.

That very rare breed — the inspirational, visionary, impactful, game-changing, transformational African leader — has finally found flesh and bones in Rwanda's Paul Kagame, who took power in 1994 after leading a guerilla force that ended a horrific genocide. Hard to believe but genocide is not a distant memory associated with Auschwitz or Dachau but something that happened in 1993, in the heart of Africa. After 20 years of Kagame's leadership, Rwanda is hitting the headlines again, but for all the right reasons this time around. Foreign visitors to Kigali, the Rwandan capital, invariably marvel at how much cleaner and more orderly the streets

[4] http://www.economist.com/news/special-report/21689871-under-recep-tayip-erdogan-and-his-ak-party-turkey-has-become-richer-and-more-confident

[5] http://www.economist.com/news/special-report/21689874-turkey-performing-well-below-its-potential-erdoganomics

are compared to other African cities. The streets are swept in Kigali, instead of serving as a repository for garbage, as in many other African capitals. Perhaps most importantly, there is a real sense of national purpose, or the dream of building a better country for future generations of Rwandans, pervading the country.

A common characteristic of strong, transformational leaders is that, by definition, they are strong, which sometimes turns into authoritarian tendencies. In an ideal world, one would like the best of both worlds — good government that delivers economic progress *and* a vibrant democracy which listens to the voice of everybody. Unfortunately, in the real world, a country often cannot have both, especially when it is at the early, take-off stage of economic growth and development. But, as the experiences of Park's South Korea, Lee's Singapore, Erdoğan's Turkey, and Kagame's Rwanda highlight, the loss of some democracy is easily a price worth paying for building a better life and a better future. Ask the long-suffering citizens of any misgoverned, mismanaged, corrupt African country whether they would sacrifice a little freedom for Rwandan levels of good government, and the answer would be overwhelmingly affirmative. Ask the citizens of Rwanda and the answer would be even more overwhelmingly affirmative.

It never ceases to amaze us how Western critics of transformational Third World leaders assume that the political, social, and economic contexts of developing countries are similar, or even remotely comparable, to those of far richer and more advanced countries, which enjoy a long history of good governance, strong institutions, and mature democracies. Rwanda 2015 is most definitely not Denmark 2015 or

> **"** In an ideal world, one would like the best of both worlds — good government that delivers economic progress *and* a vibrant democracy which listens to the voice of everybody.... But, as the experiences of Park's South Korea, Lee's Singapore, Erdoğan's Turkey, and Kagame's Rwanda highlight, the loss of some democracy is easily a price worth paying for building a better life and a better future. **"**

even Denmark 1945. For the West to lecture and hector Rwanda about lack of democracy and human rights and so forth is astounding, even ridiculous. Again, the kind of human rights that matters the most for poor Third World countries is not some abstract right to vote for the president, which, in any case, often just results in Tribe A replacing Tribe B as the main plunderers of the country, a completely meaningless change in the bigger scheme of things. Instead, human rights mean much more practical and urgent rights such as freedom from hunger, freedom from disease, and freedom from tribal genocide.

In connection with the last point, Western criticism of the Kagame government is utterly hypocritical in light of the West's deafening silence during the horrific genocide of 1992 in which bloodthirsty mobs brutally and indiscriminately killed an estimated 800,000 men, women and children, only because the victims belonged to another tribe. Where was the West pontificating and preaching about democracy and human rights and so forth back then when innocent people were being hacked to death with machetes, gang-raped, and worse, by wild-eyed, frenzied men turned monsters? If they are going to babble about democracy and human rights, that is their prerogative, but please do so when and where it matters the most. The West did not raise a single finger to stop the gruesome genocide in Rwanda, which means it lacks any moral authority whatsoever to lecture the Rwandan government about democracy and human rights.

All the more so since the post-genocide Rwandan government is a quantum improvement over the previous government that carried out the genocide. By almost any social

"

If Westerners are going to babble about democracy and human rights, that is their prerogative, but please do so when and where it matters the most. The West did not raise a single finger to stop the gruesome genocide in Rwanda, which means it lacks any moral authority whatsoever to lecture the Rwandan government about democracy and human rights.

"

and economic indicator — for example, infant mortality, literacy rate, or per capita GDP — Rwanda has changed for the better beyond all recognition.[6] In fact, according to the United Nations Human Development Index, between 1990 and 2015 Rwanda made more progress than any other country, bar none. The Kagame government's achievements are all the more remarkable in light of Rwanda's utter lack of physical infrastructure when the guerillas finally overthrew the genocidal government in July 1994. Not only did government forces and their accomplice militias kill, maim, and rape at will, they also deliberately and systematically destroyed power plants and factories as they retreated in the face of the advancing rebel forces.

[6] http://www.economist.com/news/middle-east-and-africa/21694551-should-paul-kagame-be-backed-providing-stability-and-prosperity-or-condemned

PAUL KAGAME, TEODORO OBIANG, AND AFRICA'S SAHARA-CROSSING ECONOMIC REFUGEES

42

To put it mildly, the double standards and hypocrisy of Western critics must be sickening to the survivors of the Rwandan genocide. This is not to say that the Kagame government must be given a free pass, especially for its increasingly authoritarian tendencies, but everything has to be put in proper perspective. Moreover, the proper perspective is that Rwanda is one of the best governed, if not the best governed, countries in Africa. There is progress and there is hope in Rwanda, which is more than can be said for large swathes of Africa. Ask the citizens of the many misgoverned African countries where the only hope for a better life for long-suffering citizens is to trek across the vast Saharan desert and, after that, risk life and limb to cross the Mediterranean in rickety, overcrowded boats to reach Europe. They would surely trade whatever corrupt, incompetent elite that is misgoverning and bankrupting their country for a Kagame-style government that gets things done and delivers visible progress.

Western critics of Kagame would do very well to redirect their time and energy to criticize and thus help improve the quality of governments in those miserable, wretched "crossing the Sahara Desert and the Mediterranean Sea

"

There is progress and there is hope in Rwanda, which is more than can be said for large swathes of Africa.... Africans would surely trade whatever corrupt, incompetent elite that is misgoverning and bankrupting their country for a Kagame-style government that gets things done and delivers visible progress.

"

is the only hope for a better life" countries. A classic example of such a sub-Saharan African country is Equatorial Guinea, a small West African country blessed with abundant oil reserves. Unfortunately for Equatorial Guineans, their country is run by a certain Mr. Teodoro Obiang, who came to power in 1979 and enjoys the distinction of being the longest serving president in the world. While most Equatorial Guineans live on less than US$2 a day, Obiang and his children lavish themselves with, among other things, a US$55 million Boeing 737, 32 sports cars, a mansion in Malibu near Los Angeles, and nearly US$2 million in Michael Jackson memorabilia.[1] On paper, Equatorial Guinea is the richest country in Africa, with an average income close to Japan, thanks to large reserves of oil and natural gas. In reality, thanks to spectacular misrule, three quarters of the population live below the World Bank poverty line.

Such governments are not only bad news for their own citizens; they are also bad news for the rest of the world. In particular, they are bad news for Italy and other European countries which face a massive humanitarian crisis due to the uncontrollable influx of thousands of illegal migrants. It never ceases to amaze me that many human rights advocates shrilly denounce the governments of Italy and other European countries for failing to do enough to help the boat people, but say absolutely nothing to the African governments whose corruption, incompetence, and patent disregard for the welfare of their citizens turned those citizens into boat people in the first place. The primary responsibility, including moral responsibility, for the tragedy of Africa's economic refugees lies squarely with the Obiangs, Mugabes, and other African rulers whose misrule deprive their citizens of all hope for a better tomorrow.

[1] http://www.economist.com/news/middle-east-and-africa/21694543-ordinary-folk-see-none-their-countrys-riches-palace-jungle

In this connection, pray tell me, why should the Italian government be responsible and accountable for the incompetence and corruption of some distant rotten African government? The simple answer is, it should not be. The fundamental solution for Africa's boat people problem is for more African governments to clean up their act and become decent, caring, and effective, so that their citizens can find hope and aspire to a better life in their own country, much as Rwandan citizens do under the Kagame government. It is about time that African governments take primarily responsibility for the well-being of their countries and citizens, instead of tirelessly blaming foreigners for all their problems. The causes of Africa's problems do not lie outside Africa and the answers to Africa's problems do not lie outside Africa. Both the causes and solutions lie largely in Africa. What Africa needs is more Kagames and fewer Obiangs and Mugabes and thankfully, Africa seems to be moving in that direction.

A huge first step would be for the African people to change their basic mentality, attitude, and way of doing things. Corruption does not arise in a vacuum but rather, it is the by-product of the overall social, political, and cultural milieu. Unless that milieu changes, a change of government will mean very little to the long suffering ordinary African citizen, other than the replacement of one group of crooks, belonging to Tribe A, by another group of crooks, belonging to Tribe B. There is absolute no improvement in their everyday lives. For the vast majority of African citizens, whether Tribe B took power through free elections or military coups or anything else is completely irrelevant. What is relevant is that the change of government has not brought about more jobs, put more food on the table, or delivered more and better education and health services.

"

On paper, Equatorial Guinea is the richest country in Africa, with an average income close to Japan, thanks to large reserves of oil and natural gas. In reality, thanks to spectacular misrule, three quarters of the population live below the World Bank poverty line.

"

The citizens of poor African countries where a quarter of the population lives on less than US$1 per day and half of the population lives on less than US$2 per day would prefer a strong leader, even a dictator, who builds schools, hospitals and roads, rather than a corrupt and incompetent democratically elected leaders whose only interest in gaining political power is to steal as much money possible from public coffers. What matters more for Africa and Africans, much more in fact, is not whether or not a government is democratic, it is whether or not the government gets things done and improves their everyday lives. Inconveniently for the many Western observers of Africa for whom democracy is the be all and end all of African development, the right to vote takes a distant back seat to the right to decent food, shelter and health care. Good government that makes their lives better and gives them hope, regardless of whether it is democratic or a dictatorship or whatever, is what Africans crave.

"

What matters more for Africa and Africans, much more in fact, is not whether or not a government is democratic, it is whether or not the government gets things done and improves their everyday lives. Inconveniently for the many Western observers of Africa for whom democracy is the be all and end all of African development, the right to vote takes a distant back seat to the right to decent food, shelter and health care.

"

185

THE CURSE OF FOREIGN AID, AND MEDÉCINS SANS FRONTIÈRES

43

Foreign aid can clearly help African countries, and foreign aid has done a world of good in Africa and elsewhere. It has saved millions of Africans from starvation, and saved millions from deadly tropical diseases. It has alleviated untold amount of human misery and suffering. However, as the hundreds of billions of dollars of wasted, misused, and stolen foreign aid over several decades show, it is ultimately good, honest, effective African governments that will ensure that foreign aid is used to build new roads, schools and hospitals rather than siphoned off to the Swiss bank accounts of big shot politicians and ministers. Even the most ardent advocates of foreign aid would accept that too many foreign aid dollars that are transformed into Mediterranean villas, Rolls-Royce limousines, and yachts of corrupt, greedy African officials who do absolutely nothing to improve the lives of ordinary Africans. Foreign aid works only when good governments put it to good use. Therefore, the impact of foreign aid on Africa's development, like Africa's development itself, ultimately depends on Africans themselves.

The goal of foreign aid must be to foster economic development and growth so that, at some point

> **"**
>
> However, as the hundreds of billions of dollars of wasted, misused, and stolen foreign aid over several decades show, it is ultimately good, honest, effective African governments that will ensure that foreign aid is used to build new roads, schools and hospitals rather than siphoned off to the Swiss bank accounts of big shot politicians and ministers.
>
> **"**

in time, the recipient country graduates from foreign aid and no longer needs foreign aid. Yet far too many countries in Africa and other parts of the developing world fail to graduate from foreign aid. Surely, a big part of the problem is a paternalistic tendency in the donor countries to be excessively generous toward the recipient countries. That is, rich donor countries do not monitor or care about how the poor recipient countries spend the aid that they provide them. At a minimum, the donor governments should demand a measure of transparency and accountability from the governments of recipient countries, on how their donations are being spent. They owe that much to their own country's tax payers and, more significantly, to the ordinary citizens of the poor countries whom the foreign aid is supposed to benefit.

This is probably not something the foreign aid industry wants to hear, but the ultimate goal of that industry must be its own demise. Foreign aid will be a resounding success when it is no longer necessary, and every country can stand on its own feet. That is, foreign aid must help the poor countries to learn how to fish themselves, instead of always asking for handouts of fish. It is degrading, insulting, and humiliating to have to always depend on others for your livelihood. Yet the hundreds of billions of dollars that rich-country governments threw away at incompetent, ineffective, and corrupt governments of poor countries over the past few decades suggest that teaching the poor to catch fish for themselves is a low priority, if a priority at all, for the donors. The amount of compassion is not measured by how much money you give, but by how much improvement you bring about in the lives of the ordinary citizens — i.e. more and better schools, hospitals, and roads. By that more accurate measure of effectiveness, foreign aid has been far less effective than the

> **At a minimum, the donor governments should demand a measure of transparency and accountability from the governments of recipient countries, on how their donations are being spent. They owe that much to their own country's tax payers and, more significantly, to the ordinary citizens of the poor countries whom the foreign aid is supposed to benefit.**

huge amount of money donated would warrant. Such ineffectiveness, in turn, has a lot to do with predatory, morally bankrupt poor-country leaders who have a whole lot of interest in Swiss bank accounts and much less interest in the welfare of their subjects.

Upon careful thought, there is an unmistakable element of ingrained racism in many members of the foreign aid community. Finding the meaning of your life in helping poor countries is a noble thing. But if you really care about poor countries, you should devote your time and energy to helping the poor countries help themselves, not to keep them forever dependent on your generosity. And, it is not even generosity — it is feeling good about yourself by wasting the hard-earned money of your country's tax payers on corrupt thieves who masquerade as national leaders. Contrary to the racist mentality of many foreign aid community members who believe, or would like to believe, that African countries, especially sub-Saharan African countries, are hopeless basket cases that will never amount to anything, we are seeing the dawn of an African renaissance.

The renaissance is most tangible in the best governed countries such as Rwanda and Ethiopia but the continent as a whole is growing much faster than in the past, largely as a result of better governments and better policies. Nevertheless, the continent has a long way to go before it can root out the scourge of bad government, especially corruption, and fulfill its potential. Speaking of potential, Africa has plenty of it. Anybody who has been to Africa will know that the racist stereotype of the lazy and incompetent African is utter nonsense. For one, due to the harsh environment most Africans face — for example, many of them spend two hours every day to fetch water from wells — they have

"

African renaissance is most tangible in the best governed countries such as Rwanda and Ethiopia but the continent as a whole is growing much faster than in the past, largely as a result of better governments and better policies. Nevertheless, the continent has a long way to go before it can root out the scourge of bad government, especially corruption, and fulfill its potential.

"

to work their tails off just to put enough food on the table and survive. But more fundamentally, the continent is actually home to a vast pool of entrepreneurial talent and energy.[1] What is bottling up private enterprise in Africa is government failure — government's failure to provide basic infrastructure such as roads and power and, far worse, its habit of harassing entrepreneurs and extorting bribes from them. Lack of access to finance is another major barrier for African entrepreneurs.

An important caveat is in order before we proceed any further. For sure, there are plenty of capable and caring individuals within the foreign aid community who make a big positive difference to the lives of ordinary people in poor countries. The dedicated medical doctors of Medécins Sans Frontières (MSF), or Doctors Without Borders, a global non-governmental organization (NGO) whose mission is to provide basic medical services to those without any access to medical services, is just one example. MSF volunteers sacrifice the comfortable, even plush, lifestyles of medical doctors in rich countries to serve underprivileged patients in the world's poorest, most remote, and most dangerous conflict areas. Their often life-risking dedication has saved countless lives and greatly improved the general health conditions of the world's most wretched places.

Nevertheless, both donor governments and the foreign aid community bear part of the blame for the theft and waste of hundreds of billions of dollars of their tax payers' money. Their failure to monitor how the recipient governments spent foreign aid made it possible for incompetent, ineffective, and corrupt governments to get away with theft and waste. If one thinks of the schools, hospitals and roads that were not built as a result, and the missed opportunity

189

[1] See, for example, "Opportunities galore," The Economist, 2 July 2016.

to improve the lives of hundreds of millions of Africans, the colossal theft and waste is scandalous and inexcusable, if not downright criminal. The many African rulers whose greed and corruption deprived their citizens of decent, humane lives should be tried and locked up for life, for violating basic human rights. Upon closer thought, they are not much better than the likes of Syria's Bashar Assad who butcher their own citizens by the thousands. Crushing all hope for a better tomorrow is no better, and in fact probably worse, than killing and maiming. A life devoid of hope is no life at all. This is why those corrupt, greedy, incompetent African rulers who steal money and hope from their miserable, starving citizens are, in effect, mass murderers.

"

A life devoid of hope is no life at all. This is why those corrupt, greedy, incompetent African rulers who steal money and hope from their miserable, starving citizens are, in effect, mass murderers.

"

EGYPTIAN BOYS IN ROME, TRAGEDY OF AYLAN KURDI, AND THE MEANING OF GOOD GOVERNMENT IN DEVELOPING COUNTRIES

44

B ut Africa is certainly not alone when it comes to lousy governments that waste foreign aid. More generally, it would be completely unfair to single out Africa for incompetent, ineffective, and corrupt governments that are unable or unwilling to improve the everyday lives of their citizens. In many countries of the developing world, hope is an awfully precious commodity, especially for the 99% of the population who are not part of the kleptocratic political elite that plunder their countries for their personal gain. Just as lack of hope for a better life drives Africans to cross the Sahara and take rickety boats across the Mediterranean, the same lack of hope for a better life drives Middle Easterners to flood into Europe either via the Mediterranean or over land across Turkey and the Balkans. The fundamental cause behind the influx of Middle Easterners into Europe is not Western imperialism or neocolonialism or thirst for oil or some ominous Zionist–Israeli plot or global anti-Muslim paranoia or anything else.

As with Africa, both the causes and solutions to the problem of Middle Eastern refugees lie within the Middle East, not in Europe, not in America, not in Israel — although geographically, Israel

" As with Africa, both the causes and solutions to the problem of Middle Eastern refugees lie within the Middle East, not in Europe, not in America, not in Israel.

"

is part of the Middle East — or not anywhere else. In particular, as in Africa, bad governments that fail to bring about any meaningful progress in the everyday lives of millions of Middle Easterners — be they Egyptians, Iranians, Iraqis, Syrians, Yemenis, Afghans, Tunisians, Libyans, and others — is the root cause of the region's multitude of problems. For thousands of Middle Easterners, perilous passage to Europe, either by land or sea, is the only hope for a better life. The level of their desperation is comparable to that of the Africans. Young Egyptian boys loitering around Rome's Termini station, the Eternal City's main railway station, are just one testament to the bleak hopelessness of the lives of millions of Middle Easterners. The money they send back home, often by prostituting themselves, puts food on the table for their families. Those families, despite protestations about human traffickers exploiting their children, ultimately do not care about how their children make the money they send home. It is not that they do not love their children, but survival matters more.

The specific causes of the Middle Eastern malaise differ from country to country. For example, the bloody Syrian civil war has produced 9 million refugees, a third of them abroad and two thirds inside Syria. Since the population of Syria was about 23 million prior to the outbreak of war, more than one in every three Syrian is a refugee, either at home or in foreign countries. Syrian refugees have become the biggest source of Middle Eastern migrants to Europe. The war has destroyed the lives of millions of Syrians, and even basic survival has become a tough, almost primal struggle for most Syrians. The war pits a brutal, murderous government which thinks nothing of using chemical weapons against its own citizens against a diverse array of opponents, including

In particular, as in Africa, bad governments that fail to bring about any meaningful progress in the everyday lives of millions of Middle Easterners — be they Egyptians, Iranians, Iraqis, Syrians, Yemenis, Afghans, Tunisians, Libyans, and others — is the root cause of the region's multitude of problems. For thousands of Middle Easterners, perilous passage to Europe, either by land or sea, is the only hope for a better life.

even more evil and inhumane Islamist terrorists who think nothing of beheading hostages and setting them on fire. With such evil all around, it is not hard to see that those who suffer the most are the millions of civilians caught in the middle.

The Syrian civil war was the immediate trigger of the migrant crisis that gripped Europe during the summer and fall of 2015. The picture of three-year-old Aylan Kurdi, whose tiny corpse was washed ashore after the boat which was to carry his family to safety in Europe capsized in the Aegean Sea, turned European public opinion to do more to help the thousands of Syrian and other refugees pouring into Europe. Somehow the refugee crisis came to be viewed as a European crisis. The salient questions related to the crisis were: Can and should Europe accept the refugees? If so, how many refugees should each European country accept? But this crisis is not a European crisis. It is a crisis that is 100% made in the Middle East and 100% the responsibility of Middle Eastern countries. The Syrian civil war and the breakup of Iraq are ultimately due to the failure of the Syrian and Iraqi governments to provide even the remotest hope for their citizens that tomorrow will be better than today. European governments, especially the German government, should be commended for their generosity toward the refugees, but they do not bear any responsibility for the crisis.

At the end of the day, Islamist terrorists such as those from the Islamic State would not be able to attract the thousands of recruits that it does if Middle Eastern countries were run by good governments which could give their long-suffering citizens even remote rays of hope for a better tomorrow. It is revealing that disgusting and cowardly jihadist propaganda videos showing gruesome beheadings or human burnings can

> **At the end of the day, Islamist terrorists such as those from the Islamic State would not be able to attract the thousands of recruits that it does if Middle Eastern countries were run by good governments which could give their long-suffering citizens even remote rays of hope for a better tomorrow.**

"inspire" thousands of young men from across the Muslim world to join the Islamic State. Above all, it points to the hollow meaninglessness and emptiness of their unemployed, unproductive lives. Religious fundamentalism clearly plays a role in influencing young, malleable minds toward the path of terrorism. Moreover, alienation and marginalization from the general society is a major reason why thousands of immigrant Muslim men from the UK, France, and other rich European countries — e.g. the notorious British-accented Jihadi John of the beheading videos — head to Syria and Iraq to join the Islamic State.

But young Muslim men who travel to distant lands to blow themselves up as suicide bombers are much less likely to fall prey to extremist jihadist propaganda if they had something more rewarding to look forward to than another desolate day idling around some desolate street corner of Cairo, Sanaa, Tunis, Algiers, Riyadh, the banlieues — the rough, run-down outer suburbs — of Paris, or Molenbeek,[1] the Brussels suburb which has become the most fertile breeding grounds of European jihadists. Economics is not everything, and it certainly cannot completely explain the rise of the Islamic State, but it is clearly a big factor. Unemployed young men with idle hands and restless minds are easy pickings for any propaganda machine that promises action, excitement, and a sense of purpose. It is telling that Tunisia, the birthplace of the Arab Spring and the only Arab Spring country to have made a successful transition to a functioning democracy, has become the largest source of recruits for the Islamic State. Adding insult to injury, Tunisian jihadists massacred foreign tourists at a museum and a beach resort in Tunisia itself in 2015.

Democracy and the right to vote are nice ideals, but they mean very little when you do not have

[1] http://www.theguardian.com/world/2015/nov/15/molenbeek-the-brussels-borough-in-the-spotlight-after-paris-attacks

a job, there is not enough food on the table, and tomorrow is worse than today. Predictably, Tunisia's economic conditions are no better today than they were prior to the democratic revolution, and arguably worse. Again, what matters the most for developing countries and their citizens is good government that delivers economic progress and hope for a better future. If that good government happens to be a democracy, that is a nice bonus, but purely a bonus. Furthermore, if that good government happens to be authoritarian, that is unfortunate, but that government is still far preferable to a bad government that happens to be democratic. This is an inconvenient truth for the all too numerous Western critics of effective but authoritarian developing-country governments who believe, or like to believe, that democracy is the be all and end all of progress and development. It is not, by a long shot.

One should never confuse democracy versus dictatorship with good government versus bad government, certainly not in the context of poor countries where the difference between good government and bad government can mean the difference between having two meals a day and having three meals a day. Poor people in poor countries, of which there are billions, would choose the right to have three meals rather than two meals a day over the right to vote for their president or prime minister. No doubt about it. Put differently, if they had to choose between a good government and a democratic government, the long-suffering citizens of developing countries will choose the good government, any time, any day. For example, Indians have enjoyed a vibrant multiparty democracy for a long time, but it is doubtful whether they enjoyed good governments that got things done and delivered tangible improvement in everyday life. By that

> **"** Again, what matters the most for developing countries and their citizens is good government that delivers economic progress and hope for a better future. If that good government happens to be a democracy, that is a nice bonus, but purely a bonus.... One should never confuse democracy versus dictatorship with good government versus bad government. **"**

measure, China's government has performed better since it began market reforms in 1978.

Of course, in an ideal world, the best form of government would be a good *and* democratic government, but we are living in the real world, not an ideal world. In the real world, you often have one, but not both. In judging Third World governments, the overriding comparison must be between good governments versus bad governments, not democracies versus dictatorships. By good governments, we mean governments that improve the quality of their people's lives — three daily meals rather than two — and give them realistic hope for a better tomorrow. Whether a Paul Kagame or Teodoro Obiang is democratically elected or not is a secondary and peripheral issue. The much more relevant and fundamental point is that one leader is committed to improving the lives of his countrymen while the other is committed to plundering his country to its bare bones and fattening his Swiss bank account.

"

By good governments, we mean governments that improve the quality of their people's lives — three daily meals rather than two — and give them realistic hope for a better tomorrow. Whether a Paul Kagame or Teodoro Obiang is democratically elected or not is a secondary and peripheral issue.

"

WESTERN IDEALS VERSUS THIRD WORLD REALITIES

45

More generally, it would be helpful if Westerners judged Third World governments not from the absurdly narrow and unrealistic perspective of their own countries, but based on the far different realities of the Third World. It is simply absurd to apply the perspective of the First World — where middle-class families ponder the benefits of having three cars rather than two — to the desperate on-the-ground realities of the Third World — where millions of malnourished families aspire to three meals a day rather than two. Most Westerners never set foot on a developing country and those that do often only see the poshest downtown part of the capital city, staying in a Hilton or Sheraton. Be that as it may, it would be useful if they educated themselves about the grim realities of the Third World before they start lecturing to the Third World. Most things they take for granted, such as running water or reliable electricity or schools and hospitals, are unavailable to large swathes of the population in the Third World.

Therefore, whether a government in a developing country is a good government should be judged by its effectiveness in delivering basic services as education and health care and improving the quality of life of its citizens. By that

"

It is simply absurd to apply the perspective of the First World — where middle-class families ponder the benefits of having three cars rather than two — to the desperate on-the-ground realities of the Third World — where millions of malnourished families aspire to three meals a day rather than two.

"

yardstick, the Chinese government has been an exceptionally good government. This explains why the communist party enjoys the support of the Chinese population. Getting things done and improving the quality of life of the Turkish people also explain Recep Erdoğan's electoral success and longevity in power. To return to Rwanda, the authoritarian tendencies of the Kagame government would be unacceptable in a rich, Western multi-party democracy, say Switzerland. But that is precisely the point. Notwithstanding Rwanda's aspirations to become the Switzerland of Africa, Rwanda is not and will not be, for a very long time, a Switzerland. It is an impoverished African country where a brutal, frenzied, unspeakably horrific genocide took place less than a generation ago.

What a country like Rwanda needs more than anything else is a measure of political stability, inter-ethnic harmony (or at least lack of violent conflict among different ethnic groups, one of which wanted to exterminate the other), and visible economic progress. This is precisely what the Kagame government has been delivering, and delivering superbly, for the Rwandan people since it took power in the aftermath of the genocide. In other words, Rwandans, unlike many of their fellow Africans suffering under rotten and incompetent governments, now have genuine hope and can aspire to something better than crossing the Saharan desert and the Mediterranean Sea to become an unwelcome illegal migrant in some distant European country. There is a genuine sense of nation-building and national purpose in Rwanda, and a collective sense that hard work and teamwork can deliver a better tomorrow for future generations of Rwandans.

In any case, as countries grow richer and their institutions evolve, democracy will come, slowly but surely. South Korea is a classic example

"

By the yardstick of improvement in the quality of daily life of ordinary citizens, the Chinese government has been an exceptionally good government. This explains why the communist party enjoys the support of the Chinese population. Getting things done and improving the quality of life of the Turkish people also explain Recep Erdoğan's electoral success and longevity in power.

"

of a country that successfully evolved from an authoritarian military dictatorship to a liberal multi-party democracy. The evolution was far from smooth, and often took the form of violent fits and starts. For example, President Park Chung-hee, the military dictator who was the architect of the country's economic miracle in the 1960s and 1970s, paid the ultimate price for his authoritarianism — he was assassinated by the head of the Korean national spy agency in 1979. More generally, the most common image of Korea among foreigners until the mid-1980s was violent pro-democracy riots and demonstrations in Seoul, which often adorned evening news on television sets around the world. But South Korea today has one of the most vibrant democracies anywhere in the world, with free elections, free press, and a robust civil society. South Koreans did not need the lecturing and hectoring of Western human rights and democracy advocates to overthrow dictatorship and achieve democracy. Their craving for freedom and liberty is ultimately what brought about democracy in Korea.

But that craving for freedom and liberty grew visibly stronger as the country became richer as a result of sustained rapid economic growth. In a fundamental sense, democracy is a universal value which is treasured by everybody, regardless of color, belief, race, or religion. There is nothing intrinsically Western about democracy and human rights. Asians, Africans, Latin Americans, Middle Easterners, Eastern Europeans, Pacific Islanders, and others would choose democracy over dictatorship, given a choice. The Arab Spring which erupted like a volcano in the Middle East, supposedly a barren desert of democratic values, and spread across that region like a wildfire is just one testament to the universal appeal of democracy and human rights. And there is every reason to suspect

"

South Koreans did not need the lecturing and hectoring of Western human rights and democracy advocates to overthrow dictatorship and achieve democracy. Their craving for freedom and liberty is ultimately what brought about democracy in Korea.

"

that the demands of the supposedly docile and submissive Chinese for more freedom will grow, and grow strongly, over time. Already, we are seeing plenty of evidence of a more assertive Chinese citizenry, vocally expressing their preferences and demanding their rights. One highly visible example is the emergence and diffusion of the not-in-my-backyard (NIMBY) phenomenon across the country.[1]

But even though democracy may be a universal ideal cherished by all, at another level, democracy is a luxury which is best appreciated when basic material needs have been met. The right to choose your own president or prime minister or mayor is very nice and good, but rather irrelevant to somebody whose immediate priority is to somehow secure three meals a day. A good government for the vast majority of citizens in a poor developing country is an *effective* government that gets things done. In other words, in a developing country, a good government is a government that paves roads, builds schools and hospitals, and brings about a tangible improvement in the living standards of their citizens. The enormous progress that China has achieved in almost all economic and social areas since its economic take-off points is a classic example of good government. While India has also achieved solid progress on the economic and social fronts, its progress has lagged that of China. For sure, Indians enjoy a much more democratic government than China, which is run by the communist party. But whether Indians enjoy a better government than the Chinese, that is another matter altogether.

Whether a good government is a dictatorship or a democracy is, in the broader scheme of things, secondary. The freedom that matters the most to the citizens of poor countries is most definitely NOT freedom from dictatorship. Rather,

[1] NIMBYism refers to organized local opposition to facilities which are socially necessary but may be unpleasant to local residents. Examples include prisons, homeless shelters, and waste management plants. Opposition to waste incinerators is one example of China's growing NIMBY movement, which often has an environmental dimension. See http://www.bloomberg.com/news/articles/2014-06-20/a-new-front-line-for-china-s-nimby-environmental-movement-waste-incinerators

to them, by far the most important freedom is freedom from hunger and lack of basic material necessities, or most fundamentally, freedom from hopelessness and despair. In many cases, good effective governments in developing countries were led by authoritarian but transformational leaders, like Park Chung-hee or Lee Kuan Yew. Democracy is neither a necessary nor a sufficient condition for good government in developing countries making their way into the world. It is true that democracy is, in and of itself, a valuable prize and a good thing, but in developing countries democracy takes a distant back seat to much more basic human rights, such as freedom of hunger and access to basic education and health care services.

Unfortunately for the citizens of developing countries, for every Park or Lee or Erdoğan or Kagame, there are dime-a-dozen incompetent, ineffective, and corrupt leaders who team up with equally incompetent, ineffective, and corrupt army of bureaucrats to plunder the country to the bones and set the country on the road to ruin. The ratio of transformational, game-changing, visionary leaders to uninspiring, mediocre, incompetent leaders is probably less than 1 to 10 in developing countries. The incidence of visionary leadership is unlikely to be much higher in the US and other developed countries, but the need for visionary leadership is limited. In rich countries, well-established policies, institutions, governments, rules of the game, and ways of doing things are already in place, so the damage that a weak, ineffective leader — for example, a Jimmy Carter — can inflict on the country is very limited. Precisely because policies and institutions are underdeveloped, in a flux, and still evolving, individual leaders make a much bigger difference in developing countries. In particular, a transformational leader can permanently change the script for the better.

> " In many cases, good effective governments in developing countries were led by authoritarian but transformational leaders, like Park Chung-hee or Lee Kuan Yew.... Unfortunately for the citizens of developing countries, for every Park or Lee or Erdoğan or Kagame, there are dime-a-dozen incompetent, ineffective, and corrupt leaders who team up with equally incompetent, ineffective, and corrupt army of bureaucrats to plunder the country to the bones and set the country on the road to ruin. "

MIDDLE-INCOME TRAP AND THE CURSE OF ABUNDANT NATURAL RESOURCES

46

"

The lack of visionary leadership at the top explains why many of the world's poorest countries never make it to even first base. A never-ending succession of corrupt, ineffective, and morally bankrupt presidents and prime ministers whose sole interest is to plunder their countries and fatten their Swiss bank accounts explains why those countries, especially in Africa but also elsewhere, never leave the batter's box. By the way, the disturbing tendency of many third-rate leaders of poor countries to hang on to power — e.g. Robert Mugabe of Zimbabwe, widely credited with turning one of Africa's most promising countries into one of its worst basket cases — is most definitely not motivated by any noble desire to serve the citizens of their countries. Instead, it is motivated by the selfish desire to plunder their countries for as long as possible. If you ask any Zimbabwean or the citizen of any similarly wretched country about whether public service is the main motive for their leaders' longevity in office, you will be laughed off.

Mugabe's many economic "achievements" included a fall in Zimbabwe's real income by two-thirds between 1980, when he took office, and 2008, and an inflation rate which reached $7.3*10^{22}$%

A never-ending succession of corrupt, ineffective, and morally bankrupt presidents and prime ministers whose sole interest is to plunder their countries and fatten their Swiss bank accounts explains why those countries, especially in Africa but also elsewhere, never leave the batter's box.... Mugabe's many economic 'achievements' included a fall in Zimbabwe's real income by two-thirds between 1980, when he took office, and 2008, and an inflation rate which reached $7.3*10^{22}$% in 2008.

"

in 2008, largely because the government printed money to finance spending.[1] Like his ideological soul mate and fellow economy-destroyer Hugo Chávez in Venezuela, Mugabe fixed the prices of basic goods at ridiculously low levels, in the name of "helping" the poor. Predictably, the goods quickly vanished from stores and supermarkets since no sane seller would sell his wares at a loss. Equally predictably, and like Chávez, Mugabe had blamed profiteers, traitors, and Western imperialists for the collapse of the economy. The Zimbabwe dollar was finally abandoned and mercifully replaced by the US dollar in April 2009. Unfortunately, due to continued economic mismanagement, the banks ran out of US dollars in 2016 and the government issued yet another worthless Mickey Mouse currency of its own. Mugabe's bad government had turned what was Africa's most promising economy in 1980 to a hopeless basket case. Mugabe was finally kicked out of office in November 2017, but it remains to be seen whether his successor can restore a measure of sanity to the devastated economy.[2]

The lack of visionary leadership at the top also explains why so many developing countries which are on first base never make it to second base, and why so many developing countries which are on second never make it to third base. This is a problem known among economists as the middle-income trap. Historical experience shows that it is relatively easy for countries to move up from a poor country to a middle-income country even though there are plenty of countries that fail to do even that. This unfortunate phenomenon is known as the middle-income trap, and it describes the large group of countries that are seemingly trapped forever in middle income without any hope for moving up to higher income levels. The middle-income trap countries are especially prevalent in Latin America — for example, Brazil and Mexico

[1] http://www.economist.com/news/americas/21695934-venezuela-today-looks-zimbabwe-15-years-ago-spot-difference

[2] https://www.economist.com/middle-east-and-africa/2018/05/19/zimbabwes-new-president-may-not-be-able-to-fix-the-economy

seem to be permanently middle income — but there are also well-known examples in Asia. Malaysia and Thailand in particular have not been able to make the jump to the next level.

In fact, only very few developing countries have managed to escape the middle-income trap. The handful of developing countries that made it from the batter's box all the way to home plate — e.g. South Korea or Singapore — have one thing in common — visionary, transformational leaders who permanently improved the lives of their citizens. It is difficult to overstate the contribution of Park Chung-hee to the Korean miracle or the contribution of Lee Kuan Yew to the Singaporean miracle. Another, perhaps more surprising common factor is lack of natural resources such as oil or other mineral wealth. Lack of natural resources made those countries earn their wealth the old-fashioned way — through sheer determination and hard work. Perhaps lack of natural wealth is a blessing in disguise — it makes the country work that much harder.

Perhaps abundance of natural wealth is a curse — countries like Saudi Arabia or Venezuela would have worked much harder if they did not have the luxury of oil wealth to fall back on. This phenomenon is known as the resource curse, and it afflicts virtually all developing countries that have an abundance of natural resources, be it oil, natural gas, iron ore, uranium, copper, or other natural resources. Economists have put a number of explanations for why resource-rich countries almost always underperform. For example, when a country that just struck oil starts to export the black gold, US dollars pour into the country, making the country's currency more expensive. This is good news for the country's consumers since it makes imported goods cheaper. But it is bad

"

The handful of developing countries that made it from the batter's box all the way to home plate — e.g. South Korea or Singapore — have one thing in common — visionary, transformational leaders who permanently improved the lives of their citizens.... Another, perhaps more surprising common factor is lack of natural resources such as oil or other mineral wealth.

"

news for the country's companies, who have to contend with not only cheaper imports at home, but also find it more difficult to sell abroad since their exports are now more expensive.

There is clearly an element of truth to this technical economists' explanation of the harmful impact of the natural resource boom on a country's non-oil (if the natural resource is oil) industries and firms. This explanation is often put forth to explain why oil is often the only industry in oil-rich countries, and why manufacturing, agriculture, and all other economic activities are often wiped out in oil-rich countries. Yet there is a much bigger, one-word explanation for why oil-rich countries, and more generally resource-rich countries, fail — laziness. A good analogy to an oil bonanza — e.g. suppose a dirt-poor Middle Eastern or Latin American country strikes oil and soon exports 2 million barrels of oil a day — is a penniless, alcoholic beggar who suddenly gets an unexpected million dollar inheritance from a distant uncle whom he was not even aware of. Unfortunately, all too often, in the real world, such beggars squander their unexpected windfall on booze, women and gambling, and end up where they began, penniless and on the streets. Hence, it is often the case with countries that mindlessly squander their abundant natural wealth without any regard for the future of their countries.

Instead of using the money in a sensible way, such as checking into an alcoholic rehab center, cleaning up, and getting his life back in order, the beggar goes on a drinking binge or a heroine binge or binge on whatever he was on. This may be a little harsh, but this is a fairly accurate description of what resource-rich countries have been doing with their resource bonanzas. It is true that a few, far too few in fact, resource-rich countries have used their bonanza more

"

Yet there is a much bigger, one-word explanation for why oil-rich countries, and more generally resource-rich countries, fail — laziness. A good analogy to an oil bonanza — e.g. suppose a dirt-poor Middle Eastern or Latin American country strikes oil and soon exports 2 million barrels of oil a day — is a penniless, alcoholic beggar who suddenly gets an unexpected million dollar inheritance from a distant uncle whom he was not even aware of.

"

sensibly than others — Botswana in southern Africa is a good example. But by and large, oil-rich and resource-rich countries have not used their windfall wisely and for that, they only have themselves to blame. Instead of spending at least some of the money on investments that will help create new industries and firms when the oil runs out, the governments of those countries are busy splurging money left and right engaging in buying short-term political support with cash, subsidies, public sector "jobs" where one gets paid just for showing up (and sometimes even when one does not show up), and other assorted handouts. The goodies will win votes and political support for a few years but will do precious little to prepare the country for the day when the oil or natural gas or copper or whatever runs out, and that day will eventually come.

The oil-rich countries of the Middle East are a classic example of this type of squandering natural wealth with little preparation for the future. In countries such as Saudi Arabia, the preferred modus operandi of the government is to pacify the general population with handouts, subsidies, and above all, government jobs. That is, the government uses the bulk of its vast oil revenues to buy off citizens and prevent political unrest, but makes no investment which will help the country make a living when oil runs out. Most alarmingly, there is little investment in education and human capital. Instead of teaching its own citizens to catch fish for themselves, the government is hand-feeding them fish to buy their support. This is not good for the citizens and the country's future, especially since human capital is vital for economic growth.

In oil-rich Middle East, the unskilled, low-wage jobs are done by workers from poor countries and the professional, high-wage jobs are done by Western expatriates. The locals are too lazy

The oil-rich countries of the Middle East are a classic example of this type of squandering natural wealth with little preparation for the future. In countries such as Saudi Arabia, the preferred modus operandi of the government is to pacify the general population with handouts, subsidies, and above all, government jobs.

for the former — it is also beneath their dignity to do menial jobs — and do not have the skills to do the latter. The guarantee of a well-paid government job blunts the incentives of young Arabs from oil-rich countries to work hard at school. They end up as additional workers in a bloated government sector which adds little value to the economy and does nothing to help prepare the economy for the end of oil. Some oil-rich Middle Eastern states are mandating that foreign companies operating in the country hire a certain number of local workers, as a way to boost employment. It is a measure of the abysmal quality of local education that the foreign companies subject to such regulations view local workers as a costly tax that must be paid to do business in the country. That is a sad indictment and should serve as a wake-up alarm for the petro-states.

"

Some oil-rich Middle Eastern states are mandating that foreign companies operating in the country hire a certain number of local workers, as a way to boost employment. It is a measure of the abysmal quality of local education that the foreign companies subject to such regulations view local workers as a costly tax.

"

EVITA PERÓN, HUGO CHÁVEZ, FIDEL CASTRO, AND LATIN AMERICAN BANANA REPUBLICS

It is striking how one finds hard pressed to name a single visionary leader from countries that are in seemingly endless decline — e.g. Argentina — or countries which consistently underperform — e.g. Venezuela. Evita Perón may be the heroine of a nice musical and "Don't cry for me, Argentina" may be a nice line in a nice musical, but Argentines have absolutely no reason to cry for her or her equally underwhelming husband Juan Perón. Their legacy to the country is that and only that, a nice musical with a nice line. And, their present-day spiritual successors, ex-President Cristina Fernández and her late husband and ex-President Néstor Kirchner, have been equally underwhelming. Both the Peróns and Kirchners are simply part of a long line of uninspiring, mediocre, unimpressive, and most definitely NOT transformational or visionary Argentinian leaders. They are leaders who merely stood by and did absolutely nothing to stop the century-long stagnation and decline of their country. In fact, their misguided populist policies contributed a great deal to the decline of Argentina.

When it comes to producing uninspiring, mediocre, and unimpressive leaders on a

> **"**
> They are leaders who merely stood by and did absolutely nothing to stop the century-long stagnation and decline of their country. In fact, their misguided populist policies contributed a great deal to the decline of Argentina.
> **"**

consistent basis, year in year out, decade in decade out, Venezuela is no slouch and it can easily give Argentina a good run for its money. For decades, the country was run by a kleptocratic, oligarchic elite that plundered much of the country's colossal oil wealth while delivering little, if any, improvement in the living standards of the population. Venezuela is blessed with the largest oil reserves in Latin America, and one of the largest oil reserves in the world. Instead of using this blessing to develop the country, the kleptocratic, oligarchic elite used it almost entirely to enrich themselves. All this changed when Hugo Chávez, a career military officer, won the presidential elections in 1998, promising to play Robin Hood and help long-suffering poorer Venezuelans. To be fair, his radical leftist, socialist government did bring about a sharp reduction in official poverty rates — i.e. the share of population living in poverty — although even this gain was later wiped out as a result of economic collapse, an all-too-predictable result of their economically illiterate Robin Hood policies. The central mission of the Chávez regime was to create a fairer Venezuela, and it temporarily and arguably — arguably because the regime wrecked the economy in the process — succeeded in that mission.

According to the World Bank, as a result of broad-based social programs known as Misiones, Venezuela's moderate poverty rate fell from 50% in 1998 to 30% in 2012 under Chávez's rule, which is an impressive reduction in poverty in a span of just 14 years. Moderate poverty refers to living of a person earning less than US$2 a day, or an income that is only enough to cover a family's minimum requirements for food, health care, clothing, and shelter. During the same period, Gini coefficient, the most widely

"

When it comes to producing uninspiring, mediocre, and unimpressive leaders on a consistent basis, year in year out, decade in decade out, Venezuela is no slouch and it can easily give Argentina a good run for its money.

"

used measure of income inequality, fell from 0.49 to 0.39. The value of the Gini coefficient ranges from zero, when there is perfect income equality so that everybody earns the same income, to one, when there is perfect inequality so that all income goes to only one person. The lower the value of the Gini coefficient, the more equal the economy. In short, the Chávez regime did succeed in reducing poverty and inequality, which is why the regime continues to enjoy the support of poor Venezuelans.

But critically, the achievement came at a heavy price — the obliteration of the economy due to absurd, self-destructive, economically illiterate policies such as sacking 20,000 engineers and other technocrats at the state-owned oil company and replacing them with 100,000 hacks from Chávez's political party, hacks with zero experience in or knowledge about the oil industry. All too predictably, this policy had a disastrous impact on the production of oil, the main export of a country with precious little else to sell to the rest of the world. More broadly, wholesale government takeovers of private companies and stifling harassment of the private sector have completely destroyed the confidence of the business community. In addition, price controls, or the government fixing the price at artificially low levels where no sane seller would sell, have resulted in severe shortages of basic necessities such as food and gasoline.

Considering low prices help the poor only if the goods are actually available, low prices do not help poor Venezuelans at all. A visit to any supermarket in Venezuela yields the same tragicomic outcome. No milk, no coffee, no sugar, no soap, no cornflour, no cooking oil.[1] Large crowds queue and mill around outside

[1] http://www.economist.com/news/americas/21695934-venezuela-today-looks-zimbabwe-15-years-ago-spot-difference

Venezuelan supermarkets, hoping against hope that a truck carrying anything will arrive.[2] Playing Robin Hood is fine, but most definitely NOT in the economically illiterate, Chávez-like way that ruins the economy and destroys whatever pie there is to take from the rich and give to the poor.[3] But there is no compelling reason to single out the late Hugo Chávez and his equally destructive successor Nicolás Maduro.[4] Both are merely part and parcel of a long line of uninspiring leaders who have wasted their country's vast oil wealth, and left no lasting positive legacy from that wealth to Venezuelans, especially poor Venezuelans.

Not surprisingly, given the collapse of the economy due to economically illiterate policies, even the reduction in poverty was short-lived. By 2015, 81% of Venezuelans lived in poverty and 87% of Venezuelans did not have enough money for food. Furthermore, over 13% of Venezuelans could afford only one or two meals per day. The shortage of food and medicine is so widespread that it resembles a country in the immediate aftermath of a war.[5] Poverty and hunger have become so extensive that even middle-class Venezuelans have been reduced to dumpster diving,[6] or sifting through trash for food to survive. This economic catastrophe, which forced hundreds of thousands of Venezuelans to flee to Colombia, Brazil and other neighboring countries, was entirely due to the absurd ruinous economic policies of the Chávez and Maduro governments. In short, the catastrophe was entirely manmade and underlines the unparalleled destructive power of socialism.

It is simply mindboggling to think what Venezuela would be like today if the governments had used the colossal oil wealth even half, make

[2] Predictably, Venezuela's insane price controls created a thriving smuggling industry in the Colombian–Venezuelan border area. It does not take a Colombian genius to figure out that buying, say, toothpaste in Venezuela for, say, $1 and selling it in Colombia, which is free from insane price controls, for $3 will deliver a nice tidy profit. The Colombian genius can even afford to give the Venezuelan toothpaste seller a bribe to get his hands on the artificially cheap toothpaste, further worsening the shortage and misery for Venezuelans, especially poor Venezuelans. "Venezuela's economic crash has led to a vast smuggling industry," TIME magazine, by Ezra Kaplan, 25 April 2016; and "Requiem for Venezuela," TIME magazine, by Ioan Grillo, 22 August 2016.

[3] Venezuela's inflation rate was expected to hit 481% by end of 2016 and 1,642% by 2017. http://time.com/4348972/venezuela-goes-from-bad-to-catastrophe/ Inflation, of course, hits the poor harder than the rich since the poor do not have access to sophisticated financial products which protect them from inflation. Furthermore, when inflation is so high, anybody with any money will try to change as much of their increasingly worthless local currency into US dollars and send them abroad. Unfortunately, the poor do not have any money to send abroad and are stuck with their bolívares, which buy them less and less goods and services with every passing day. Venezuela under Chávez and Nicolás Maduro is a classic example of how economically illiterate, populist, socialist governments hurt the poor the most, ironically. http://time.com/4348972/venezuela-goes-from-bad-to-catastrophe/

[4] In May 2016, Venezuelans set their clocks ahead by 30 minutes to save power in the face of severe power shortage, on President Maduro's orders. According to the Venezuelan government, the 30 extra minutes of daylight would reduce the use of lights and air conditioning. Government workers were ordered to come to work only on two weekdays, and schools were closed on Fridays. These are just some examples of the government's absurd efforts to undo the damage done by its own farcical economic policies, which created the power shortage in the first place. https://sg.news.yahoo.com/crisis-hit-venezuela-push-clocks-forward-save-power-221919207.html?nhp=1

[5] https://panampost.com/pedro-garcia/2016/07/04/venezuela-hunger-poorest-widespread/

[6] http://www.cbsnews.com/news/venezuela-economic-crisis-middle-class-dumpster-diving-food/

that one fourth, as effectively as they actually did — for example, by investing in education and health care. Instead the oil-rich country has become a banana republic and a laughing stock. The wasted opportunity is downright criminal, especially for the millions of poorer Venezuelans who would have benefited the most from better use of the oil wealth. In other words, what Venezuela would be like today if it had its own Lee Kuan Yew or Park Chung-hee instead of the long line of mediocre, uninspiring duds. Forget game-changing, transformational leaders like Lee or Park. That is perhaps too much to ask. But if Venezuela had at least half-decent leaders, rather than Chávez, Maduro or their kleptocratic predecessors, the country would be in immeasurably better shape today.

Of course, since countries get the governments they deserve, the Venezuelan people themselves are partly to blame. After all, Venezuela is a country where the Miss Universe beauty pageant is the top national obsession. If Venezuela is to become a serious country with a serious government, Venezuelans themselves must change their mentality and way of life, and demand an effective government that invests the country's oil wealth in a productive way. The same is true for all other countries which suffer from seemingly perennial bad government. At the end of the day, if you are willing to settle for a lousy government that pilfers your country's natural wealth while delivering lousy roads, lousy schools, and lousy hospitals, then that is exactly the government you deserve and you have no right to complain about lousy government. If the top leader is always a dud, and there is not even a remote chance of a visionary, transformational, game-changing leader, then the people themselves are a big part of the problem.

By the way, decreeing low prices which only creates shortages and 10-hour waits for a loaf

"

At the end of the day, if you are willing to settle for a lousy government that pilfers your country's natural wealth while delivering lousy roads, lousy schools, and lousy hospitals, then that is exactly the government you deserve and you have no right to complain about lousy government.

"

of brain or a few rolls of toilet paper does not help anybody, least of all the poor who are unable to afford the bribes that the better off can pay to get their hands on the basic necessities. More fundamentally, if the government simply announces that the price of a loaf of bread will be US$1 instead of US$3, then the supply of bread will dry up. Bread makers will not sell bread which costs US$2 to make at US$1. Governments, even economically illiterate socialist governments, cannot force the private sector to sell goods and services at a loss, except perhaps at gunpoint. The alternative is for the government to take over production and produce the goods and services, but we all know where that story ends — e.g. endless queues for a few rolls of low-quality, seeping toilet paper, as in the Soviet Union. In this kind of socialist policy environment, private entrepreneurs will simply close shop, pack their bags, and leave the country.

This is exactly what happened in Cuba when Fidel Castro decided to turn his Caribbean island into a Soviet satellite. To be fair, the Cuban revolution did have some notable achievements, such as better health care than the rest of Latin America, but it was an unmitigated economic disaster. In fact, without massive Soviet subsidies, the Cuban economy would have collapsed, which is why, at the end of the day, Castro will be remembered by history as just another mediocre, uninspiring, mundane leader, notwithstanding his own self-delusions of greatness.[7] Soviet satellite is an accurate description of Cuba despite the futile efforts of its supporters, especially starry-eyed leftists in Western countries, to romanticize and glorify the Cuban revolution. Standing up to US imperialism is all nice and good, but if the government cannot even feed its own people

[7] In addition to economic misery, Castro delivered political dictatorship, locking up political prisoners without even any pretense of trial. There is nothing romantic about the Cuban revolution, notwithstanding the misguided tendency of many foreigners to romanticize it. Just ask the Cuban people, who have lived through almost six decades of economic hardship and political authoritarianism. Worst of all worlds.

without Soviet handouts, then basically it is a beggar, and certainly no role model for other developing countries. In the extreme case of Cuba, virtually the entire middle class and private sector fled to the US. Cuba's loss was America's gain, and Cuban-Americans have become a highly successful immigrant group, in Florida and elsewhere.

Venezuela's economic meltdown under the economically illiterate, populist tag team of the late Chávez and Maduro is a good summary of the perils of socialism, which is, to repeat, the single biggest man-made disaster in the history of mankind, without any doubt and by a long distance. Bar none. In short, socialism amounts to a group of mediocre politicians and bureaucrats stealing the hard-earned money of the country's most productive entrepreneurs and companies, keeping a large share of the stolen money for themselves and their supporters, and giving away the remainder to the poor. There is absolutely nothing heroic, noble, generous, dignified, humane, compassionate or uplifting about stealing other people's money to enrich yourself and your supporters, and acting like a noble savior of the poor people by giving out various goodies before the money runs out. Indeed it is utterly hypocritical and disgusting. The money will run out, as in Venezuela, as a result of illiterate policies such as unaffordable subsidies which bankrupt the government and devastate the economy. Socialist governments tend to spend money right and left for the same reason that thieves spend their loot left and right. It is because the money is not theirs.

Most damningly, at the end of the day, it is the poor, the very people the Chávezes and Maduros of the world purport to "help," who suffer the most from their economy-destroying

"

In the extreme case of Cuba, virtually the entire middle class and private sector fled to the US. Cuba's loss was America's gain, and Cuban-Americans have become a highly successful immigrant group, in Florida and elsewhere.

"

populist socialist policies. Populism refers to economic policies that are popular and hence vote winners, especially among poor voters, in the short run but harm the economy beyond the short run. It has to be said that populism is a terrible misnomer because populist socialist policies do not benefit poor people at all. In fact, to the contrary, the poor suffer the most under such economically illiterate, politically motivated policies. Rich Venezuelans can and often do send their money, their children, or both to Miami to escape the economic catastrophe. Poor Venezuelans do not have that luxury. A classic example of shortsighted and self-destructive so-called populist policies is giving out handouts, for example subsidy for food or fuel, when the government cannot afford such handouts. The late Chávez was able to carry on such insane policies only because the global price of oil, the only thing that Venezuela can sell to the world, was sky-high during his rule. If the man-made disaster that is Venezuela makes for depressing reading, the man-made miracle of China is infinitely more inspirational and uplifting.

"

In fact, to the contrary, the poor suffer the most under such economically illiterate, politically motivated policies. Rich Venezuelans can and often do send their money, their children, or both to Miami to escape the economic catastrophe. Poor Venezuelans do not have that luxury.

"

215

THE STUNNING RISE OF CHINA, AND MANDARIN-SPEAKING GUIDES IN PARISIAN SHOPS

48

The single most significant global economic trend since the second half of the 20th century has been the phenomenal rise of China. The country has transformed itself from a stagnant, over-populated, hopeless basket case to the world's most dynamic, fastest-growing, most exciting major economy within a generation. China overtook Japan to become the world's second largest economy in 2010, and is on course to overtake the US to become the world's biggest economy in the foreseeable future. Its GDP or gross domestic product, the total amount of goods and services produced by an economy in one year, exploded from US$186 billion to US$12 trillion between 1978 and 2017. The size of the Chinese economy thus grew by an astonishing 65 times in 39 years. It is as if a dwarf morphed into a giant within a generation! One would be hard pressed to think of a more powerful testament to the unparalleled superiority of capitalism as an engine of economic growth and progress than the stunning economic transformation of China. As a result, more than a billion Chinese enjoy far more productive, abundant, and humane lives.

China was hardly relevant to the world economy 40 years ago, but now China is at the very front

> **" One would be hard pressed to think of a more powerful testament to the unparalleled superiority of capitalism as an engine of economic growth and progress than the stunning economic transformation of China. As a result, more than a billion Chinese enjoy far more productive, abundant, and humane lives. "**

and center of the world economy. To name just one example, China's seemingly insatiable appetite for raw materials drove the decades-long commodity boom which lifted commodity-rich economies as distant as those in Africa and Latin America. Indeed China's robust demand had a powerful impact on global commodity prices, from oil to iron ore to soya beans. Conversely, when China's growth slowed down after the Global Financial Crisis, those same distant economies deeply felt the reverberations of the slowdown. A popular saying is "When the US sneezes, Asia catches a cold" but the same thing can be said about China's growing economic influence over its Asian neighbors and many developing countries farther afield.

Nor are rich, advanced countries such as the US, Japan and Western Europe immune from the growing imprint of China on the global economy. For example, China is, in effect, helping to finance the US federal government's deficit by buying massive amounts of US government bonds. There is a great deal of China bashing in the US, including ridiculous attempts by populist US politicians to legislate China's exchange rate. But at the end of the day, the China–US relationship is not a one-way street where the US bears all the costs and China gains all the benefits.[1] The US exports a lot to China, which creates thousands of American jobs, and most importantly, US consumers benefit hugely from the sharp reduction in the price of the goods they buy. "Made in China" may still be a byword for poor quality in the US, but made in China adds thousands of dollars to the real incomes of American consumers by reducing prices. Moreover, Japan depends heavily on huge amounts of exports to China to sustain its feeble economy, despite geopolitical tension between the two Asian giants.

[1] This is, of course, exactly how Donald Trump portrays the US–China trade relationship. The US does run a large and persistent trade deficit with China, which reached a record US$566 billion in 2017, and this is fueling trade tension between the two giants. The tension is reaching fever pitch under the Trump administration. See, for example, https://www.nytimes.com/2018/02/06/us/politics/us-china-trade-deficit.html

Furthermore, while foreign investment, in particular foreign direct investment — i.e. building new factories and other productive facilities, as opposed to just lending money to Chinese firms — contributed a lot to China's industrialization and growth, China has now turned the tables and become one of the world's largest investors in other countries. Indeed countries, rich and poor, are scrambling for a piece of China's huge and growing foreign investment, in the hopes that it will lift their economies and create jobs. China's investment, combined with its foreign aid, has become a powerful engine of growth for Africa. While Western and African critics bemoan China's unscrupulous exploitation of Africa's natural wealth and blatant disregard for the environment and workers' rights, China is investing in countries where there are few other foreign investors. That is, while Chinese investors may not be saints, their investments in corrupt, poor, wretched "no go" countries contribute to the growth and development of those countries. In short, China has become a genuine global economic superpower with influence in all corners of the world. No doubt about that.

However, China is still a long shot from being a rich country and it is important not to confuse China's sheer economic size with the average living standards of its citizens. Of course, China's capitalist revolution has produced plenty of millionaires and billionaires, including tech tycoons such as Jack Ma, Pony Ma, Lei Jun, and Robin Li, but the average Chinese remains much poorer than the average American. China's population is much larger than that of the US, so it will be decades before it catches up with the US in terms of living standards. In 2014, the average income of the Chinese was US$7,400, far below the US figure of US$55,200.[2] But even

[2] This is a difference of around 7.5 times. Even if we account for the fact that the prices of non-tradable goods and services such as haircuts are cheaper in China than America, the difference is still more than four times — US$13,170 versus US$55,860.

living standards, measured by GDP per capita or the amount of goods and services produced by each person, have skyrocketed. Average income grew by more than 40 times between 1978 and 2015, and the proportion of those living in poverty fell sharply as well. Just 40 years ago, China was a poor, low income country by any measure, comparable to the poorest African countries. Now China is comfortably a middle-class country and according to the World Bank's classifications, it is an upper middle-income country.

The skylines of Beijing, Shanghai and even smaller provincial cities have changed beyond all recognition, and millions of Chinese are buying their first car, taking their first airline flight, and enjoying their first vacation abroad. While locals outside of China laugh at the crude, uncouth, and unsophisticated behavior — e.g. spitting on the streets, talking loudly inside museums, or taking shower robes as souvenirs from five-star hotel rooms — of Chinese tourist hordes descending upon Paris, New York or Bangkok like locusts, they stop laughing when they open their fat wallets. Big spending Chinese tourists are not just a stereotype; statistics show that they are often the biggest spending nationality of tourists. This explains why the flagship stores of European luxury brands such as Louis Vuitton, Salvatore Ferragamo or Burberry, in Paris, Milan or London usually have Mandarin-speaking guides on hand. Uncouth and uncivilized they may be,[3] but Chinese tourists add much more to the local economy[4] than beer-swilling, gum-chewing, penny-pinching multinational backpacker hordes who can be equally obnoxious, but provide far fewer benefits for the local economy.

[3] The behavior of some Chinese tourists has become so embarrassing that in September 2014, during an official visit to the Indian Ocean island-state of the Maldives, Chinese President Xi Jinping personally implored Chinese tourists to behave themselves when traveling abroad. For example, in December 2014, a China-bound Thai AirAsia flight had to return to Bangkok airport after a hot-headed Chinese female passenger threw hot water on a flight attendant during an altercation over service. http://edition.cnn.com/2015/01/11/travel/china-eastern-air-rage-2015/?iid=ob_lockedrail_bottommedium

[4] In 2015, 109 million Chinese tourists armed with purchasing power of US$229 billion traveled abroad. Their most popular destination was Asia, followed by Europe. http://edition.cnn.com/2016/05/03/travel/chinese-police-italy-rome-milan-tourists/index.html

TRANSFORMATIONAL LEADERS, DENG XIAOPING, RONALD REAGAN, AND CHINESE HUMAN RIGHTS

49

As you might have already guessed, China's explosive economic growth was set off by a transformational leader, Deng Xiaoping. More precisely, his momentous decision in 1978 to free the Chinese economy from the shackles of central planning — i.e. government bureaucrats deciding how much of what gets produced by which firm — and allow market forces to play a much bigger role in how resources are allocated. That unleashed the colossal entrepreneurial energy of the Chinese people which had been artificially bottled up for decades by Mao Zedong and his fellow comrades who were busy indoctrinating the masses with socialist — more accurately, Maoist or mass peasant egalitarian — ideology, wrecking the economy in the process. As noted earlier, the Chinese are by nature an exceptionally entrepreneurial lot, and this is probably the single most common denominator linking the Chinese and the Americans, another famously entrepreneurial lot. When Deng decided to endorse the profit motive and private enterprise by uttering the famous, game-changing dictum "To get rich is glorious," the Chinese entrepreneurial genie was out of the bottle and the rest, as they say, is history, and

> " When Deng decided to endorse the profit motive and private enterprise by uttering the famous, game-changing dictum 'To get rich is glorious,' the Chinese entrepreneurial genie was out of the bottle and the rest, as they say, is history, and the Chinese economy took off like a supersonic rocket. "

the Chinese economy took off like a supersonic rocket.

Some historians and economists doubt whether the diminutive Deng, who ran China from 1978 to 1992, contributed any concrete or specific ideas to China's capitalist revolution. Others argue that many of the reform plans attributed to Deng actually came from other top communist party officials such as Zhou Enlai. Such criticisms, even if they are true, are beside the point. The genius and vision of Deng was not that he chose this specific reform plan or that specific reform plan, but that he realized, at a big-picture strategic level, that the centrally planned socialist economy was not working, the lives of hundreds of millions of Chinese people were not getting better, and it was time to change course and espouse the market. Since the socialist model which delivered equal poverty for all was clearly failing the Chinese people, Deng decided to ditch it and catch the capitalist bus to economic progress and prosperity. His visits to prosperous, capitalist East Asian countries, in particular Singapore, a multi-racial city-state which is now one of the richest countries in the world, left an indelible mark on his psyche. If tiny Singapore, three quarters of whose citizens are descended from Chinese immigrants, can succeed, why not China?

The role of a national leader, especially the national leader of a big country like China or America, is to set forth a grand vision for their countries. The greatest leaders are those who have a clear vision and follow through with that great vision. Ronald Reagan, who is now widely regarded as one of the greatest American leaders in the postwar era, was never known for sharp intellect or detailed grasp of policy, but he had a clear vision — that of a strong America standing up to and

> **"**
> Deng realized that the centrally planned socialist economy was not working, the lives of hundreds of millions of Chinese people were not getting better, and it was time to change course and espouse the market. Since the socialist model which delivered equal poverty for all was clearly failing the Chinese people, Deng decided to ditch it and catch the capitalist bus to economic progress and prosperity.
> **"**

defeating the Soviet empire — and he followed through with that vision. His famous dictum "Mr. Gorbachev, tear down this wall," uttered when he expressed his wish for the removal of the Berlin Wall which divided East and West Germany, best expresses his unyielding, visionary, game-changing leadership. Reagan's leadership helped free millions of Russians, East Germans, Poles, Czechs, and others from socialist slavery. Likewise, Deng's famous dictum "It doesn't matter if a cat is black or white, so long as it catches mice" reflects his practical philosophy and above all, his determination to put ideology aside and use the magic of capitalism for the benefit of his people.

If there is one historical episode that captures the immense power of capitalism to foster economic growth and improve the lives of people, it is the meteoric rise of China as an economic superpower. Deng's momentous decision to ditch the sterile socialism that artificially impoverished the talented, industrious, and entrepreneurial Chinese people — hence his angry dictum "Poverty is not socialism" — for the infinitely more fertile capitalism set China on its way. The average Chinese today eats much better, has a better home, wears better clothes, has access to better health care, and attends better schools than his counterparts 40 years ago could have even imagined. Western critics of China, of which there are a dime a dozen, tend to dwell on China's lack of Western democracy and poor human rights record. Fair enough, but surely, better nutrition, health care, education, and overall quality of life is part of human rights too. Indeed for poor countries, they are the more important human rights.

Nor has China's economic growth just benefited the better off, such as the large and growing middle class in Beijing, Shanghai, Guangzhou,

> " Deng's momentous decision to ditch the sterile socialism that artificially impoverished the talented, industrious, and entrepreneurial Chinese people — hence his angry dictum 'Poverty is not socialism' — for the infinitely more fertile capitalism set China on its way. The average Chinese today eats much better, has a better home, wears better clothes, has access to better health care, and attends better schools than his counterparts 40 years ago could have even imagined. "

and other big cities. According to the World Bank, based on the widely used poverty measure of living on less than US$1.25 a day, the number of poor Chinese fell from 689 million in 1990 to 84 million in 2011. Moreover, the poverty rate, or share of the poor in total population, fell from 60.7% to 6.3%. Yes, gaping inequality is a major problem, but that is a global problem, not a China-specific problem. In short, post-Deng China is the one-word, exclamation-point rejoinder to any doubts about capitalism as the greatest invention of mankind. By the same token, the crushing poverty of pre-Deng China serves a powerful testament to the unparalleled destructive capacity of socialism as an impoverishing, immiserizing, and dehumanizing economic system. To repeat, socialism is by far the biggest man-made disaster in the history of mankind. Bar none.

"

In short, post-Deng China is the one-word, exclamation-point rejoinder to any doubts about capitalism as the greatest invention of mankind. By the same token, the crushing poverty of pre-Deng China serves a powerful testament to the unparalleled destructive capacity of socialism as an impoverishing, immiserizing, and dehumanizing economic system. To repeat, socialism is by far the biggest man-made disaster in the history of mankind. Bar none.

"

MARKETS OVER MAO

50

Somewhat perversely and completely inaccurately, China's economic success may be seized upon by anti-capitalists who advocate a larger role for the state or the government in the economy, and a correspondingly smaller role for the market or the private sector. The government continues to play a much larger role in the Chinese economy than in full-fledged market economies such as America. For example, when Beijing dismantled socialist commune farms in 1978 in one of the most important market-oriented economic reforms and gave farmers the freedom to manage their individual plots of land, it kept ownership of land and gave the farmers 30-year leases. State ownership of farm land is just one example of the state's dominance of many parts of the economy. The visible hand of the government still remains all too obvious in China, and China has a long way to go before it becomes a market economy.

The Chinese financial system, in particular, is tightly controlled by the state and its banks' lending decisions are heavily influenced by the state. In other words, Chinese banks decide to lend not on the basis of purely commercial considerations, as American banks would,

> **"**
>
> The government continues to play a much larger role in the Chinese economy than in full-fledged market economies such as America.... The Chinese financial system, in particular, is tightly controlled by the state and its banks' lending decisions are heavily influenced by the state.
>
> **"**

but partly on the basis of the government's preferences. In a market economy, the financial system channels savings to the most productive investments which, in turn, is determined by market forces. For example, if the rapid expansion of the Chinese middle classes brings about a surge in demand for automobiles, as it actually has, a well-functioning financial system should channel savings toward the automobile industry. In stark contrast, in the case of China, due to the extensive interference of the government, the financial system ends up directing resources toward industries, firms, and activities favored by government bureaucrats. The lack of a market-based financial system is one of the key features of China's unique brand of capitalism. It also shows that China still has yet to become a full-fledged market economy.

Above all, Chinese banks, themselves state-owned, allocate far too much capital to state-owned enterprises (SOEs). These firms are relics from China's socialist past, but they still play a major role in the Chinese economy. At the end of 2014, China's 12 largest companies — a diverse list that includes the country's four largest banks, three energy companies, an energy utility, a car manufacturer, a construction company, a railway operator, and a mobile telecom — were all owned by the government.[1] The top five were Sinopec — the world's largest oil refiner, China National Petroleum — China's biggest oil producer, State Grid — the world's largest energy utility, and two large state-owned banks — Industrial and Commercial Bank of China and China Construction Bank. Agricultural Bank of China, China State Construction Engineering, Bank of China, China Mobile Communications, SAIC Motor, China Railway Engineering, and China National Offshore Oil (CNOOC) round out the top twelve. These large state-owned giants are

225

[1] http://fortune.com/2015/07/22/china-global-500-government-owned/

known as red chips — the blue chip companies of state capitalism — and are viewed by Chinese and foreigners alike as advertisements for the success of state capitalism.

Indeed most of the 100 or so Chinese firms on the Fortune 500 list of the world's biggest companies are state-owned companies,[2] which still account for a large share of output and employment even though their share has declined steadily since 1978. For example, according to *Markets over Mao*, an excellent scholarly account of the rise of private business in China by Nicholas Lardy of the Peterson Institute for International Economics, a world-renowned China expert, the share of state firms in total industrial output was still substantial at 26% in 2011. In some industries such as tobacco and cigarettes, state firms account for almost 100% of output.

But appearances are completely deceiving in the case of Chinese SOEs. Notwithstanding their huge size and glossy headquarters in Beijing or Shanghai, they are largely bloated and inefficient, and owe their apparent "success" to government protection.[3] They are not and never will be the engines of China's economic growth and process. This explains why very few foreigners ever heard of China's top 12 companies, mentioned earlier. To the contrary, they subtract from rather than add to China's economic dynamism, and the sooner they give way to the more efficient, productive and innovative private sector, the better it will be for China's future.

State capitalism refers to China's unique brand of capitalism under which the government plays a big role in the economy and the transition to a fully market-based economy is far from complete. In other words, state capitalism means that the basic economic system is capitalism, but the

[2] http://www.economist.com/news/special-report/21663329-it-private-sector-not-state-capitalism-responsible-modern-chinas

[3] http://www.economist.com/news/business-and-finance/21679360-and-its-no-longer-certain-government-will-bail-them-out-creditworthiness-chinas

state continues to exert significant control over the economy — which firms and industries gets how much bank loans, the interest rate that banks can charge for loans, how a plot of land is to be used, and so forth. A key attribute of state capitalism is that the "state" in "state capitalism" is usually a strong state, although not necessarily authoritarian. For example, although Turkey is a multi-party, Western-style parliamentary democracy, Prime Minister Recep Tayyip Erdoğan is widely viewed as a strong leader running a strong government. On the other hand, China is clearly not a Western-style democracy and it is ruled by a single political party. Furthermore, the links between politics and business are so tight that the line between the two is blurred. Many local governments, for example the governments of China's 31 provinces, own a large number of companies in a wide range of industries.

China's combination of state capitalism and rapid growth can be interpreted as evidence that the visible hand of the government, as opposed to the invisible hand of the market — or Adam Smith's classical description of how individual greed under capitalism promotes the social good — can deliver economic progress, improvement in general living standards, and massive reduction in poverty. Yet nothing could be further from the truth, as explained convincingly by Lardy in *Markets over Mao*. China has done so well not *because of* the government's visible hand, but *despite* the government's visible hand. A much more accurate reading of China's phenomenal growth reveals that the country's explosive growth closely parallels the growth of the private sector. For example, to return to an earlier statistic, while the share of state firms in total industrial output stood at 26% in 2011, it stood at 78% in 1978. Therefore, what explains China's astonishing transformation into

> **"** Yet nothing could be further from the truth, as explained convincingly by Lardy in *Markets over Mao*. China has done so well not *because* of the government's visible hand, but *despite* the government's visible hand. A much more accurate reading of China's phenomenal growth reveals that the country's explosive growth closely parallels the growth of the private sector. **"**

an economic superpower is not the 26% share of the state in 2011, but rather the steady decline in the share of the state from 78% in 1978 to 26% in 2011. The story of China's remarkable success is ultimately the story of the rise of the private sector.

All other indicators tell exactly the same story. The private sector has been growing, and growing relentlessly, in China. Take employment for example. According to *Markets over Mao*, almost all the 250 million jobs created in Chinese cities since 1978 have been in the private sector. The share of the urban labor force working for the state collapsed from 99% in 1978 to 18% by 2011.[4] Private firms also contribute an ever-growing share of China's exports. The share of China's domestic private sector, as opposed to foreign firms or China's state-owned firms, in China's exports rose from virtually nothing as recently as 1995 to 39% in 2012. Conversely, the share of state-owned firms plummeted from almost two-thirds in 1995 to only 11% by 2012.

Foreign firms in China tend to assemble imported parts and components for exports, to take advantage of China's abundant pool of cheap labor — although that abundant pool is disappearing and workers' wages are rising now. For such exports, China's value added — the value that China adds to the exported good — is limited to the low wage of the assembly line worker. In striking contrast, the exports of private Chinese firms are less likely to be assembled goods. In other words, China's value added is higher for those exports, which helps China move up the value chain. That is, it is the private sector that is spearheading China's technological upgrading into higher value-added industries and activities. This suggests that if China succeeds in making the difficult jump from

[4] http://www.economist.com/news/business-books-quarterly/21627564-private-companies-have-been-hugely-underestimated-china-unstated-capitalism

middle income to high income — a feat achieved by only South Korea and a tiny handful of other countries — it will be credited to dynamic, risk-taking private entrepreneurs, not self-important, risk-averse government bureaucrats.

"

China's jump from middle income to high income will be credited to dynamic, risk-taking private entrepreneurs, not self-important, risk-averse government bureaucrats.

"

AMERICA AND CHINA, THE TWO BEST HOPES FOR TOMORROW'S CAPITALISM

In short, China's recipe for economic success is not a new alternative model which combines capitalism with an extensive economic role of the government — a model popularly known as state capitalism — but good old-fashioned, muscular, profit-driven, risk-taking capitalism fueled by individual greed for material gain. Common sense alone tells us that "state capitalism" is an oxymoron. Government bureaucrats may be good at lots of different things, but creating wealth and jobs is not one of them. This is true for even the most capable, honest, hardworking bureaucrats who work their tails off for the public good. The reason is that wealth creation is not, and never will be, part of the government bureaucrats' job description. If a bureaucrat was any good at taking risks and making money, he would not be a risk-averse bureaucrat in the first place. He would be out in the real world, taking risks and making money, creating wealth and jobs in the process.

In fact, China's meteoric rise can be viewed as definitive proof of the colossal benefits of the invisible hand of the market. It is the greedy, profit-driven, risk-taking Chinese entrepreneur sniffing out profitable opportunities in the streets of Shanghai or Guangzhou or Chengdu who

❝

... China's recipe for economic success is not a new alternative model which combines capitalism with an extensive economic role of the government — a model popularly known as state capitalism — but good old-fashioned, muscular, profit-driven, risk-taking capitalism fueled by individual greed for material gain.

❞

expanded the Chinese economy many times over and improved the lives of more than a billion Chinese. Contrary to the wishful thinking of the anti-capitalist crowd, China owes its remarkable economic transformation to these heroes of capitalism, not the hordes of bribe-seeking government bureaucrats and communist party cadres running around the country. What fueled China's economic miracle was capitalism and entrepreneurs, not state capitalism and bureaucrats. The Chinese miracle does NOT show that state capitalism — that unholy, unworkable alliance between the government and capitalism — works. To the contrary, it proves that it was the "capitalism", not the "state", in "state capitalism" that propelled China forward.

To be fair, and to give credit where credit is due, the Chinese government did make some vital contributions to the rise of China's exceptionally productive and dynamic private sector. Beijing has invested massively in infrastructure, building up a network of impressive (parts of it world-class) roads, railways, ports, airports, power plants, telecommunication systems, water supplies, and other facilities. As a result, China has a lot of infrastructure and much of it is high quality. Good infrastructure contributes to the productivity of all firms and industries. For example, reliable power supply enables factories to run without disruptive stoppages due to blackouts. Likewise, good transportation networks reduce the cost of moving goods from one city to another. In fact, more and better infrastructure has been widely viewed as a major factor why China outperformed India. So yes, the state did contribute to China's success, but strictly as a supporting actor. The star of the movie was, is, and will be the private sector.

The fact that capitalism has been the engine of China's sustained rapid growth since 1978

> **"**
> In fact, more and better infrastructure has been widely viewed as a major factor why China outperformed India. So yes, the state did contribute to China's success, but strictly as a supporting actor. The star of the movie was, is, and will be the private sector.
> **"**

provides ample cause for optimism about China's future economic prospects. Along with the rest of the world, China's growth has slowed down visibly since the Global Financial Crisis. Prior to the crisis, China was growing at breakneck speed of 10% or more per year — doubling in size in eight years — but by 2015, reaching even 7% had become a struggle. While China's slower growth is a natural and normal phenomenon — economic growth typically slows down as countries get richer, and there is no obvious reason why China should be exempt from this economic law of gravity — it has spawned widespread concerns about China's economic future. Those concerns are largely misplaced. The reason is that despite the relentless onslaught of the Chinese revolution, China still has a long way to go before it becomes a full-fledged market economy, which means that there is plenty of room for the Chinese economy to grow.

The good news for China, and the rest of the world, is that as the market advances further in China, and the state retreats further, further shrinking the "state" in "state capitalism", China will inch ever closer to a full-fledged market economy. In the process, the efficiencies of the public sector will melt away, boosting economic growth. Those inefficiencies are substantial, which means that the erosion of those inefficiencies will give China a healthy growth dividend. For example, according to *Markets over Mao*, in 2012, the rate of return on assets was a healthy 13.2% in the private sector, but a measly 4.9% in the state-owned sector. That is, investing in a privately owned company yielded more than two and a half times profits as investing in a state-owned company. In other words, a dollar invested is much more efficient and productive in the private sector. Yet between 2010 and 2012, private firms received 52% of all corporate loans from banks, but produced around 70% of China's GDP (gross

> **"**
>
> The good news for China, and the rest of the world, is that as the market advances further in China, and the state retreats further, further shrinking the 'state' in 'state capitalism', China will inch ever closer to a full-fledged market economy. In the process, the efficiencies of the public sector will melt away, boosting economic growth.
>
> **"**

domestic product). Merely shifting corporate loans from the state sector to the private sector will thus yield a sizable increase in output. Do not be fooled by size. China's biggest and most visible companies may be in the state sector, but the engine room of the Chinese locomotive lies firmly in the private sector.

What makes capitalism an especially potent tool for China's economic progress is that the Chinese people are highly entrepreneurial, natural capitalists. Many Chinese, especially the younger ones, are eager to start their own businesses and be their own bosses, rather than be salaried employees toiling for others all their lives. It is this kind of people who are the true heroes of capitalism, who create wealth and jobs, and who move societies forward. The contrast between China, the rising Asian sun, and Japan, the setting Asian sun, cannot be any starker. In Japan, entrepreneurship is almost an alien concept, even among the young. Many explanations have been put forth for Japan's interminable recession since 1990 but surely, lack of adventurous, risk-taking, greedy capitalist spirit must rank near the top. Team spirit and decision-by-consensus — the hallmarks of the Japanese national character — are nice and good, but someone has to build the team in the first place. Perhaps this explains why Japan did just fine when it largely borrowed advanced technology from the US, but when it had grown rich enough that it had to innovate on its own, it started to falter. Nobody was there to build the team. Without a team, team spirit becomes irrelevant.

If the can-do, not-afraid-to-fail, why-not-me attitude of China and the Chinese sounds eerily similar to another country, that is because it is — America and the Americans! For sure, there is rising geopolitical tension between the two giants. When there is initially only one superpower, and

> **What makes capitalism an especially potent tool for China's economic progress is that the Chinese people are highly entrepreneurial, natural capitalists. Many Chinese, especially the younger ones, are eager to start their own businesses and be their own bosses, rather than be salaried employees toiling for others all their lives.**

233

a new aspiring superpower appears on the horizon, it is only natural that the incumbent feels threatened and the newcomer feels stifled. America's concern about the rise of China is thus understandable, but it sometimes borders on the hysterical and irrational.[1] At the same time, America has more legitimate concerns. For example, China's overly aggressive behavior in its territorial disputes with smaller Asian neighbors in the South China Sea — for example, building air strips on artificial islands in contested waters — casts doubt on whether China's rise is entirely peaceful. Moreover, America and China have completely different political systems. Yet the two giants are much more alike than they realize.

Above all, they are bound by the boundless and optimistic "tomorrow will be better than today" energy of raw, muscular, dynamic entrepreneurial capitalism. Together, China and America are the best hopes for tomorrow's capitalism. China's own Silicon Valley in Shenzhen is a long way behind the original Silicon Valley in California, and it may be years before China produces a revolutionary innovator like Steve Jobs or Elon Musk. But the sheer raw vitality of China's tech startups is a promising sign of bigger, better things to come.[2] Also, China has already produced its own bevy of tech tycoons, including Jack Ma. The future of Chinese capitalism can be seen in the streets of Shenzhen, where there is an incredible amount of entrepreneurial buzz and energy. For technological entrepreneurs, Shenzhen is "a nirvana — a vibrant, multi-colored landscape of possibility, opportunity, and creative exploration."[3] As in Silicon Valley, the possibility, opportunity, and creative exploration is driven by innovative, risk-taking, profit-seeking entrepreneurs, not risk-averse, paper-pushing bureaucrats. Despite their differences, America and China are set to carry the capitalist torch in the 21st century.

[1] For example, America inexplicably opposed tooth and nail the 2016 creation of Asian Infrastructure Investment Bank (AIIB), a Chinese-led multilateral development bank — a kind of World Bank — dedicated to building infrastructure in developing countries. Other than the fact that the bank was a Chinese-led initiative, there was no compelling or logical reason for the American opposition. This kind of American behavior, in turn, fuels Chinese suspicion that America is blindly hostile to China, even when China leads peaceful and beneficial pursuits, such as building roads and ports in poor countries.

[2] China boasts the second largest number of unicorns, or tech startups valued at more than US$1 billion, after the US and its Silicon Valley. http://www.chinadaily.com.cn/business/2016top10/2016-03/03/content_23716285.htm

[3] http://www.theguardian.com/cities/2014/jun/13/inside-shenzen-china-silicon-valley-tech-nirvana-pearl-river

Surprisingly, popular support for capitalism is, if anything, even stronger in China, which is still nominally socialist after all, than in America, the cradle of entrepreneurial capitalism. For sure, there is wide and worsening inequality in China, as in the rest of the world, and gathering public indignation toward inequality. But a good measure of the depth of popular support for capitalism in China is the universal admiration for Jack Ma, the founder of Alibaba, China's answer to Alibaba, and China's richest man.[4] There is a genuine sense among ordinary Chinese that anybody with talent, drive, and courage, can aspire to be the next Jack Ma. Yes, the late Steve Jobs is lionized by Americans and remains big in America, but Jobs is nowhere near as big as Ma, who is a genuine rock star in China. More worryingly, the rumblings of anti-capitalist sentiment are audible and growing louder in America, fueled by growing public anger toward widening inequality. Donald Trump and Bernie Sanders personify the ugly public mood. In contrast, the Chinese are too busy making money to ponder the ills of capitalism. China has become a cauldron of capitalism, producing millions of new entrepreneurs every year.[5]

While America and China offer the best hope for capitalism, both giants face threats to their capitalism. Let us start with China, which is still in the midst of a transition from socialism to capitalism. As stated earlier, China is not yet a full-fledged market economy and still retains some legacies from its pre-1978 socialist days. Most China watchers who worry about China are concerned about the risk of a hard landing. That is, while China's slower growth rate in recent years — from over 10% in 2010 to 6.9% in 2015 — is part of a healthy and natural transition to more sustainable growth, there is a risk that growth will slow down much more sharply than expected. Financial crisis, perhaps

[4] http://www.economist.com/news/books-and-arts/21696495-how-jack-ma-conquered-chinas-internet-crocodile-yangzi

[5] http://www.economist.com/news/books-and-arts/21696495-how-jack-ma-conquered-chinas-internet-crocodile-yangzi

compounded by bursting of a property bubble, will be the most likely catalyst of a hard landing. China also faces other structural challenges, most notably a rapidly aging population. But by far the biggest threat to Chinese capitalism would be the failure of the government to boldly complete the transition to a full-fledged market economy. In particular, further expanding the role of the private sector — and thus reducing the role of state-owned firms and banks — is vital for the future health of Chinese capitalism.

Alas, threats against capitalism are mounting even in America, the undisputed global bastion of entrepreneurial capitalism. Increasingly, the optimistic popular belief that America is a land of opportunity where anybody with drive, talent and creativity can make it big, become the next Steve Jobs, Elon Musk or Ted Turner, is giving way to growing popular suspicion that the economic game is unfairly rigged in favor of powerful vested interests. That is, perhaps to a greater extent than ever before, Americans feel that America is no longer a land of opportunity for all, but a land of opportunity only for the rich elite. This groundswell of anger is eroding popular support for capitalism in America.[6] It also propelled the surprisingly successful presidential candidacies of Donald Trump and Bernie Sanders, both of whom ran on populist, anti-establishment platforms. While Trump is a Republican and Sanders is a Democrat, both posed as anti-elite outsiders standing up for the 99% and against the 1% during their election campaigns. Indeed Trump's campaign was so successful that he became the Republican nominee and staged a stunning upset over Hillary Clinton on 8 November to become the 45th president of the US.

A potent piece of evidence which supports the popular suspicion is that large US firms are

[6] Related to the rise of anti-capitalism, popular sentiment against free trade is also on the rise in the US. Both Donald Trump and Bernie Sanders railed against free trade during their 2016 presidential election campaigns, outdoing each other in making promises to protect the American worker with tariffs and other protectionist barriers. There is a close link between anti-capitalism and anti-globalization.

earning record profits year after year.[7] Record profits themselves are not a problem, especially if they are due to superior products that consumers love — e.g. Apple's iPhone. But what is a problem is that the sky-high profits of the large US firms tend to persist and show no signs of declining over time. Under healthy competition, profits will be competed away over time as new, innovative firms enter the market. Therefore, to restore the health of capitalism and popular support for capitalism, Washington should make a concerted effort to make American markets more competitive. For example, while patents and copyrights are critical for innovations and inventions, the government should monitor and prevent their misuse by large incumbent firms to impede new and smaller firms and thus stifle competition.

Another important set of measures has to do with making life easier for startups and smaller firms, for example by reducing red tape and excessive regulation. The mind-numbing fine print of Obamacare is just one example. Alarmingly, the rate of small-company creation in America is at its lowest since the 1970s and, alarmingly because startups are the lifeline of entrepreneurial capitalism.[8] The number of startups per 100,000 people in the US had dropped from 257 in 1977 to 185 in 1983 to 181 in 1992 to 165 in 2001 and 129 in 2013.[9] In 2015, 50% of American small businesses could not secure the financing they needed. As a result, 32% of growing firms had to delay their expansion and 21% had to turn to personal funds to finance their business.[10] In short, the current malaise of American capitalism is due to stifling overregulation which saps the very life out of new and small firms as well as the grotesque transformation of the financial industry from a nurturer of businesses into a self-serving monster.

[7] http://www.economist.com/news/leaders/21695392-big-firms-united-states-have-never-had-it-so-good-time-more-competition-problem

[8] For example, administrative compliance with laws like Obamacare places a disproportionately heavy burden on small firms, which do not have legal departments and other administrative departments that handle such issues. Similarly, the share of American professions requiring occupational licensing, a major barrier to startups, has shot up from 5% in the 1950s to 29% now. http://www.economist.com/news/leaders/21695392-big-firms-united-states-have-never-had-it-so-good-time-more-competition-problem

[9] http://time.com/4327419/american-capitalisms-great-crisis/

[10] http://time.com/4327419/american-capitalisms-great-crisis/

237

SINGAPOREAN STATE CAPITALISM, AND SINGAPORE AIRLINES

52

C hina is by no means the only successful developing country that combined a strong state and vibrant market forces to achieve rapid economic growth on a sustained basis. In fact, some might argue that the blueprint for China's growth strategy was laid out by two other highly successful East Asian economies — South Korea and Singapore. Those two countries started industrializing much earlier than China and as a result, they are much richer than China. Singapore is one of the world's richest countries although one may question the relevance of the Singaporean experience for China. After all, Singapore is a small city-state of 5 million people while China is a continental country of more than 1.3 billion people. Singapore would not even be one of the biggest, top-tier cities in China. South Korea, on the other hand, is a real country of 50 million, although its land area is relatively small, about the size of Iceland or Kentucky. Nevertheless, Chinese policymakers have looked at both countries as role models to follow and emulate.

Above all, in both countries there were strong governments at the time of the economic take-off. In the case of Singapore, the political party that ruled the country when the economy

" In fact, some might argue that the blueprint for China's growth strategy was laid out by two other highly successful East Asian economies — South Korea and Singapore.... Above all, in both countries there were strong governments at the time of the economic take-off. "

took off — the People's Action Party or PAP — remains in power to this day. In the case of South Korea, as noted earlier, an army general turned civilian dictator named Park Chung-hee laid the foundation of the country's economic miracle. A few years after his assassination, South Korea has blossomed into a full-fledged Western-style democracy with power changing hands between right-wing conservatives and left-wing progressives. On the other hand, while Singapore is a parliamentary democracy, the PAP, the political party founded by Lee Kuan Yew, continues to dominate politics and government. Nevertheless, the big-picture takeaway from South Korea and Singapore is identical as far as China's rulers are concerned — that a strong government is consistent with, and even necessary for, economic progress.

This is wishful thinking which fits rather nicely with China's current situation — politically, it is ruled by the communist party but economically, the private sector and market forces are in control. However, it would be a grave mistake for the Beijing elite to draw the wrong lessons from South Korea and Singapore. They may be tempted to conclude that the success of the two countries proves that state capitalism works. Yet nothing could be further from the truth. Clearly, a strong state — in particular, capable and honest government bureaucrats — contributed to the success of both countries. Singapore in particular has the cleanest, most corruption-free civil service in the world, the result of two things — zero tolerance policy toward corruption and high pay for civil servants. The contrast with the civil service of many other developing countries, where huge hordes of incompetent, lazy, corrupt bureaucrats ruin the country, is stark. But at the end of the day, the decisive contribution of the state to economic growth in South Korea and Singapore was not that it

" However, it would be a grave mistake for the Beijing elite to draw the wrong lessons from South Korea and Singapore. They may be tempted to conclude that the success of the two countries proves that state capitalism works. Yet nothing could be further from the truth. **"**

239

replaced the market, but rather that the state created an environment in which the market flourished and capitalism worked its magic.

The experiences of Singapore, a city-state whose experience has only limited relevance for the Chinese giant, should nevertheless dispel the myth, held by Beijing, that state capitalism offers a viable third-way alternative to capitalism and socialism. First of all, Singapore's growth was powered to a large extent by foreign investors who built factories that produced manufactured goods for exports. Those foreign investors were often large multinational companies, from the *private* sector. China, of course, also relied heavily on foreign *private* companies and their investments to fuel its industrialization. Both countries, in effect, imported industrial entrepreneurship and private enterprise, besides the usual benefits of foreign investment — capital, technology, and managerial and marketing knowhow. Singapore had plenty of entrepreneurs but they were traders — Singapore is a port city with an excellent location between Asia and Europe — not manufacturers. China, for its part, had a billion would-be entrepreneurs — again, the Chinese are an exceptionally entrepreneurial lot. But that huge reservoir of wealth-creating capitalist energy was bottled up under decades of communist rule, and it took some time for the Chinese to rediscover their entrepreneurial mojo.

But there is another part of the Singaporean growth model which gives more heart to the many adherents of state capitalism among China's ruling elite. One pillar of the Singapore economy is the large, well-established foreign multinational companies. The second pillar is the state-owned sector, which consists of companies in which the Singaporean government owns a substantial stake. What is missing in Singapore is a vibrant domestic private sector. It is true

"

The experiences of Singapore, a city-state whose experience has only limited relevance for the Chinese giant, should nevertheless dispel the myth, held by Beijing, that state capitalism offers a viable third-way alternative to capitalism and socialism.

"

that Singaporean state companies, known as government-linked companies or GLCs, are managed better than their counterparts elsewhere. The negative stereotype of inefficient state-owned companies with overpaid, bloated workforce with lifetime job security, making losses year after year after year, clearly does not apply to Singaporean GLCs. Singapore is not Greece, and Singaporean state firms are not Greek state firms.

But a number of factors suggest that what works for a city-state like Singapore will not work for big countries like China. First, in Singapore, the small population and hence the limited talent pool, in combination with the lack of a domestic private sector, means that the state sector is able to get the lion's share of the talent that is not scooped up by foreign multinationals. In contrast, in China, there are plenty of private sector opportunities for bright, young talent. In fact, such talent is driving the explosive rise of China's dynamic private sector. Second, Singapore's GLCs are run along purely commercial lines, much like private sector firms, with a firm focus on minimizing costs and maximizing profits. But in China and most other countries, state-owned firms are saddled with social or political objectives, such as boosting employment in a depressed region. The burden of such additional objectives explains why they tend to be inefficient and unprofitable.

Above all, for a small city state like Singapore, the domestic market is too small to be viable. Therefore, all firms, whether state or private, have to compete in the global market, which means they have to be efficient. The best Singaporean state firms are those that are most exposed to foreign competition — most notably the world-class Singapore Airlines. Chinese state companies, on the other hand, can milk a

"

The negative stereotype of inefficient state-owned companies with overpaid, bloated workforce with lifetime job security, making losses year after year after year, clearly does not apply to Singaporean GLCs.... But a number of factors suggest that what works for a city-state like Singapore will not work for big countries like China.

"

241

large domestic market, which explains why they can survive despite their inefficiencies. To sum up, Singapore gives false hope to supporters of state capitalism, in China and elsewhere, because its state-owned companies are relatively well managed — false hope because the success of those companies is rooted in the tough discipline of international competition, not in the fact that they are owned by the Singaporean government.

"

To sum up, Singapore gives false hope to supporters of state capitalism, in China and elsewhere.

"

KOREAN INDUSTRIAL POLICY, HYUNDAI CAR JOKES, AND SAMSUNG GALAXY PHONES

53

South Korea also offers false hope to believers of state capitalism, but for a fundamentally different reason — industrial policy, which refers to extensive government interference in the allocation of resources. In any economy, resources such as capital and labor are scarce and finite. In a market economy, those scarce resources flow according to demand — if consumers buy more cars, more machines and workers will flow to the auto industry. Broadly speaking, industrial policy means that the state, rather than market demand, dictates the allocation of resources. That is, government bureaucrats identify promising firms and industries, and direct resources toward their favored firms and industries. Under industrial policy, the government rather than the market picks winners — which firms and industries prosper — and losers — which firms and industries shut down. South Korea, and Japan earlier, are sometimes viewed as having actively and successfully pursued industrial policy.

South Korea' success in particular gave hope to developing countries that they too can industrialize and grow rapidly if the government channeled resources to the "right" firms and industries. Even countries on the other

> " South Korea, and Japan earlier, are sometimes viewed as having actively and successfully pursued industrial policy. South Korea' success in particular gave hope to developing countries that they too can industrialize and grow rapidly if the government channeled resources to the 'right' firms and industries. "

side of the world from South Korea, in Latin America, are dreaming the Korean dream of forceful government intervention to foster the development of high-productivity industries and activities.[1] It is certainly true that in South Korea powerful government bureaucrats in charge of the economy had a major say in the allocation of resources, in addition to the market. It is also true that South Korean firms and industries favored by the government received substantial preferential treatment, which included access to more and cheaper credit as well as tariffs and non-tariff barriers which kept out imports and thus protected those firms from more efficient foreign firms. Such important protection was crucial to many Korean industries, especially their growing up from infants and becoming internationally competitive.

For example, South Korea's automobile industry, which is now the fifth largest in the world, would never have had a chance to grow up if it bore the full brunt of foreign competition early on. Back in the 1960s, superior foreign cars would have had shoddy South Korean cars for breakfast, lunch and dinner. The practice of protecting infant industries from foreign completion with trade barriers until they can grow up is known among economists as the infant industry argument. Korean automobile industry is a poster child for the infant industry argument. Hyundai was once the butt of wisecracks on late-night US television shows. Yes, those of who are old enough have all heard a Hyundai joke or two. Some of them are actually quite funny.

Q. How do you upgrade a Hyundai?
A. Put in an engine.
Q. How do you make a Hyundai go faster uphill?
A. Throw out the passenger.

244

Well, nobody is laughing at Hyundai now, least of all in the boardrooms of GM (General Motors)

[1] "Latin America's Korean Dream," http://www.economist.com/news/americas/21618785-case-modern-industrial-policy-latin-americas-korean-dream

or Toyota. It is now a top 10 carmaker in both the US and global markets.

Since South Korea closely followed Japan's footsteps toward industrialization and both countries were characterized by activist industrial policies, a short comparison of their industrialization policies is in order. South Korean industrial policy was more intense than its Japanese counterpart for the simple reason that Japan started industrialization much earlier than South Korea and thus had a larger pool of industrial entrepreneurs. Even the most ardent opponents of industrial policy would accept that the South Korean government's helping hand aided in the transformation of South Korea into the manufacturing powerhouse that it is today. In particular, South Korea's flagship industrial companies or chaebols, which include global powerhouses such as Samsung Electronics, Hyundai Automobiles and POSCO, a steelmaker, received considerable support from the government as they grew from infancy to national champion to world champion. There is a popular perception that the chaebols owe their success largely to government help.

In fact, such a perception would be largely a misperception. Yes, competent, hardworking, and relatively honest government bureaucrats laid the foundation for the South Korean miracle. We should also acknowledge that the chaebols received assistance from the government and that assistance contributed to their success. However, we should be careful not to give too much credit to South Korean industrial policy and South Korean government bureaucrats. At the end of the day, the true heroes of the South Korean miracle, the people who made it happen, were bold, visionary, risk-taking *private sector* entrepreneurs such as Samsung founder Lee Byung-chul, who entertained the crazy idea that a South Korean firm could make electronics

> **"**
>
> At the end of the day, the true heroes of the South Korean miracle, the people who made it happen, were bold, visionary, risk-taking *private sector* entrepreneurs such as Samsung founder Lee Byung-chul.
>
> **"**

goods or Hyundai founder Chung Ju-yung, who entertained the equally crazy idea that a South Korean firm could build cars. True, government assistance did help them get started, but it was their own sheer determination, relentless drive, and keen business sense that transformed their companies from national champions into global champions. In fact, even the achievement of being national champions had more to do with their own efforts than government help.

This is because South Korean industrial policy, widely admired by those who downplay the role of the market and private sector (and correspondingly, exaggerate the role of the government) in economic growth, had some unique features which set it apart from the industrial policies of other developing countries. In particular, South Korean industrial policy was noticeably more ruthless than elsewhere.[2] More specifically, government support for private firms was temporary and closely linked to their performance in exports and innovation. In other words, government helped only private firms that succeeded in selling abroad and moving up the technology ladder. Exporting subjects firms to the often brutal discipline of global competition, and firms have to raise their games to global standards — i.e. become highly productive and efficient — to achieve export success. Likewise, innovation requires that firms invest in building up their technological capabilities, so they can move up the value chain. South Korea's industrial policy was an altogether different animal than the unsuccessful industrial policy of Latin American countries and elsewhere. Above all, it was a "tough love" industrial policy, which limited government support to firms that were eventually able to export.

South Korea was fortunate in that it had bold, dynamic, visionary entrepreneurs who had the guts and smarts to build up their companies from scratch into world-class companies. They

[2] "Latin America's Korean Dream," http://www.economist.com/news/americas/21618785-case-modern-industrial-policy-latin-americas-korean-dream

were the Michael Jordan and LeBron James of the South Korean miracle, the star players whose teams were eventually able to compete in tough global markets. Their entrepreneurship transformed Hyundai cars from the butt of jokes of late-night television shows into a global top 10 carmaker, and Samsung Galaxy mobile phones into Apple's number one competitor. It is much more accurate to say that industrial policy worked in South Korea because there was a latent pool of industrial entrepreneurs, rather than to say that South Korea's industrial entrepreneurs succeeded because of industrial policy. That is, industrial policy worked in South Korea because, and only because, it was able to catalyze latent entrepreneurs into actual entrepreneurs. The achievement of those private sector entrepreneurs is truly breathtaking. If anybody in 1950, or even 1975, predicted the sophistication and diversity of goods made by South Korean companies today, he would have been shipped off to a mental hospital.

"

That is, industrial policy worked in South Korea because, and only because, it was able to catalyze latent entrepreneurs into actual entrepreneurs. The achievement of those private sector entrepreneurs is truly breathtaking.

"

LESSONS FROM KOREA AND SINGAPORE

54

To sum up, the experiences of South Korea and Singapore do not, in any way, shape or form, suggest that government bureaucrats can substitute private sector entrepreneurs as the engines of economic progress, and creators of jobs and wealth. Only an extremely biased interpretation of the experiences of the two exceptionally successful countries, among the rare group of countries that went from Third World to First World, would produce that conclusion. This is not a knock against South Korean and Singapore government bureaucrats, who are among the world's best. But taking big risks, making bold decisions, and thinking outside the box are not part of their DNA or job description.

Toeing the line and flattering powerful senior staff may be useful for bureaucratic promotions, but it is no recipe for starting or running your own business. Common sense alone tells us that if bureaucrats did have a knack for identifying profitable industries and activities, they would go into business themselves and become millionaires. The South Korean and Singaporean experiences suggest, much more plausibly, that competent, honest, and dedicated bureaucrats can create a conducive

> " ... the experiences of South Korea and Singapore do not, in any way, shape or form, suggest that government bureaucrats can substitute private sector entrepreneurs as the engines of economic progress, and creators of jobs and wealth. "

environment for the private sector and market to flourish. They can set the tables but far better to let private sector entrepreneurs do the cooking. To put otherwise, they are great supporting actors, but not the stars.

Not that setting the table is an easy task, which explains why most governments are terrible at doing it. Creating a conducive environment for private entrepreneurship requires good government, but good governments are a scarce commodity in developing countries, which is why so few of them succeed in building dynamic, job- and wealth-creating private sectors. To the contrary, far too many of them succeed, and succeed spectacularly, in strangling the life out of the private sector and entrepreneurship, and thus wrecking the economy. For every rare South Korea or Singapore, the Greeces, Nigerias, and Venezuelas are a dime a dozen. Bad government is detrimental for the countries themselves, and it is also harmful for the rest of the world. The hordes of economic and political refugees, which are creating a major headache across Europe and contributing to the rise of extremist right-wing parties, and the millions of potential recruits for the Islamic State, which is threatening global security, are just two examples.

State-owned firms in most countries, in stark contrast to their Singaporean counterparts, are rife with fraud, waste, cronyism, nepotism, and more generally, inefficiency. They deprive the private sector of valuable resources and subtract from, rather than add to, economic growth. By the same token, the industrial policy of most developing countries, in stark contrast to the South Korean version, did nothing to encourage the private sector to become more efficient and productive. In fact, it did exactly the opposite, allowing inefficient, unproductive firms to survive, with the help of handouts. Industrial

> **“**
>
> Government bureaucrats can set the tables but far better to let private sector entrepreneurs do the cooking. To put otherwise, they are great supporting actors, but not the stars.
>
> **”**

policy thus contributed directly and massively to economic stagnation.

South Korea and Singapore belong to a tiny elite group of countries that made the rare jump from Third World to First World within a generation. Many Third World countries cannot even get to second base and remain perpetually mired in poverty. Much of Africa falls into this category. Many others make it to second base but remain stuck there forever, in what is known as the middle-income trap. Brazil, Mexico and many other Latin American countries are classical example of countries that are seemingly middle income forever. For both groups of countries, the South Korean experience is much more relevant because most countries are not small city-states like Singapore. But in any case, the key takeaway from South Korea and Singapore is that good governments matter hugely for economic growth. In fact, good government is what separates South Korea and Singapore from most developing countries. Critically, good government means a government that creates a conducive environment for risk-taking, profit-seeking private entrepreneurs to thrive. It most definitely does not mean a government that is itself an entrepreneur, something which risk-averse bureaucrats are incapable of anyway.

❝

In fact, good government is what separates South Korea and Singapore from most developing countries. Critically, good government means a government that creates a conducive environment for risk-taking, profit-seeking private entrepreneurs to thrive.

❞

GOVERNMENT BUREAUCRATS AS PARASITES OF BUSINESS, BUSINESSMEN AS PARASITES OF THE GOVERNMENT

55

I n short, even in developing countries with the best governments, such as South Korea and Singapore, run by honest and capable government bureaucrats dedicated to improving the lives of their citizens, such as from the aforementioned countries, it is ultimately the private sector that creates jobs and wealth, and drives the economy forward. It is a pipe dream for developing countries to believe that good government alone can transform them into the next South Korea or Singapore, in the absence of a productive private sector. Where there is no private sector to speak of or only an embryonic private sector, it is the government's job to grow and nurture a dynamic and efficient private sector, for example, by investing in physical infrastructure such as roads and electricity and social infrastructure such as schools and hospitals that benefits all firms and industries. But the government, even the best government, can only be a Steve Kerr, never a Michael Jordan, if the economy is to grow and prosper.[1]

It is the job of the risk-taking private sector entrepreneur to create wealth and jobs, and drive economic progress, not the risk-averse government bureaucrat. "High risk, high reward" is usually used to describe an

[1] This is no knock against Steve Kerr, who was a good National Basketball Association (NBA) player in his own right, but even he would admit that he would not have had wide-open shots if it were not for Michael Jordan attracting all the defenders.

251

investment strategy — for example, picking relatively unknown stocks that may turn out to be a dud (95% probability) or the next Apple (5% probability) — but it is an equally apt description of career choice. It is infinitely safer to work for somebody and draw a monthly salary than to start your own business. Anybody who has done both know this fact only too well. Most bureaucrats do not have the temperament or the ability to start a business, which is why they are bureaucrats rather than businessmen. Of course, some bureaucrats do become successful businessmen, especially in developing countries. But a large number of these bureaucrats-turned-businessmen receive a lot of help from the government — for example, subsidies, cheap bank loans, preferential tax treatment, and a monopoly position which protects them from competition. The government's Visible Hand enables those so-called "successful" state capitalists to survive and even thrive despite selling shoddy products at inflated prices.

A breed closely related to the "successful" bureaucrat-turned-businessman, who owes his success entirely to the unfair advantages he enjoys as a result of extensive government help, is the politically well-connected private sector entrepreneur whose only entrepreneurial skill is to gain special favors from the government. These are not private sector capitalists in any meaningful sense. A more accurate term for them would be government parasites. One common way to gain government favor is by bribing greedy, grasping government bureaucrats, of which there are a dime a dozen. Another common way is to be born as the son, daughter, wife, brother, or nephew of powerful politicians. Yet another common way is to be the best buddy of a powerful politician or failing that, the best buddy of the best buddy of a powerful

"

A breed closely related to the 'successful' bureaucrat-turned-businessman, who owes his success entirely to the unfair advantages he enjoys as a result of extensive government help, is the politically well-connected private sector entrepreneur whose only entrepreneurial skill is to gain special favors from the government. These are not private sector capitalists in any meaningful sense. A more accurate term for them would be government parasites.

"

politician, or failing that, the best buddy of the best buddy of the best buddy of a powerful politician. These parasites do not invest in new factories or technologies, but in building up relationships with influential political leaders and government bureaucrats. Those wining and dining investments — known as rent seeking in economists' jargon — are profitable for the well-connected, so-called capitalist, but they do not benefit the society at large.[2]

In fact, those relationships are privately profitable — not only for the so-called capitalist but also for the politician or bureaucrat who receives a nice, fat cash packet in exchange for a nice, fat tax break or subsidy or loan — but socially harmful — consumers and workers end up paying the bill, in the form of higher prices and lower quality and fewer and lower-paying jobs. To illustrate, for decades, developing countries around the world protected their firms and industries with high tariffs and other trade barriers to promote industrialization and economic growth. The one big problem, actually one huge problem, was that the protected firms and industries were politically well-connected firms and industries which had nothing to fear and no incentives to improve their game. They were thus able to get away with producing over-priced garbage year after year, and their chance of growing up into internationally competitive firms was zero. This growth strategy is known as import substitution — i.e. substituting importing goods with domestically produced goods — and all too often succeeded only in substituting good capitalism with bad capitalism. Latin America's heavy reliance on import substitution helps explain why it stagnated, while export-oriented Asia thrived.

Above all, unhealthy ties between corrupt politicians/bureaucrats and businessmen with

[2] Rent seeking increases one's share of existing wealth but does not increase total wealth. That is, it increases one's share of the pie without increasing the size of the pie. An economy characterized by a lot of rent seeking behavior will be stagnant. This is because companies will invest in bribing politicians and officials rather than invest in creating better products and technologies. Resources are used to influence the referee rather than build stronger teams.

no desire or ability to deliver good value for the consumers strangle the very life out of the dynamic, muscular, best-man-wins capitalism — the Steve Jobsian sort of capitalism that propels mankind forward to greater heights. Millions, perhaps even hundreds of millions, of genuine capitalists are deprived of an opportunity to create new products and technologies that can benefit society because the playing field is tilted against them. For example, they cannot get bank loans at reasonable interest rates because the banks will only lend to well-connected firms that produce overpriced shoddy products. Yet such socially harmful firms often not only survive but thrive because they are protected from competition due to their political connections. The source of their market power — in fact, such firms are often monopolists, or the only firm in a market — is not superior product or technology but the government's keeping out other firms from the market. If GovTel is the only telecom service provider in the market, GovTel will be successful and profitable even if it is the world's worst telecom service provider.

Both bureaucrats-turned-businessmen and government parasites destroy value rather than create value. They are the exact opposites of Steve Jobs. Their vision has absolutely nothing to do with creating a new product or a new technology that benefits society. In fact, the bureaucrats-turned-businessmen and government parasites embody the very worst of capitalism. Actually, if you think about it, it is hard to view these state capitalists, which is what both these breeds are, as capitalists at all. Furthermore, they are identical twins — both breeds owe their success entirely to extensive connections with the government rather than any talent in creating new, socially beneficial wealth based on new, socially beneficial products or technologies. These so-called capitalists, who

"

> Both bureaucrats-turned-businessmen and government parasites destroy value rather than create value. They are the exact opposites of Steve Jobs. Their vision has absolutely nothing to do with creating a new product or a new technology that benefits society. In fact, the bureaucrats-turned-businessmen and government parasites embody the very worst of capitalism.

"

are anything but capitalists in the true sense of risk-taking, value- and job-creating capitalists, give capitalism a bad name. They succeed not because they are the better team, but rather because they have the referee in their pocket. Capitalism fails miserably when it is not allowed to be capitalism, and is instead captured, subverted, and degraded beyond all recognition by corrupt and greedy government bureaucrats and their equally corrupt and greedy friends in the private sector.

State capitalism is not capitalism at all. The very concept of state capitalism is utter nonsense. Capitalism can work its magic and create wealth, jobs and prosperity only when the government and bureaucrats get out of the way and let the market, private sector, and entrepreneurship to do their thing. Nothing has changed since the days of Adam Smith. What drives mankind forward, and what creates new, socially useful products, services and technologies — e.g. CNN (Cable News Network), Tesla, Google, iPhone, and Amazon — is the risk-taking, profit-seeking entrepreneur driven by material gain, not the risk-averse, paper-pushing bureaucrat seeking a side payment. There are plenty of dedicated, capable, hardworking government workers doing plenty of good things, but creating and running business is not one of them. If they had the temperament and knack for business, they would have been businessmen in the first place, not bureaucrats sitting in their desks and basking in lifetime job security. The only thing that enables bureaucrats, especially politically powerful ones, to "succeed" in business is not any natural ability to spot good profit opportunities, but government connections that give them a leg up on the competition.

"

State capitalism is not capitalism at all. The very concept of state capitalism is utter nonsense. Capitalism can work its magic and create wealth, jobs and prosperity only when the government and bureaucrats get out of the way and let the market, private sector, and entrepreneurship to do their thing.

"

A SUBURBAN GARAGE IN LOS ALTOS, CALIFORNIA, USA

56

Silicon Valley, that globally admired paragon of American capitalism, is the ultimate testament to the superiority of the private sector and individual greed over the government and bureaucratic risk-aversion in creating wealth and jobs. Paper-pushing bureaucrats could not have created Silicon Valley if their lives depended on it. Apple, Google, Amazon, Microsoft, and eBay are all brainchildren of dynamic, innovative, creative, risk-taking, profit-seeking entrepreneurs, not some bureaucrats sitting in their cozy offices, bored out of their wits and looking for something to do. This is not to belittle the many valuable contributions of government workers, but they should not be in the business of business. In fact, they should get out and stay out. If there is a gold standard for capitalism — an ideal vision of how capitalism should work — it is Silicon Valley, where entrepreneurs compete vigorously with each other, based on new products and technologies, and deliver a great deal of joy and satisfaction to consumers.

The iconic image of Steve Jobs building the foundations of Apple with Steve Wozniak and other collaborators in a suburban garage in Los Altos, California, may be too iconic for

"

If there is a gold standard for capitalism — an ideal vision of how capitalism should work — it is Silicon Valley, where entrepreneurs compete vigorously with each other, based on new products and technologies, and deliver a great deal of joy and satisfaction to consumers.

"

some, but it captures the essence of Silicon Valley. Rugged, individualistic capitalism is often derided by many non-Americans as symptoms of America's excessive materialism, but it embodies the very best of America — its optimistic, can do, tomorrow is better than today spirit. Moreover, those fierce critics of American materialism are often the first to lap up the latest version of iPhones as soon as they come out. It is no accident that America is the home of Silicon Valley rather than in Europe, Japan or elsewhere. The raw, pulsating entrepreneurial energy that permeates America is, above all, the consequence of its uniquely welcoming environment for entrepreneurs. Yes, even America can do much more to further improve the business environment, but relative to the rest of the world, America is a veritable entrepreneurial nirvana which continues to attract the best and brightest talent from around the world. More than anywhere else, anybody armed with nothing but a good idea can make it big in America.

This brings us to another major strength of Silicon Valley, which is also a major strength of the American economy as a whole — the huge economic contributions of immigrants who come from all corners of the world. The American Dream still remains a powerful magnet to millions of non-Americans. Immigrants' contribution to the rise of Silicon Valley is well documented. For example, Sergey Brin, a Russian immigrant, co-founded Google with Larry Page, and in 2014, Indian-born Sundar Pichai was appointed the search engine giant's CEO (chief executive officer).[1] Thousands of highly skilled Chinese and Indian scientists and engineers are indispensable to Silicon Valley. It is not just much-needed technical skills that such immigrants bring to the table. Their entrepreneurial energy (indeed many

[1] http://www.forbes.com/sites/gregoryferenstein/2015/08/14/ceos-of-silicon-valleys-top-firms-are-often-non-white-immigrants-or-women-in-1-graph/

of them set up tech companies) adds a lot to the manic cauldron of entrepreneurship that is Silicon Valley. They bring fresh blood to the body of American capitalism, helping to renew, fortify, and revitalize American capitalism in the process.

To us, it is simply mindboggling that America has not had a sensible, intelligent political debate on immigration reform. Such a debate should clearly recognize the value of immigrants to America's economic dynamism and open the doors to at least some immigration, especially the highly skilled, entrepreneurial immigrants — e.g. Chinese and Indian engineers in Silicon Valley — that create wealth and jobs. Even less skilled immigrants bring a lot to the table. A well-known example is backbreaking farm work such as picking strawberries in California, performed by Mexican migrants because no American workers would do such work. Furthermore, the determination of first-generation immigrants to give their children a better future — something better than bending almost 90 degrees to pick strawberries under a hot sun[2] — drives them to work their tails off. Moreover, many of their children do indeed become doctors, lawyers, engineers, architects, and yes, strawberry field owners.

Instead of reasonable debate, presidential candidates and other politicians, especially Republicans, try to outdo each other in talking tough on immigration. Walls, barbed wires, and mass deportations are just some of the proposed "solutions" to the immigration "problem". Such irrational rhetoric predictably reaches hysteric fever pitch whenever a Mexican migrant commits a burglary or a Muslim couple goes on a terrorist killing spree, as happened in San Bernardino in December 2015. If nativist American politicians — e.g. Donald Trump — were to succeed in sharply

[2] http://www.latimes.com/local/great-reads/la-me-strawberry-pick-20130503-dto-htmlstory.html

curtailing immigration by playing on the public's fear, ignorance and prejudice, America would deprive itself of an invaluable economic asset. That would be downright criminal. Expensive strawberries would be the least of the costs of blocking immigration. It is sad and ironic that Republicans, the self-claimed champions of private enterprise and entrepreneurship, blindly oppose the influx of immigrants, a highly entrepreneurial and hardworking lot.

"

It is sad and ironic that Republicans, the self-claimed champions of private enterprise and entrepreneurship, blindly oppose the influx of immigrants, a highly entrepreneurial and hardworking lot.

"

SILICON VALLEYS IN RUSSIA AND MALAYSIA, SHENZHEN, DIDI CHUXING, AND WECHAT

57

Many countries around the world are aspiring to build their own Silicon Valleys. For example, Malaysia has its Cyberjaya, a town with a science park that was set up by the Malaysian government in May 1997 and is located 30 kilometers south of Kuala Lumpur, the capital. The explicit goal of Cyberjaya was to become the Silicon Valley of Malaysia. Even Russia, not exactly a paragon of entrepreneurship and private enterprise, envisions a Silicon Valley of its own. To this end, the Russian government has established the Skolkovo Innovation Center, just outside Moscow. The Center is a huge high-tech research campus which hosts startups and industry. Very few of these Silicon This or Silicon That, or Cyber North or Cyber South, have succeeded so far, and very few are likely to succeed in the future. The common thread running through the often quixotic efforts of countries around the world to create their own Silicon Valleys is the central role of the government.

Unfortunately, no amount of bureaucratic effort will succeed in creating a Silicon Valley, or anything close to a Silicon Valley. This is why government-led efforts to create Silicon Valleys, whether in Malaysia, Russia or elsewhere,

> " Unfortunately, no amount of bureaucratic effort will succeed in creating a Silicon Valley, or anything close to a Silicon Valley. This is why government-led efforts to create Silicon Valleys, whether in Malaysia, Russia or elsewhere, are doomed to fail. "

are doomed to fail. Silicon Valley is a powerful testament to the vast potential of capitalism, what capitalism can achieve if innovative entrepreneurs bursting with fresh ideas are left alone and allowed to do their business. The paper-pushing bureaucrat, even the most public-spirited and talented pen-pushing bureaucrat, is no match and no substitute for Steve Jobs and Steve Wozniak tinkering in their Los Altos garage. It is true that other countries lack the scale and depth of the American market and, yes, market size gives American technology startups a big advantage. But Silicon Valley is in America not because the American market is big. It is in America because America remains the cradle of dynamic, muscular, risk-taking capitalism, bursting with raw entrepreneurial energy. The closest thing to Silicon Valley in the rest of the world is in Israel, where private entrepreneurs have created a thriving tech industry, known as the Silicon wadi.[1]

China's colossal reservoir of entrepreneurial energy suggests that it may just succeed in creating an Asian Silicon Valley. As noted earlier, China already has its own bevy of highly valuable IT companies — Baidu, Alibaba, Tencent, NetEase, and Xiaomi, and a growing number of IT billionaires — Robin Li, Jack Ma, Pony Ma, William Ding, and Lei Jun. Impressive as China's achievements are, Chinese companies are basically knockoffs of more famous American companies. For example, Baidu is the Chinese equivalent of Google. Furthermore, they enjoy substantial government assistance, as many foreign visitors who tried to unsuccessfully access Google in their Beijing or Shanghai hotel rooms can attest. Baidu dominates the Chinese market for search engines, and only the Chinese market, but it is no match for Google outside China. Firms whose success is predicated on

[1] The Silicon wadi has propelled Israel's rapid growth in recent years. While the Silicon wadi was created by private entrepreneurs, many of those entrepreneurs honed their skills and found future business partners during their mandatory military service in Israel Defense Forces (IDF). "Tales from Silicon wadi," The Economist, 4 June 2016.

government protection from competition, such as Baidu, rarely grow up to be world-class.

If Chinese IT companies are to move beyond copycatting Silicon Valley, and become true innovators in their own right with original products and services that can wow the entire world (and not just China), it is best for the Chinese government to get out of the way, stop "helping" their companies (for example, by blocking Google in China), and let the private sector take over. Only then will China have a good shot at producing its own Silicon Valley and its own Steve Jobs. But China's huge reservoir of entrepreneurial energy bodes well for China's dreams of its own Silicon Valley. In particular, the amazing entrepreneurial buzz of Shenzhen, where creative, risk-taking, profit-seeking entrepreneurs, many of them young, compete and network with each other, suggests that the first viable Silicon Valley outside the United States is likely to be in China. This is achievable as long as Beijing moves to the back stage and allows bold Chinese entrepreneurs work their capitalist, wealth-creating magic.

In fact, there are already some promising signs of world-class Chinese tech companies that are not merely Silicon Valley knockoff but innovative enough to compete against the best of Silicon Valley. One such Chinese company is Didi Chuxing, China's answer to Uber, the fast-growing taxi-hailing app.[2] Didi Chuxing was the product of the 2015 merger of rival taxi-hailing apps of two Chinese tech giants, Alibaba and Tencent. The Chinese upstart arranged more than 1.4 billion rides in China in 2015 alone, more than Uber's global total in its entire history. Didi Chuxing's success is not due to Beijing's help but due to its own ingenuity, innovation, and business sense. The firm is expanding its range of services well beyond its core of

[2] Didi Chuxing's former name is Didi Kuaidi. http://www.economist.com/news/business-and-finance/21689487-companys-ambitions-go-far-beyond-taxi-hailing-didi-Chuxing-dominating-uber-chinas

arranging rides. In January 2016, for example, it announced a tie-up with a major Chinese bank to offer car loans to its drivers.

Another highly innovative Chinese internet firm is messaging app WeChat, which dwarfs WhatsApp, the world's most popular messaging app, in China. In contrast to Baidu, a mediocre search engine which owes its success to the Chinese government's blocking of Google, or Renren, an inferior knock-off of Facebook, which is unavailable in China, WeChat dominates the Chinese market due to its superior features. Indeed WhatsApp is freely available in China. WeChat's functions include messaging, voice calls, browsing, gaming, and payment. In fact, it is an entire mobile operating system which allows users to pay parking tickets, book hospital appointments, or order food and pay for a cup of coffee. WeChat is light years ahead of most Western apps.[3] The sooner the Chinese government comes to its senses and gets out of the way, the sooner it will realize its dream of a Chinese Silicon Valley, with many more Didi Chuxings and WeChats, companies that can compete globally, unlike Baidu or Renren.

[3] See "China's tech trailblazers," The Economist, 6 August 2016; and "WeChat's world," The Economist, 6 August 2016.

THE VAST UNFULFILLED PROMISE OF INDIA: WILL HISTORY BE KIND TO NARENDRA MODI?

58

N o discussion of Silicon Valley and future Silicon Valleys would be complete without a discussion of India. The country has probably the largest number of IT experts in the world, which explains the prominence of Indians in Silicon Valley[1] and the global IT industry. The immense concentration of IT scientists, engineers, technicians, and other IT brain power means that India is well-positioned to become the home of the next Silicon Valley. To be sure, India has already enjoyed a great deal of success in the global IT industry, in particular as the world's most successful exporter of IT services. Furthermore, Bangalore and Hyderabad have emerged as globally important IT hubs, and some Indian IT companies — most notably TCS (Tata Consultancy Services), Infosys and Wipro — have become globally recognized names. But the much bigger question is, given its cornucopia of IT talent, why has not India yet produced its own Apple or Google or Amazon, in other words a world-class tech giant?

The two-word answer is government regulation. Despite some progress under the government of Prime Minister Narendra Modi, who was elected in 2014, India remains a highly regulated economy, with nosy government bureaucrats

[1] http://www.firstpost.com/business/more-than-just-pichai-and-nadella-indians-now-the-biggest-power-players-in-silicon-valley-2387058.html

poking their noses into almost every facet of economic life. While Prime Minister Modi won a comfortable parliamentary majority by promising to cut red tape, make it much easier for businessmen to do business, and revive economic growth, the sheer amount of bureaucracy and regulation in place makes it difficult for even such a strong leader with a strong political mandate to tame bureaucrats and tackle overregulation. Nevertheless, if Modi keeps his central electoral promise and follows through on key economic reforms — for example, making it easier for businesses to acquire land so they can build factories — then India has every chance to host the next Silicon Valley.

If India is serious about producing the next Steve Jobs, then its government will have to get out of the way and provide a much more conducive business environment for millions of Indian entrepreneurs and would-be entrepreneurs. Anybody who has tried to do business in India will tell you that it is very difficult to do business there. To name just one prominent example, Korea's POSCO, one of the world's largest steelmakers, threw its hands up in frustration and eventually dropped plans to build a steel plant in the eastern Indian state of Odisha after trying in vain (for more than a decade!) to acquire the land for the plant.[2] The US$12 billion project would have been India's single biggest foreign direct investment (FDI) project. The cancelation of the project is bad news for POSCO, but it is even worse news for India, which stands to lose thousands of well-paid jobs and millions of rupees in taxes.

If the Modi government caves in to political opposition and fails to deliver the promised reforms, India's only connection to Silicon Valley will be the one it already has with the Californian

[2] http://timesofindia.indiatimes.com/business/india-business/Poscos-12-billion-Odisha-project-on-hold/articleshow/48105882.cms

Silicon Valley — as a supplier of IT brainpower and talent. Reforms are much more difficult in a vibrant multi-party democracy such as India than in one-party states since opponents to reform have to be dealt with in a democratic way rather than arrested, beaten up, or worse. Moreover, reforms always produce vocal losers, such as nosy bureaucrats who lose their power to meddle and extort bribes, and they will cause a ruckus and make noise. Count on it. Nevertheless, if Modi shows political courage, seizes the moment, and pushes through the reforms that will transform the economy and turn India into the next China, then he will be forever remembered as India's transformational leader, as India's Deng Xiaoping.

Given the grinding poverty that still traps much of India, the stakes are enormous. The harsh reality is that India has a long way to catch up with China. India's average income is less than half that of China, even if we account for the fact that Indian prices for non-tradable products such as haircuts are lower than Chinese prices, precisely because India is much poorer. According to 2014 IMF estimates, for example, China's average income stood at US$13,224 while the corresponding figure for India was a much lower US$5,808.[3] And, according to 2014 World Bank estimates, India is home to 180 million who live on less than US$1.25 a day, which is about 20% of the global total. Indians abroad have been exceptionally successful, not only in Silicon Valley but throughout the world — from Fiji to Kenya to Canada — and in all kinds of different industries — from retail to hotels to diamond-cutting.[4] All it takes to unlock the vast promise of India is a transformational leader who can take the country up to the next level. It still remains to be seen whether Modi will be that transformational, game-changing leader who can leave a lasting imprint on the country.

[3] These incomes are purchasing power parity (PPP) incomes, which means that they are adjusted for the fact that the prices of haircuts (and, more generally, goods and services which are not internationally traded) are lower in poorer countries.

[4] http://www.economist.com/news/christmas-specials/21683983-secrets-worlds-best-businesspeople-going-global

The challenge for Modi is all the more daunting because India has underperformed, and underperformed dismally, in the past. In particular, a comparison with China, the other Asian giant, illustrates the magnitude of India's underperformance. For the first time in decades, the Indian economy is projected to grow faster than the Chinese economy in 2015. It is a measure of India's past failures that Indians and foreign fans of India — especially, Westerners enamored with Indian democracy — are jumping up and down at this underwhelming news as if they just won the lottery. But this news is no cause for celebration. Economic history tells us that poorer countries, and India is much poorer than China, typically grow faster than richer ones. For one, investment tends to be more productive in poorer countries since they have less machines and factories than richer countries. What is remarkable is not that India is growing faster than China. Rather, it is that India underperformed China for so long.

The fact that India grew slower than China for years and years when economics predicts the opposite is due to many factors. One popular explanation for India's underperformance is its rickety infrastructure — roads, ports, airports, electricity, water supply, and so forth. Infrastructure affects the productivity of all firms and industries — for example, power blackouts disrupt the entire economy and poor roads raise the cost of moving all goods from one place to another. In contrast, China boasts high-quality infrastructure which is often world-class, for example the Beijing–Shanghai bullet train, which covers 1,318 kilometers (819 miles) in about five hours. This kind of high-speed railway will remain a pipe dream for India for a long time to come. But an even bigger reason for why India lagged far behind China

> **"**
>
> For the first time in decades, the Indian economy is projected to grow faster than the Chinese economy in 2015.... But this news is no cause for celebration. Economic history tells us that poorer countries, and India is much poorer than China, typically grow faster than richer ones.
>
> **"**

up to now is the mind-numbing, patience-testing, business-strangling overregulation and excessive intervention of its vast government bureaucracy. The secret to unlocking India's vast potential is to fundamentally change the mentality and culture of bureaucrats from obstructing business to helping business. History will remember Modi kindly indeed if he makes good progress on this front.[5]

[5] There are promising signs that the Modi government is moving in the right direction. For example, India attracted more greenfield foreign direct investment (FDI) — i.e. new factories — than any other country in 2015, a clear sign of growing foreign investor confidence in the country. Furthermore, India's strong growth prospects do not depend on top policymakers. Not even the departure of Raghuram Rajan, India's widely respected top central banker who was formerly IMF Chief Economist, announced for September 2016, is likely to significantly affect India's growth momentum. "India's success is built to last," TIME magazine, 4 July 2016.

CHINA'S GROWTH SLOWDOWN, THE GROTESQUE MUTATION OF CAPITALISM, AND RISK PARASITES

59

India may aspire to be the next China and Narendra Modi may aspire to be the next Deng Xiaoping, but the capitalist revolution is far from complete in China itself. The sooner that China and developing countries that look to China as a role model of "state capitalism", disabuse themselves from the ludicrous notion that "state capitalism" offers a viable third way, neither capitalism nor socialism, for economic progress, the better it will be for their economic future. Again, China grew so rapidly despite the government, not because of the government. The only part of state capitalism that fueled China's phenomenal economic ascent was the capitalism, not the state. China itself would grow faster if it further reduced the role of the state in the economy, in particular by reducing the role of state-owned firms, which deprive the more productive and dynamic private sector of scarce capital and labor. Shifting machines and workers from the state-owned firms to the private sector will create more jobs and more wealth, and help China regain its economic momentum at a time when economic growth in 2015 slowed down to its slowest pace in a quarter-century.

By the way, China's growth slowdown is causing concerns inside and outside China. Businessmen

> Again, China grew so rapidly despite the government, not because of the government. The only part of state capitalism that fueled China's phenomenal economic ascent was the capitalism, not the state. China itself would grow faster if it further reduced the role of the state in the economy, in particular by reducing the role of state-owned firms, which deprive the more productive and dynamic private sector of scarce capital and labor.

269

and government officials outside China are concerned because China is now the world's second largest economy, which means that what happens to the Chinese economy matters, and matters greatly, for the global economy. However, while there are certainly risks surrounding the Chinese economy, concerns about China's slowdown are overdone. The historical experience of other countries suggests that economic growth typically slows down as countries become richer. There is no reason why China alone should defy the economic law of gravity, which has pulled down economic growth in all other countries, especially since China grew at double-digit pace for almost 40 years. Precisely because it grew so rapidly, China has now reached an income level at which growth typically starts to slow down.

Therefore, China is simply following the earlier footsteps of other countries and slowing down to more normal growth rates. In that sense, China's slowdown is not a cause for concern but instead, a healthy, natural and welcome transition to more sustainable growth. But in order for China to grow at healthy rates, it will have to disabuse itself from its infatuation with state capitalism. That is, China will have to further reduce the role of the state in the economy, and more fully unleash the entrepreneurial energy of the private sector. Above all, the slowdown means that China can no longer bear the costly burden of inefficient, unproductive state-owned firms sapping the vitality of its wealth- and job-creating private sector. We saw earlier that the role of the state in the Chinese has been steadily declining since the market-oriented reform of 1978. If the Chinese miracle is to continue, the role of the state will have to decline further.

Government parasites are clearly a major problem in today's capitalism. They owe their success to their close ties to politicians and

"

But in order for China to grow at healthy rates, it will have to disabuse itself from its infatuation with state capitalism. That is, China will have to further reduce the role of the state in the economy, and more fully unleash the entrepreneurial energy of the private sector.

"

bureaucrats, who give them unfair advantages in exchange for bribes, rather than to any talent in creating value for society. But an even bigger problem, in fact the root of the problem, is those same politicians and bureaucrats whose corrupt greed imposes a heavy tax on private sector entrepreneurs. The bribes they demand and extort out of the private sector amount to stealing part of the fruits of risk-taking done by entrepreneurs. In other words, they bear none of the risks but earn a sizable chunk of the profits generated by those who bear the risks. All in the name of serving the public interest and protecting the public from the rapacious greed of the private sector! The only interest they are interested in serving is in lining their own pockets. The bribes are not always explicit — for example, cushy post-retirement jobs in the insurance industry for government bureaucrats who regulate the insurance industry. But whether explicit or not, the bribes impose a crushing burden on the private sector all the same.

Risk parasite is an apt description for the hordes of politicians and bureaucrats who benefit from entrepreneurial risk-taking without taking any risk themselves. Those hordes are especially prevalent in developing countries where they create and impose all kinds of absurd regulations as tools for extorting bribes from risk-taking, wealth- and job-creating entrepreneurs. In exchange for waving off the absurd regulation, entrepreneurs pay off the risk parasites. The hordes of risk parasites go a long way toward explaining why private sector and entrepreneurship never grow up in developing countries. Anybody who quit a regular salaried job to start his or her own business knows how tough it is to start and run one's own business. Moreover, the chances of success are small, as evidenced by the countless startups that fail within one year. Starting and running one's

> " ... in fact the root of the problem, is those same politicians and bureaucrats whose corrupt greed imposes a heavy tax on private sector entrepreneurs. The bribes they demand and extort out of the private sector amount to stealing part of the fruits of risk-taking done by entrepreneurs. In other words, they bear none of the risks but earn a sizable chunk of the profits generated by those who bear the risks.... Risk parasite is an apt description for the hordes of politicians and bureaucrats who benefit from entrepreneurial risk-taking without taking any risk themselves. "

own business is a risky venture. It must be demoralizing to be robbed by some salivating bureaucrat when the entrepreneur finally makes it. It must be a killer, in fact.

Risk parasitism clearly reduces the returns to risk-taking and thus reduces risk-taking, entrepreneurship, and private sector development. The result is far fewer jobs and far less wealth than would be the case in the absence of risk parasitism. More insidiously, the prevalence of politicians and bureaucrats armed to the teeth with regulations and with their bribe-expecting hands wide open alters the very nature of capitalism for worse. Instead of investing their time and energy in producing new, better products and technologies, those who are courageous enough to start their own business even in the presence of risk parasites spend all their time and energy in cultivating relationships with the risk parasites in the hopes of limiting regulations and greedy demands to reasonable levels. In a world where politicians and bureaucrats give unfair advantages to the firms they favor, the "best" firms are those that curry favor with politicians and bureaucrats, rather than those that give the consumers the best value for money. Such a world is clearly bad for consumers (lousy products), bad for workers (too few jobs), and bad for the economy as a whole (slow growth).

Unfortunately, excessively close ties between government and business are the rule rather than the exception in today's world economy. The problem is universal and by no means limited to China and other countries associated with state capitalism. Even in the US, that paragon of muscular, dynamic, Steve Jobs-ian capitalism, firms spend hundreds of billions of dollars on lobbying politicians and bureaucrats to bend rules and regulations in their favor. Those dollars

"

Risk parasitism clearly reduces the returns to risk-taking and thus reduces risk-taking, entrepreneurship, and private sector development. The result is far fewer jobs and far less wealth than would be the case in the absence of risk parasitism.

"

have spawned a major industry, nicknamed K Street after the Washington, D.C., street where many top lobbying firms are located. Those precious dollars would have been much better spent on finding a cure for cancer, eradicating hunger in the Third World, or building decent public housing for the hundreds of millions of people who live in squalid, dehumanizing slums across the world.

In a fundamental sense, cozy ties between business and government are an unavoidable feature of any liberal, multi-party, Western-style democracy. Politics is an expensive business. Running for office takes a lot of money. In a mature democracy, politicians do not literally buy votes — i.e. bribe voters — but getting votes is expensive all them same. Forming a political party and keeping it going takes even more money. Moreover, in a capitalist economy, big business has the most money. The predictable result is that big business exerts a disproportionate influence on politics. In the US, for example, politicians from both main political parties — Republicans and Democrats — receive huge amounts of political donations from big business. It is naïve to believe that big business expects nothing in return for its hefty donations. For example, the US government rewarded the US financial industry, among the biggest sources of political donations, with a massive bailout during the Global Financial Crisis, which had its origin in the US subprime mortgage crisis. Those donations are, in effect, insurance premiums and they paid off handsomely since the bailout saved many financial firms from bankruptcy.

The truth is, today's capitalism is a grossly mutated form of capitalism which bears little relation to true capitalism. In true capitalism, the government is an honest, fair and capable referee that efficiently and effectively presides

"

In a fundamental sense, cozy ties between business and government are an unavoidable feature of any liberal, multi-party, Western-style democracy.... Running for office takes a lot of money.

"

273

over an unpredictable, dynamic, and vigorous contest between private sector players competing vigorously with each other to deliver the most value to the consumers. Instead the visible hand of the government is increasingly replacing the invisible hand of the market across the world. In other words, whether private sector players succeed or fail depends less on how good they are at satisfying the consumer and more on how good they are at currying favor with politicians and bureaucrats. It is as if the football team which has better connections to the referee always wins, rather than the team with superior talent, motivation, and teamwork. The quality of both capitalism and football would suffer, and suffer hugely, if competition was rigged in this way. But then this is not football. And, it is definitely not capitalism. In fact, Adam Smith would roll in his grave if he saw how his benign vision of capitalism has been grotesquely mutilated beyond all recognition.

❝

Instead the visible hand of the government is increasingly replacing the invisible hand of the market across the world. In other words, whether private sector players succeed or fail depends less on how good they are at satisfying the consumer and more on how good they are at currying favor with politicians and bureaucrats.

❞

RISK TAX, ENTREPRENEURIAL CAPITALISM, AND ENTREPRENEURSHIP 101

60

The essence of healthy, dynamic, wealth- and job-creating capitalism is risk-taking entrepreneurship and private enterprise. If everybody were content to be a salaried worker, the economy would be permanently stuck in first gear. Even worse, if everybody were salaried workers working for the government, there would be mile-long queues for basic necessities such as bread and toilet paper, nightmares that occurred on a regular basis in Moscow, Warsaw and elsewhere under communism. In the absence of risk-taking entrepreneurship and private enterprise, there would be no plethora of new products, services and technologies, there would be no iPhones, and there would be no material abundance. In short, a world where everybody is content to work for somebody else would be a much poorer and much less interesting world. In fact, such a world would feel like a puddle of stagnant water, listless, lifeless and hopeless.

It is impossible to exaggerate the critical role of risk-taking in entrepreneurial capitalism, the kind of capitalism that creates jobs and wealth and moves mankind forward. Yet from an individual perspective, it is far easier and less risky to work for somebody else and draw a regular salary,

> **It is impossible to exaggerate the critical role of risk-taking in entrepreneurial capitalism, the kind of capitalism that creates jobs and wealth and moves mankind forward.**

275

than to start your own business. Success is anything but guaranteed and, in fact, far more businesses fail than succeed. We are not even talking about Apple or Tesla or CNN (Cable News Network). Even in mundane business ventures such as opening a restaurant or convenience store, the risk of failure is high. Too high for most people, which is why most individuals, including the author of this book, choose to work for others than for ourselves. It is far safer. When businesses fail, the owners bear the costs, often in the form of debts that take years to pay back. When businesses succeed, the owners keep the profits, which is only fair since they are the ones who took the risk. But their risk-taking benefits not only themselves, it benefits others and society at large. In economists' jargon, they generate a positive externality.

The positive externality is obvious in the case of entrepreneurs who produce innovative and useful new products and technologies like mobile phones or laptops or electric cars that enrich and improve our lives. However, even mundane and ordinary entrepreneurial capitalists, the guy who owns a popular street corner pizza shop, or the lady who runs a reliable dry cleaner, or the auto shop owner whose mechanics fix your car, generate positive externalities. At a minimum, they hire workers and thus create jobs, and pay taxes that help to finance public services. In addition, small businesses are the often under-appreciated lifeblood of cities and towns. This explains why small businesses disappear in mass when cities and towns — for example, Detroit — start to die. By the same token, the revival of run-down urban areas is complete only when small businesses begin to return. More generally, entrepreneurial capitalists are not only the lifeblood of cities and towns, they are the lifeblood of the entire economy.

"

The positive externality is obvious in the case of entrepreneurs who produce innovative and useful new products and technologies like mobile phones or laptops or electric cars that enrich and improve our lives.

"

Since entrepreneurial capitalists are the engines that drive forward a market economy, there is a case for governments to subsidize or help them. The government subsidy or assistance should be limited since the risk-taking entrepreneurs keep most of the profits when their businesses succeed (and bear all of the losses when their businesses fail). Nevertheless, their risk-taking benefits others and society at large and not just themselves, which is why the government should help them. One potentially effective means of encouraging entrepreneurship is to revamp the education system so that students have more opportunities to learn about starting and running their own business. Entrepreneurship 101 would not be some theoretical class completely detached from the practical challenges of real-world entrepreneurship. Instead entrepreneurship education, which can start as early as high school, should focus on teaching the students the hands-on skills to become successful entrepreneurs, such as drawing up viable business loans, the ABCs of financial literacy, or the mechanics of taking out a loan from a bank.

One very promising trend in university education is the growing efforts of the world's elite universities to help their students become entrepreneurs. For example, MIT (Massachusetts Institute of Technology), one of the world's top science and engineering universities, set up the Martin Trust Center for MIT Entrepreneurship, which has a stated mission of providing the expertise, support, and connections needed for MIT entrepreneurs to become effective entrepreneurs. The center not only imparts knowledge to its students, but also actively helps them to put their acquired knowledge to good use by starting their own startups. The center has helped MIT, which boasts more than 40,000 firms founded by its alumnus and around 900 startups set up by its graduates every year, to

> **"**
> Since entrepreneurial capitalists are the engines that drive forward a market economy, there is a case for governments to subsidize or help them. The government subsidy or assistance should be limited since the risk-taking entrepreneurs keep most of the profits when their businesses succeed.
> **"**

277

become one of the two most fertile cradles of startups in the US, along with Stanford, which has its own, equally well-renowned school. Top US universities are competing fiercely with each other to produce the next Mark Zuckerberg. In light of the entrepreneurial buzz of elite Chinese universities, where many students aspire to start their own business, it is only a matter of time before they travel the same path as the elite American universities.

In the real world, unfortunately, governments provide precious little help to would-be entrepreneurs. For example, to our knowledge, there is no government that has a systematic entrepreneurship education strategy. This is downright scandalous given the indispensable role of entrepreneurial capitalists in the economy. To the contrary, the tendency of governments to force the private sector to cough up bribes amounts to a hefty tax on risk-taking. The entrepreneur bears all the risk and he bears all the cost if he fails, but has to give the grasping government bureaucrat a cut if he succeeds. For the bureaucrat, who bears none of the risk, it is easy money. For the entrepreneurial capitalist, the bribes he coughs up amount to a hefty tax on his risk-taking — a risk tax. Even in the absence of bribes, meddling and overregulation by bureaucrats with too much time on their hands amount to an equally harmful risk tax. Rather than encouraging risk-taking, the key ingredient of entrepreneurial capitalism, governments around the world discourage it by taxing it heavily. Besides overregulating and the presence of bribe-seeking bureaucrats, financial capitalism poses another mortal threat to entrepreneurial capitalism, an issue we explore over the next few pages.

"

In the real world, unfortunately, governments provide precious little help to would-be entrepreneurs. For example, to our knowledge, there is no government that has a systematic entrepreneurship education strategy.... For the entrepreneurial capitalist, the bribes he coughs up amount to a hefty tax on his risk-taking — a risk tax.

"

US SUBPRIME MORTGAGE CRISIS AND GLOBAL FINANCIAL CRISIS, 2008-2009: A SHORT HISTORY

61

Within the broader worldwide wave of growing disenchantment with and hostility to capitalism, one industry in particular has been singled out as the root of all evil. That industry is the global financial industry, epitomized by Wall Street in New York and The City in London. Criticism of Goldman Sachs, J.P. Morgan, Citibank, and the financial industry in general has grown louder by quite a few decibels since the Global Financial Crisis of 2008–2009. That crisis originated from the US subprime mortgage crisis and almost paralyzed the US financial system, before spreading like wildfire across the Atlantic and paralyzing the European financial system. In a nutshell, US banks and other US financial institutions were lending large amounts of money to subprime borrowers — i.e. borrowers with poor credit histories and low creditworthiness — to buy homes. To put it bluntly, the banks were giving out mortgage loans to homebuyers who should not be buying homes.

The banks then repackaged the mortgage loans into complicated, sophisticated financial products such as mortgage-backed securities (MBS)[1], credit default swaps (CDS)[2], and collateralized debt obligations (CDO)[3], and

[1] MBS refers to the packaging of mortgages into securities that investors can buy.

[2] The seller of CDS agrees to compensate the buyer in the event of a loan default by the debtor.

[3] CDO is an asset-backed security whose collaterals in the run-up to Global Financial Crisis were increasingly dominated by high-risk tranches recycled from other asset-backed securities, whose underlying assets were typically subprime mortgages. CDOs gave lenders a false sense of security and encouraged them to make more subprime mortgage loans.

279

sold them to investors. But no amount of repackaging, splicing and dicing can reduce the huge amount of risk inherent in banks' funneling huge amounts of loans to high-risk homebuyers. The banks' desperate search for yield, evident in MBS, CDS, CDO, and other innovations, was largely motivated by the lack of profitable opportunities in a low interest rate environment. The low interest rates, in turn, were due to the large pool of liquidity sloshing around global financial markets, due to lax monetary policy in the US and other major advanced economies. The financial industry's behavior amounted to excessive risk-taking which tried to create profit where there was no inherent profit — i.e. giving out mortgage loans to homebuyers who should not be buying homes.

Clearly, the reckless subprime mortgage lending was not motivated by Wall Street's altruistic concern for the welfare of the homebuyer with poor credit history. It is motivated by one thing and one thing only — pure, unadulterated greed or greed gone mad. Our best guess is that one fine day, some Wall Street whiz kid with an advanced mathematics degree from MIT or Caltech probably came up with the "brilliant" notion of engineering subprime mortgage into seemingly respectable, "innovative" financial products such as MBS and CDO, got handsomely rewarded for it, and patted himself for his cleverness. But this kind of innovation and risk-taking has nothing to do with the innovation and risk-taking of Steve Jobs, Ted Turner, Elon Musk, and the other heroes of capitalism. Yes, Jobs, Turner and Musk were motivated by greed too, but their greed is a socially valuable kind of greed that creates socially valuable products and services that actually benefit society. On the other hand, the so-called innovations of Wall Street circa 2006 and 2007 were the socially destructive kind that fattened the paychecks of Wall Street

> **"**
> But no amount of repackaging, splicing and dicing can reduce the huge amount of risk inherent in banks' funneling huge amounts of loans to high-risk homebuyers.... The financial industry's behavior amounted to excessive risk-taking which tried to create profit where there was no inherent profit — i.e. giving out mortgage loans to homebuyers who should not be buying homes.
> **"**

fat cats but yielded no obvious benefits for the larger society. Forget benefits, the innovations brought ruin to all.

In effect, Wall Street's so-called financial innovations such as MBS, CDS, and CDO were privately profitable but socially destructive greed-driven efforts to artificially fabricate profits. Unfortunately, no amount of financial engineering, even by brilliant world-class minds with advanced mathematics degrees from MIT and Caltech, can turn lead into gold, junk into value. Shoveling mortgages down the throats of borrowers with subprime credit histories and turning those mortgages into securities, it is impossible to see where the profit is in this shenanigan. The 2015 Hollywood movie *The Big Short* provides an excellent account of Wall Street's blind, crazed, frenzied pursuit of profits without any regard for the social good. The movie correctly suggests that Wall Street's greed-driven pre-2008 profit fabrication amounts to one colossal financial fraud which benefited Wall Street but almost brought down the global economy. A fraud of this scale would simply not be possible without help from the government, and that was indeed the case. Alarmingly, Wall Street was back at it soon, creating a financial product which seemed suspiciously similar to CDOs in 2015.

The rising chorus of anti-finance criticism since the global financial crisis is rooted in two factors. First, the reckless greed and excess of the US financial system was the immediate cause of the crisis. It is certainly true that the US financial regulators failed to do their job. They were asleep at the wheel while the financial industry was going haywire in its quest to fabricate profits when profits were not there. The regulators' casual, laissez-faire attitude to so-called financial innovation — so-called because

> " In effect, Wall Street's so-called financial innovations such as MBS, CDS, and CDO were privately profitable but socially destructive greed-driven efforts to artificially fabricate profits. Unfortunately, no amount of financial engineering, even by brilliant world-class minds with advanced mathematics degrees from MIT and Caltech, can turn lead into gold, junk into value.... The movie *Big Short* correctly suggests that Wall Street's greed-driven pre-2008 profit fabrication amounts to one colossal financial fraud which benefited Wall Street but almost brought down the global economy. "

281

real financial innovation should generate real benefits — allowed the financial industry to get away with MBS, CDO, and other privately profitable but socially disastrous shenanigans. Nevertheless, the first and foremost culprit of the global crisis was the financial industry that came up with those shenanigans in the first place. Blaming the financial regulators for the Global Financial Crisis is akin to blaming policemen and judges for burglaries, rapes, and murders, rather than the burglars, rapists, and murderers. There is simply no two ways about it — the blind quest of talented, arrogant, and super-rich bankers on Wall Street to make even more money so they can buy another Lamborghini or Porsche lay at the heart of the crisis.

There is a second, equally compelling case against the financial industry. The Wall Street fat cats did not care one iota about the social good when the going was good, and they were raking in billions of dollars. Yet those same Wall Street fat cats suddenly became champions of the public good when their own blind greed precipitated the US subprime mortgage crisis, and cried out for the US government — i.e. US tax payers — to bail them out. They argued that the collapse of the financial system would devastate the economy, which is why the government should bail them out. The amount of financial assistance the US financial industry received from the US government was staggering. More specifically, under the Troubled Asset Relief Program (TARP), signed into law by President George W. Bush on 3 October 2008, the US government spent over US$420 billion to purchase assets and equity from financial institutions which sought to bolster their distressed balance sheets. The list of TARP beneficiaries reads like a who's who of Wall Street — Citigroup, Bank of America, AIG

"

The Wall Street fat cats did not care one iota about the social good when the going was good, and they were raking in billions of dollars. Yet those same Wall Street fat cats suddenly became champions of the public good when their own blind greed precipitated the US subprime mortgage crisis, and cried out for the US government — i.e. US tax payers — to bail them out.

"

(American International Group), J.P. Morgan Chase, Wells Fargo, Goldman Sachs, Morgan Stanley, American Express, and others.

To be sure, the program succeeded, and succeeded beyond the most optimistic expectations, in stabilizing the US financial system. A widely feared meltdown of banks, insurance companies and other financial institutions, along with stock markets and bond markets, was decisively averted. Perhaps more importantly, TARP prevented a repeat of the Great Depression, which was the deepest and longest-lasting economic downturn of the Western world. That mother of all recessions was kicked off by the crash of the US stock market on 29 October 1929 (Black Tuesday), and spread like wildfire across the Atlantic to Europe and subsequently across the entire world. Unemployment reached 25% in the US and as high as 33% in some countries. Nearly half of all US banks failed as a result of bank runs — i.e. panicking depositors fearful of losing their savings rushing to their banks to withdraw their money. Between 1929 and 1932, the world economy shrank by an estimated 15%. In addition, global trade plummeted by 50%, further denting global growth. The Great Depression persisted until the outbreak of the Second World War, when governments' massive military spending finally lifted the global economy out of its doldrums, albeit at a horrific human cost.

At the onset of the US subprime mortgage crisis, there were genuine and almost universal fears about a meltdown of the global financial system and the world economy. After all, the US is not a small Third World economy but the world's biggest economy, the central hub of the global financial system, and one of the world's richest economies. Therefore, a severe

> **“**
>
> Perhaps more importantly, TARP prevented a repeat of the Great Depression, which was the deepest and longest-lasting economic downturn of the Western world.... At the onset of the US subprime mortgage crisis, there were genuine and almost universal fears about a meltdown of the global financial system and the world economy.
>
> **”**

283

financial crisis which originated in the US and crippled its economy was bound to have huge repercussions for the rest of the world. That is, the US matters, and matters hugely, for the global economy. The US is not a mismanaged Third World economy, which used to be the sources of most financial crises prior to the Global Financial Crisis. When a crisis erupts in, say, Argentina or Venezuela, that is bad news for the thousands of Argentinians and Venezuelans who lose their jobs, savings, or both, but it does not matter for the rest of the world except for foreign investors who were stupid or greedy (or both) enough to invest money in the mismanaged economy.

Furthermore, many European banks invested heavily in the aptly called toxic US subprime assets — the fancy, sophisticated, complex financial products which repainted, varnished, and repackaged the underlying garbage American assets of American mortgage loans to American borrowers with subprime credit ratings. Again, no amount of repainting, varnishing, and repackaging will turn lead into gold, which is, in effect, exactly what greed-crazed US bankers purported to do. The heavy exposure of European banks to the toxic US assets spread the financial turmoil across the Atlantic and transformed the US subprime mortgage crisis into the Global Financial Crisis which threatened to bring down the global financial system and world economy. Therefore, TARP was a desperate response to a desperate situation and, to the extent that it staved off Great Depression II and the end of the global economy as we know it. TARP was an unqualified success.

"

Again, no amount of repainting, varnishing, and repackaging will turn lead into gold, which is, in effect, exactly what greed-crazed US bankers purported to do. The heavy exposure of European banks to the toxic US assets spread the financial turmoil across the Atlantic and transformed the US subprime mortgage crisis into the Global Financial Crisis which threatened to bring down the global financial system and world economy.

"

THE FREE BAILOUT, TOO BIG TO FAIL, AND ARSONIST BANKERS

62

In addition, there is some truth to the argument that TARP (Troubled Asset Relief Program) paid for itself, which means that it cost the US government and the US tax payers nothing in actual money. While the precise estimates vary, there is general agreement that the US government recovered all or most of the money it lent to financial institutions, which were able to repay their loans much sooner than expected. Many banks, including J.P. Morgan Chase, Morgan Stanley, American Express, Goldman Sachs, and Wells Fargo, fully repaid TARP money. TARP effectively came to an end on 19 December 2014, when the US government sold its remaining holdings in Ally Financial. The popular, widely accepted narrative of TARP is that the US government decisively and forcefully rescued the US financial institutions at a time when they were on the brink of collapse, at almost no cost to the US tax payers.

For example, according to one widely cited estimate, the US government spent US$426.4 billion on TARP and earned US$441.7 billion, suggesting that TARP even turned a profit. Even if we account for various hidden costs, such as implicit subsidies that TARP provided the financial institutions — for example, the difference between

> **The popular, widely accepted narrative of TARP is that the US government decisively and forcefully rescued the US financial institutions at a time when they were on the brink of collapse, at almost no cost to the US tax payers.**

285

the market value of the loans and the lower, actual cost of the TARP loans, most experts agree that the financial cost of TARP to the US government and thus US tax payers was quite small and limited.[1] Furthermore, TARP spent significantly less than the originally authorized US$700 billion in October 2008 and, on top of that, most of what it did spend was recovered. At the same time, TARP delivered almost incalculable benefits — it prevented a global financial meltdown and a rerun of the Great Depression. In short, according to the prevailing benign narrative, the rate of return on TARP investments was exceptionally high. Those investments cost little but, in effect, saved the world.

There are a number of big holes in this absurdly generous narrative of TARP. In particular, TARP's so-called success does not absolve the Wall Street fat cats of their greed-driven economic crime against the millions of ordinary folks on Main Street. Above all, while TARP prevented the global financial system and the world economy from collapsing, which would have brought on untold human misery and suffering, the costs of the global financial crisis remain high and persistent. In particular, the global economy remains stuck on first gear since the outbreak of the global crisis. Financial crises tend to have large and long-lasting effects on the real economy. Above all, banks and other financial institutions whose balance sheets have been badly damaged by mounting piles of loans gone sour are reluctant to lend to firms, especially the small and medium-sized firms that generate the bulk of jobs in most economies. Lack of finance cripples the ability of firms to invest in factories and production capacity.

It does not take an economist to figure out that the lack of investment and jobs will slow down the economy. Indeed there has been an unmistakable

[1] http://www.theguardian.com/commentisfree/2013/may/28/bank-bailout-cost-taxpayers

slowdown of economic growth around the world since 2008. At first, the slowdown was limited to the advanced economies of US, Europe, and Japan. The US was the epicenter of the Global Financial Crisis, Europe's banks were hit hard, and Japan depended heavily on exports to the US and Europe. The malaise had subsequently spread to developing countries, even high-flying China, turning the rich-country slowdown into a global slowdown. Widespread concerns about the global slowdown since the Global Financial Crisis have even given rise to the Secular Stagnation hypothesis, championed by ex-Harvard University President Larry Summers and other prominent economists. According to the hypothesis, since the Global Financial Crisis, the world economy faces an extended period of slower growth.

The Global Financial Crisis is not, by a long shot, the be-all and end-all of the global economic slowdown. For example, population aging is set to reduce the workforce and economic growth of many countries, especially in the rich world. When the entire country grows older, fewer workers have to support growing numbers of elderly. Indeed some countries such as Germany, Italy, Japan, South Korea, and Russia are facing demographic apocalypse, largely due to a collapse in fertility (number of children per woman), with dire economic and social consequences. Furthermore, as noted earlier, the deceleration of growth in China — the world's second biggest economy — reflects a normal, natural and welcome transition to a slower but still healthy and more sustainable growth path. Nevertheless, the Global Financial Crisis and the disruption of global finance clearly contributed to the visible loss of momentum in the world economy. Therefore, the economic cost of the Global Financial Crisis is large indeed.

> **"**
> Nevertheless, the Global Financial Crisis and the disruption of global finance clearly contributed to the visible loss of momentum in the world economy. Therefore, the economic cost of the Global Financial Crisis is large indeed.
> **"**

While TARP helped to prevent Great Depression II, it did nothing to mitigate the high and persistent economic costs of the Global Financial Crisis. This should give cause for the US financial industry and US government to pause before they congratulate themselves. But the first and foremost cost of TARP is that it entrenched moral hazard in the financial industry. Moral hazard is an economists' term for incentives that encourage undesirable behavior. In the case of TARP, the US government is encouraging banks to continue to recklessly take risk in search of profit. It does so by bailing them out when they were about to go out of business during the global crisis, as a result of their reckless risk-taking fueled by blind greed. When Wall Street does not pay for its excessive greed, Wall Street will engage in the same kind of reckless behavior once the memories of the crisis fade. You can count on it.

The US government bought — lock, stock and barrel — Wall Street's arrogant and self-important argument that it was too important to fail. If the banks failed, the financial system failed, and if the financial system failed, the economy would go belly up, or so the argument went. There is certainly an element of truth to Wall Street's "we are too important to fail," as self-serving as it is. Finance is the lubricant which turns the wheels of industry and business. Without finance, the economy would come to a screeching halt since all firms, old and new, big and small, need finance to invest and pursue other productive activities. Budding entrepreneurs with even the greatest business ideas could not get off the ground without access to adequate amounts of reasonably priced credit.

The "too important to fail" argument, along with the associated "too big to fail" argument (i.e. if

"

The US government bought — lock, stock and barrel — Wall Street's arrogant and self-important argument that it was too important to fail. If the banks failed, the financial system failed, and if the financial system failed, the economy would go belly up, or so the argument went.

""

Citigroup or Bank of America or J.P. Morgan or some other big banks fail, credit will freeze and the entire US economy goes down the toilet), may be superficially enticing. However, upon closer thought, both arguments are nothing more than gigantic self-serving hogwash. The logic behind TARP and, more generally, government assistance for banks in trouble, is ludicrous because it does not penalize the financial industry for reckless risk-taking. The financial industry puts the economy at its risk through its blind quest for profit — lending out billions in mortgages to substandard borrowers — and it is rewarded with billions of dollars in tax payers' money to clean up the mess created by that blind quest! Yes, putting out the fire is important, but it is much more important to punish the arsonist so that he does not set fire again. By the same token, preventing a big-time financial crisis from morphing into a financial and economic Armageddon matters a lot, but punishing the greed-crazed banks that caused the crisis in the first place matters even more.

"

The logic behind TARP and, more generally, government assistance for banks in trouble, is ludicrous because it does not penalize the financial industry for reckless risk-taking. The financial industry puts the economy at its risk through its blind quest for profit — lending out billions in mortgages to substandard borrowers — and it is rewarded with billions of dollars in tax payers' money to clean up the mess created by that blind quest!

"

PRIVATE GAIN, SOCIAL PAIN: THE BLATANT GREED AND ARROGANCE OF WALL STREET

63

If you think about it, Wall Street's self-serving argument that it is too important to fail — the argument with which it extorted a multi-billion dollar bailout package out of the US government and US tax payers — reveals an unbelievable degree of arrogance, self-importance, and condescension. Following the logic of Wall Street's self-serving argument, striking subway operators who are demanding 100% wage hikes should be granted every penny of their exorbitant wage demands. After all, public transportation is indispensable for the smooth functioning of large cities such as New York, London, or Tokyo. Those cities are thrown into utter chaos whenever public transportation workers go on strike, costing millions of dollars in economic damage. By the same token, policemen, firemen, teachers, doctors, and a whole host of other occupations are also indispensable, and their every demand should be humored by the government and the general public.

Of course, those who work in most of the other occupations do not make anything close to what Wall Street fat cats make. Nor do they have finance PhDs from Harvard or economics PhDs from MIT (Massachusetts Institute of Technology) or mathematics PhDs from Caltech, as many

> " Following the logic of Wall Street's self-serving argument, striking subway operators who are demanding 100% wage hikes should be granted every penny of their exorbitant wage demands. After all, public transportation is indispensable for the smooth functioning of large cities such as New York, London, or Tokyo. "

of the Wall Street fat cats do. The fundamental problem with Wall Street is that it is full of rich, talented people who believe that their wealth and talent make them far superior to the dumb, poor masses. That arrogance would be less unforgivable if they actually created something valuable, like Steve Jobs or Ted Turner or Elon Musk. The sad truth is that they do not. High-tech financial wizardry may have delivered 500% bonuses for the fortunate financial industry professionals on Wall Street during the pre-2008 go-go boom years, but it is not clear what benefits it delivered for the economy at large. Forget benefits, the high-tech financial wizardry precipitated a catastrophic financial crisis which almost brought the global financial system and the world economy to their knees.

Again, very few people would begrudge Jobs the millions he made by creating superior products such as the iPhone or iPad or Mac. On the other hand, most people would begrudge the millions raked in by greedy, grasping, money-crazed Wall Street professionals who create nothing of social value. It is difficult, if not impossible, to point to a single concrete, specific benefit from the frenzy of financial speculation that immediately preceded the Global Financial Crisis. The frenzy was not all that different from a school of hungry piranha going after and going through an injured fish floating limply on the Amazon River, leaving only the bones behind, the kind of footage you see on National Geographic or Animal Planet. The pre-2008 greed-crazed human frenzy on Wall Street was, if anything, far more frightening. The 500% bonus raked in by the Wall Street piranha with a finance degree was certainly good for himself, but not good at all for everybody else. In fact, it brought nothing but pain and grief.

Quite clearly, the profits from Wall Street's feeding frenzy prior to 2008 were purely personal profits

"

It is difficult, if not impossible, to point to a single concrete, specific benefit from the frenzy of financial speculation that immediately preceded the Global Financial Crisis. The frenzy was not all that different from a school of hungry piranha going after and going through an injured fish floating limply on the Amazon River, leaving only the bones behind, the kind of footage you see on National Geographic or Animal Planet. The pre-2008 greed-crazed human frenzy on Wall Street was, if anything, far more frightening.

"

in the sense that they benefited nobody but those who took part in the frenzy. The frenzy benefited very few outside the financial industry. It does not take a genius to figure out that shoveling billions of dollars of mortgage up the throats of people who, to put it bluntly, should not be buying homes does not create any value to society. It did not even benefit the hordes of subprime homebuyers who saw their homes foreclosed when the bubble collapsed, as it inevitably did. The ultimate irony here is that although Wall Street's profits were purely private, Wall Street cried out for the nationalization of losses when the shit hit the fan. Wall Street kept all the profits when the party was in full swing, yet asked the US government and US tax payers — i.e. US society — to foot the bill when the party ended. Private profits, social losses.[1] Private gain, social pain. The unhealthily close, almost incestuous, links between the US government and Wall Street embodies the very worst of American capitalism. It is no coincidence that Hank Paulson, the US Treasury Secretary who led the TARP (Troubled Asset Relief Program) bailout, was CEO (chief executive officer) of Goldman Sachs before he moved to Washington, D.C.

At a deeper level, there is something fundamentally unsavory about TARP and, more generally, the government's financial assistance to the financial industry. Pray tell me, why in the world should Joe Doe on Main Street pay for the greed of Richie Rich on Wall Street? Why should the working stiffs uncomplainingly toiling through eight-hour shift at a Walmart or a steel factory subsidize the champagne and caviar lifestyle of Wall Street fat cats? This is not fair. Nor is it logical. Yet this is exactly what the TARP bailout package amounted to, the poor giving money to the rich, Robin Hood in reverse. What is even more galling is that Wall Street cloaked its appeals for government help in terms of the public good. That is, the government

[1] Nobel Prize-winning economist Joseph Stiglitz coined the term "private profits, social losses" to denote the notion that investors make purely private profits from excessive risk-taking but the government steps in to bail them out when their excess risk-taking causes a crisis.

should help out Wall Street when Wall Street is in trouble because Wall Street is vital for Main Street.

More specifically, what the distressed banks told the US government and US general public was, in effect, "If you don't help us out, the entire financial system will go down, the economy will collapse, and millions of workers will lose their jobs." While Wall Street's sudden altruism and concern for Main Street was touching, it is a little too rich. What endangered the jobs of millions of Main Street workers in the first place was the unbridled greed of Wall Street. It is as if an arsonist suddenly cared about burn victims. Well, if one cared so much about the burn victims, one should not have set the building on fire in the first place. As outrageous as Wall Street's self-serving justification of TARP was, there was an element of truth to Wall Street's arguments. A healthy and well-functioning financial system is an indispensable ingredient of a healthy and well-functioning market economy. In particular, if entrepreneurship is the lifeblood of capitalism, finance is the lifeblood of entrepreneurship.

But the problem with today's financial system is precisely that it has wandered off, and wandered off a long way, from its core mission of providing capital to the real economy — i.e. to entrepreneurs, companies, and industries. In other words, far too little money goes to the would-be Steve Jobses and Elon Musks who create socially useful goods and services, and far too much stays within the financial system for speculative investments with no obvious social benefits. The financial industry no longer serves the real economy, but serves itself instead. According to experts such as Adair Turner, the former head of financial regulation in the UK, only around 15% of all capital flows within the

> **But the problem with today's financial system is precisely that it has wandered off, and wandered off a long way, from its core mission of providing capital to the real economy — i.e. to entrepreneurs, companies, and industries. In other words, far too little money goes to the would-be Steve Jobses and Elon Musks who create socially useful goods and services, and far too much stays within the financial system for speculative investments with no obvious social benefits.**

American financial system end up in the real economy.[2] The remaining 85% stay within finance, especially high finance, making the rich even richer, as they buy and sell financial assets with each other, bidding up asset prices in the process, while investing precious little in innovation, products, and workers. That is, the financial industry is much more preoccupied with trading financial assets — i.e. making itself rich and the rich even richer — than channeling credit to entrepreneurs and economic activity.

[2] http://time.com/4270359/billions-continues-to-reveal-whats-really-wrong-with-wall-street/

GOOD FINANCE, EVIL FINANCE, OCCUPY WALL STREET, AND MIKE MARKKULA

64

The preceding discussion should make it abundantly clear that poorly regulated, greed-crazed financial systems can cause serious damage to the economy. The Great Depression, which was initially triggered by a stock market crash and later exacerbated by a massive wave of run on banks by depositors desperate to get their money before the banks went out of business, painfully illustrated the scope for colossal damage. A frenzy of greed-driven financial speculation drove up stock prices to unsustainably high levels, and it was only a matter of time before they came crashing down to earth. The failure of the US government to decisively help the banks made things much worse. Similarly, the greed-driven wave of so-called financial innovation — the kind of innovation that tries to repackage garbage into gold — that preceded the Global Financial Crisis devastated the global financial system and severely disrupted the flow of credit to the real economy. Thankfully, the US and the rest of the world learned well the lessons of the Great Depression, and intervened boldly and forcefully to shore up the banks, averting a re-run of that apocalyptic horror show.

> **"**
> Similarly, the greed-driven wave of so-called financial innovation — the kind of innovation that tries to repackage garbage into gold — that preceded the Global Financial Crisis devastated the global financial system and severely disrupted the flow of credit to the real economy.
> **"**

Clearly, there is a negative dimension to finance and the financial industry. Therefore, we have every right to criticize, and criticize in the harshest possible terms, the excesses of Wall Street, in the hope that they will be corrected. However, precisely because finance is so vital to the real economy, we have to be clear-headed about what is wrong with finance in the 21st century. Wholesale, blanket criticisms of banks and financial system are unhelpful and unproductive. One line of misguided criticism has to do with the fact that banks produce nothing tangible. In fact, in a modern market economy, most of what we produce and consume, from air travel to education to health care, are intangible services rather than tangible manufactured products such as cars or televisions or laptops. Another line of misplaced criticism has to do with the sky-high salaries of bankers and finance professionals. In and of itself, this is not a problem. Above all, the fiercest critics of finance argue that it is all pain and no gain, that finance provides no benefits to the real economy while imposing significant costs, especially when a financial crisis breaks out and disrupts economic activity.

The chorus of anti-finance criticism has grown visibly louder since the Global Financial Crisis. After all, that crisis came close to pushing the global economy over the cliff, and inflicting untold suffering and misery on billions of people. Anti-finance sentiments did not appear overnight, and plenty of people outside finance harbored grave doubts about the benefits of finance well before the Global Financial Crisis. But, for sure, the crisis gave a firm push to those sentiments. In addition, some studies by economists found that the financial sector does not contribute to economic growth, and may even harm growth. To the anti-globalization, anti-capitalism crowd, Wall Street is the poster child for everything

"

Clearly, there is a negative dimension to finance and the financial industry.... However, precisely because finance is so vital to the real economy, we have to be clear-headed about what is wrong with finance in the 21st century. Wholesale, blanket criticisms of banks and financial system are unhelpful and unproductive.

"

that is wrong with capitalism and the market economy — producing no useful service or product, lining the pockets of greed-crazed bankers, and costing the tax payers billions of dollars. The Occupy Wall Street movement best captured the anti-capitalist, anti-finance mood. A common refrain among the adherents of the movement is that while the richest 1% of the global population is getting richer, the remaining 99% is getting poorer.

While Occupy Wall Street and their supporters have many legitimate concerns, a sound and efficient financial system is in fact indispensable for economic growth. The financial system consists primarily of banks and capital markets — i.e. stock markets and bond markets. Banks take deposits from savers and lend them to borrowers. A large part of bank borrowing is used by firms to finance their investments. Firms also issue stocks and bonds to directly access savings to finance their investments. Both banks and capital markets thus channel savings into investments. Both the quantity and quality of investments, which are central to economic growth, would suffer in the absence of a well-functioning financial system. Growth requires building factories, infrastructure such as road and power plants, and investing in R&D (research and development) and other innovative activities. The fundamental role of the financial system is to mobilize and allocate capital to those growth-conducive investments.

Above all, finance is indispensable for dynamic, risk-taking, entrepreneurial capitalism that creates socially useful innovations — not the kind that Wall Street churned out prior to 2008 — and drives mankind forward. For example, financing from venture capitalists and angel investors catalyzed Silicon Valley, the capital of the global information and communication technology (ICT) revolution. Venture capital funds invest in

"

> While Occupy Wall Street and their supporters have many legitimate concerns, a sound and efficient financial system is in fact indispensable for economic growth.... Above all, finance is indispensable for dynamic, risk-taking, entrepreneurial capitalism that creates socially useful innovations — not the kind that Wall Street churned out prior to 2008 — and drives mankind forward.

"

new companies with a new technology, business model, product or service in exchange for equity. Angel investors are similar except that they tend to be rich individuals who invest their own money in exchange for a stake in the startup. Despite the brilliance of Steve Jobs and Steve Wozniak, Apple would never have gone far beyond the suburban garage in Los Altos without the critical seed money provided by the angel investor Mike Markkula, who also helped the company get additional funding — credit and venture capital — and served as CEO in the 1980s and 1990s. Not surprisingly, angel investing and venture capital are much better developed in the US than elsewhere, and contribute a lot to the dynamism of the US economy.

But forget Steve Jobs and Mike Markkula. Even more mundane entrepreneurs with more mundane business ideas cannot start their business without a bank loan or some other funding. Indeed access to finance is an indispensable ingredient of entrepreneurship and equivalently, lack of access to finance is a serious barrier to entrepreneurship. In many developing countries with underdeveloped banks and financial markets, far too many businesses fail to get off the ground due to lack of finance. In particular, new firms and smaller firms, which are the regenerative lifeblood of economic dynamism and a vital source of competition, innovation and jobs, cannot get enough credit on reasonable terms. In those countries, there is a strong case for expanding and deepening banks and stock and bond markets, in order to promote the underdeveloped private sector. In rich countries with large, well-developed financial systems, such as the US, the urgent challenge is to get the banks to return to their core business of lending to entrepreneurs and firms, rather than investing in financial markets

“

Despite the brilliance of Steve Jobs and Steve Wozniak, Apple would never have gone far beyond the suburban garage in Los Altos without the critical seed money provided by the angel investor Mike Markkula, who also helped the company get additional funding — credit and venture capital — and served as CEO in the 1980s and 1990s.

”

and inventing risky, privately profitable but socially useless financial products.

More generally, the financing of new entrepreneurs and smaller firms allows for the entry of new players into the market and fosters competition, which spurs new and old firms to create new products and technologies. But far too often, it is very difficult for entrepreneurs who want to start their own companies to obtain credit at reasonable interest rates. The problem is especially severe in developing countries, where state-owned firms or large, politically well-connected corporations enjoy preferential access to credit. In China, for example, the largest banks are state-owned banks, and these banks still shovel a disproportionate share of their loans to inefficient state-owned firms. As a result, smaller firms and entrepreneurs with bright ideas are starved of the capital they need to grow, and the economy is starved of new products and technologies and fresh blood. China must develop a more efficient financial system that allocates credit on the basis of commercial merit rather than political connections to sustain healthy economic growth. All over the world, and not just in China, far too many Steve Jobses do not have a Mike Markkula to help their business ideas get off the ground.

Another major contribution of the financial system to the real economy is that it helps firms and households manage risk. Insurance companies help firms and households better cope with all kinds of contingencies, from natural disasters to automobile accidents to ill health. As we saw earlier, taking risk is the heart and soul of entrepreneurial capitalism. Services that help entrepreneurs to better manage risk will encourage them to take more risk, and thus create more new companies, products, services, jobs, and wealth, to everybody's benefit. The financial system provides the bulk

> **But far too often, it is very difficult for entrepreneurs who want to start their own companies to obtain credit at reasonable interest rates. The problem is especially severe in developing countries, where state-owned firms or large, politically well-connected corporations enjoy preferential access to credit. In China, for example, the largest banks are state-owned banks, and these banks still shovel a disproportionate share of their loans to inefficient state-owned firms.**

of such services. For example, when companies sell their products abroad or make investments abroad, they want to protect themselves against changes in the exchange rate. When Apple sends iPhones in Japan, its Japanese revenues will suffer in US dollar terms if the Japanese yen strengthens against the US dollar. Global foreign exchange markets, where 5 trillion dollars' worth of international currencies is traded every day, allow Apple to protect itself by betting beforehand that the yen will rise. Those markets make possible global trade and cross-border investments.

The financial industry also provides a host of other valuable services which are essential for both firms and households. More formally, according to Stephen Davis, Jon Lukomnik and David Pitt-Watson, the four main roles of finance are providing (1) safe custody for assets, (2) a payments system, (3) intermediation between savers and borrowers, and (4) risk reduction or insurance.[1] A good financial industry performs those functions well whereas a bad financial industry performs those functions poorly. The industry sometimes does a terrible job of providing such services. For example, the reckless, greed-crazed risk-taking of banks prior to the Global Financial Crisis jeopardized the lifelong savings of countless depositors — i.e. very unsafe custody of their assets. More damningly, recent research suggests that the financial industry, measured by the cost of providing financial services, is no more efficient today than it was at the end of the 19th century![2] That is, most so-called financial innovations benefit the financial industry, but not the economy as a whole. Even worse, such "innovations" often trigger crisis, such as the Global Financial Crisis of 2007–2008 which almost brought on Great Depression II.

[1] Stephen Davis, Jon Lukomnik, and David Pitt-Watson, "What They Do with Your Money: How the Financial System Fails Us and How to Fix It," 2016, Yale University Press.

[2] Thomas Philippon, "Has the US Finance Industry Become Less Efficient? On the Theory and Measurement of Financial Intermediation," 2016, http://pages.stern.nyu.edu/~tphilipp/papers/Finance_Efficiency.pdf

ENDING SUBSIDIES FOR WALL STREET, AND RETURNING FINANCE TO ITS ROOTS

65

Nevertheless, demonizing the financial industry itself on account of financial crisis is equivalent to demonizing the automobile industry itself on account of automobile accidents. Finance delivers enormous benefits to society notwithstanding financial crisis, even catastrophic ones such as the Global Financial Crisis, just as the automobile delivers enormous benefits to society notwithstanding automobile accidents, which cause a great deal of human pain and suffering across the world. Therefore, radical solutions to financial crisis, such as wholesale nationalization of the entire financial system, are unlikely to work. Government bureaucrats are not good at, in fact they are terrible at running business, and there is no reason why banks should be an exception. Even worse, state ownership of banks and other financial institutions will channel credit toward state-owned firms or politically well-connected private firms at the expense of more efficient firms. This is exactly what we observe in China, for example. In short, private banks pose plenty of risks and problems for the economy, but replacing them with state-owned banks is most definitely not the solution.

Yet, much more than in the automobile industry or most other industries, there is a

> " Therefore, radical solutions to financial crisis, such as wholesale nationalization of the entire financial system, are unlikely to work. Government bureaucrats are not good at, in fact they are terrible at running business, and there is no reason why banks should be an exception. Even worse, state ownership of banks and other financial institutions will channel credit toward state-owned firms or politically well-connected private firms at the expense of more efficient firms. "

compelling case for government intervention in the financial industry. More specifically, since the Global Financial Crisis was the consequence of inadequate regulation, the regulatory authorities — i.e. government agencies that oversee the banks and financial markets — need to effectively regulate the financial industry, in particular to prevent it from taking excessive risks which may bring about instability and even crisis. It is true that the automobile industry, for example, also requires effective regulation, as evident in the infamous Volkswagen emissions scandal which erupted in September 2015. However, the stakes are much higher for the financial industry; after all, regulatory failures led to the Global Financial Crisis of 2008–2009, which almost precipitated another Great Depression. The Dodd–Frank Act, mentioned earlier, and Basel III guidelines for banks, which will force banks to set aside more capital against their lending, are steps in the right direction. However, Dodd–Frank needs to be greatly simplified and, more fundamentally, regulation needs to be strengthened without going overboard and impeding credit flows to the real economy.

If governments need to do more in terms of regulating the financial industry, they need to do much less in terms of bailing out the financial industry whenever it gets into trouble. On balance, the Troubled Asset Relief Program (TARP), the financial rescue of banks during the Global Financial Crisis, was the right call because it averted a global financial and economic meltdown. However, TARP is just part of a much broader trend — unhealthily close links between Washington and Wall Street. For example, according to Bloomberg News, the top 10 US banks receive government subsidies amounting to a staggering US$83 billion every

" The Dodd–Frank Act, mentioned earlier, and Basel III guidelines for banks, which will force banks to set aside more capital against their lending, are steps in the right direction. However, Dodd–Frank needs to be greatly simplified and, more fundamentally, regulation needs to be strengthened without going overboard and impeding credit flows to the real economy. If governments need to do more in terms of regulating the financial industry, they need to do much less in terms of bailing out the financial industry whenever it gets into trouble. **"**

year.[1] In the absence of subsidies, which is a particularly harmful form of corporate welfare, those banks would just break even. In other words, all their profits are due to subsidies. This incestuous relationship between government and finance is replicated across much of the world.

Well before TARP, there was a popular assumption within Wall Street that the government would bail it out if it got into trouble, an assumption that TARP only confirmed. The assumption is ultimately grounded in the bankers' arrogant self-belief that banks are too important to fail, too big to fail. Unless the government imposes much stricter conditions for future bailouts — for example, high interest rate on its loans — the banks will continue to take excessive risk, safe in the knowledge that the government will help them out again when their greed causes the next crisis. Moreover, in their blind pursuit of profit, they may return to the senseless so-called financial innovation that generates fat bonuses for themselves for a few years, but eventually brings tears for everybody. Unconditional bailouts of the financial industry are, in effect, a subsidy for risk-taking by the banks. In contrast to socially beneficial risk-taking by entrepreneurs like Steve Jobs, the banks' risk-taking only benefits the banks. Private profits, social losses. Private gain, social pain. Any sensible reform of finance must attach stringent conditions to future bailouts, so that banks that play with fire pick up the bill themselves, not the tax payers.

The rapid expansion of the financial industry prior to the Global Financial Crisis was driven by a surge of investment in financial assets, which drove up their prices and thus fattened the industry's profits. The surge of investment, in turn, was driven to a large extent by a sharp decline

[1] http://www.bloombergview.com/articles/2013-02-20/why-should-taxpayers-give-big-banks-83-billion-a-year-

303

in the real interest rate, or the nominal interest rate adjusted for inflation. Larry Summers, a prominent US economist and former Treasury Secretary, put forth a number of explanations for the record low real interest rates.[2] For one, slower population growth reduces economic growth and demand for loans. Massive accumulation of reserves by central banks around the world expands global supply of savings and thus helps to reduce global interest rate. Worsening inequality also expands global savings since the rich tend to save a larger share of their income than the poor. Finally, demand for loans may be declining because the new generation of tech companies needs less capital than old economy, smokestack companies.

[2] http://www.economist.com/blogs/
buttonwood/2014/11/secular-stagnation

THE FED'S EASY MONEY, THE GREENSPAN PUT, AND THE BERNANKE PUT: ANOTHER MASSIVE SUBSIDY FOR WALL STREET

66

While the aforementioned structural factors played a major role in the decline of real interest rates which, in turn, fueled investment in financial assets and the expansion of the financial industry, another key culprit was monetary policy. More precisely, monetary policy was too loose prior to the Global Financial Crisis, unleashing a flood of money into the financial markets and property markets. The crisis was, in short, the predictable result of too much money searching for profit and the consequent fabrication of profit opportunities. Where on earth, pray tell me, is there a profit in lending mortgage loans to subprime borrowers who should not be buying homes? There is perhaps a case for the government to provide low-cost social housing for those borrowers, but the only possible profit opportunity in this scenario is a fabricated, manufactured profit opportunity, the kind that ends up in asset price bubbles and crisis.

At a deeper level, US monetary policy has become hostage to Wall Street's self-interest, and a similar capture of the central bank by the financial industry can be observed in many other countries. The clearest example of this disturbing trend of the financial industry dictating monetary

> "
> The crisis was, in short, the predictable result of too much money searching for profit and the consequent fabrication of profit opportunities.... At a deeper level, US monetary policy has become hostage to Wall Street's self-interest, and a similar capture of the central bank by the financial industry can be observed in many other countries.
> "

policy is a disturbing asymmetry in monetary policy. When the economy slows down, the US Federal Reserve cuts the interest rate to boost investment. But when the economy speeds up, the Fed does not raise the interest rate even though it is prudent to do so to prevent overheating. The most likely explanation for the asymmetry is that the Fed is caving in to pressure from Wall Street, which likes lower interest rate but hates higher interest rate, for obvious reasons. Lower interest rates tend to push up stock and other asset prices, higher interest rates pull them down. The predictable result of the US Fed's one-way interest rate is the build-up of potentially dangerous asset price bubbles.

One has to wonder why financial newspapers, which tend to be Wall Street mouthpieces, always raise a ruckus when the Fed is mulling an interest rate hike but always raise the loudest cheers when the Fed cuts rates. Federal Reserve Board chairman Alan Greenspan had a habit of reducing interest and providing ample liquidity whenever the stock market fell sharply. His successor Ben Bernanke had a similar habit. This type of monetary policy encourages investors to believe that the Fed will always step in to bail them out, which, in turn, encourages investors to take excessive risk in the belief that with the Fed standing ready to help, things could never go wrong. In effect, the Greenspan put and the Bernanke put[1] limited the amount of losses that investors could suffer when markets fell. In the aftermath of the Global Financial Crisis, the Federal Reserve, as well as the central banks of the Eurozone and Japan, embarked on a massive expansion of the money supply under unconventional monetary policies known as quantitative expansion (QE).[2] Predictably, much of the QE money ended up sloshing around in global stock markets, pushing up global stock prices.

[1] Greenspan's habit was called the Greenspan put by the financial markets, which also coined the term the Bernanke put for Bernanke's identical habit. Such monetary policy behavior encourages moral hazard or reckless risk-taking by investors, who are safe in the knowledge that the Fed will always come to their rescue when the markets fall. In technical finance terminology, a put option gives the holder the right to sell an asset at a pre-specified price to another party, thus protecting the holder from additional losses when the markets tank. Both Greenspan and Bernanke were viewed as lowering the interest rate whenever the stock market fell by a large margin, thus limiting the losses of investors.

[2] Under QE, which is an unorthodox type of monetary policy, the central bank buys up large amounts of financial assets from commercial banks, which raises the prices of those assets and lowers their yields, and expands the money supply. Central banks were forced to resort to such policies because with interest rate at or close to zero, conventional monetary policy — i.e. rate cuts — was no longer effective.

Lower interest rates push up stock and property prices, which fatten Wall Street's profits, while higher interest rates do the opposite. The predictable result is a ratcheting down of interest rate, huge increase in liquidity, upward spiral of asset prices, and the formation and bursting of an asset bubble. When there is a glut of money chasing stocks and property, it does not take a genius to figure out which way their prices will go. Moreover, why bother to work hard and look for the next Steve Jobs when you can earn easy money by piling into stocks, property and other financial assets, courtesy of the Fed's easy-money monetary policy and one-way interest rates? Indeed, this is exactly what the banks did prior to the Global Financial Crisis of 2008–2009. The Fed's lax monetary policy amounted to a massive subsidy for Wall Street, and it also distorted Wall Street's investments away from the real economy and toward financial assets.

The result of the aforementioned trends is that finance is moving away from its roots — of serving the real economy by channeling resources to productive investments. Wall Street's greed-crazed, liquidity-fueled speculation in financial assets and property — evil finance — is so far removed from the textbook picture of banks and financial markets allocating capital to firms and industries — good finance — that it is hard to reconcile the two. The Global Financial Crisis was the logical and predictable culmination of evil finance, or finance for the sake of finance. A hugely important global challenge facing the world's governments, no less important than, say, fighting climate change, is to return the banks and financial markets to their original domain of serving the real economy, rather than themselves. Tougher regulation, tougher bailouts, and sensible monetary policy are the first steps of the difficult but necessary reform

"

The Fed's lax monetary policy amounted to a massive subsidy for Wall Street, and it also distorted Wall Street's investments away from the real economy and toward financial assets. The result of the aforementioned trends is that finance is moving away from its roots — of serving the real economy by channeling resources to productive investments.

"

process. The rewards of successful reform — many more Steve Jobses and fewer hedge funds — will be enormous.

Successful financial reform that returns banks to their core business of lending to firms and industries will generate more Steve Jobses by expanding the flow of credit to entrepreneurs with innovative ideas. But there will be a more direct impact of financial reform on socially beneficial entrepreneurship that produces socially useful products and technologies. Too many of the best and the brightest young talent flock to Wall Street because of the sky-high salaries. After four grueling years at MIT or Caltech, you feel like you deserve a fat paycheck and nobody can blame you for that. But the problem is that those sky-high Wall Street salaries are, to some extent, the result of excessive risk-taking made possible by government subsidies. Removing those subsidies will bring down those salaries to levels more comparable to other occupations, and thus help unleash a large pool of talent to socially more beneficial work. For example, would not it be wonderful if many of Wall Street's best and brightest devoted their minds to fighting environmental destruction and global warming instead?[3] Maybe they can start a Green Valley, a vibrant cluster of innovative environmental startups!

[3]A more specific example is improving and reducing the cost of renewable energy such as solar power and wind power. Given the growing demand for renewable energy and, more generally, a cleaner environment, there will be plenty of profit opportunities and high-wage jobs in the green industries. It is unrealistic to expect talented men and women to join green industries purely out of a sense of idealism. Reducing the artificially inflated salaries of the financial sector by removing explicit and implicit government subsidies will encourage more and better talent to shift from finance to socially more productive sectors such as green industries.

ELON MUSK, BOYAN SLAT, AND GREEN GROWTH

67

A Green Valley or a Silicon Valley for startups that specialize in products and technologies that help to protect the environment, is more than just a pipe dream. There is a widespread belief that there is a difficult tradeoff between economic growth and environmental protection. That is, a country can achieve a cleaner environment only by sacrificing some growth or, conversely, a country can grow faster only at the cost of higher environmental costs. Many businesses view environmental regulations as a burdensome additional cost, which is why they tend to oppose those regulations. But upon closer thought, the growing demand for a cleaner environment also presents opportunities for businesses. In particular, since environment-friendliness is now a key dimension of competition, entrepreneurs and firms that produce greener products will gain market shares at the expense of those that do not. Moreover, just as demand for faster and better transportation gave rise to the railway, automobile and airplane, we can expect the demand for cleaner environment will give rise to entirely new products and industries, fostering growth in the process. Green may be good for growth, after all!

> " There is a widespread belief that there is a difficult tradeoff between economic growth and environmental protection.... But upon closer thought, the growing demand for a cleaner environment also presents opportunities for businesses. In particular, since environment-friendliness is now a key dimension of competition, entrepreneurs and firms that produce greener products will gain market shares at the expense of those that do not. "

A prominent example of a new high-impact green product is the electric car.[1] There are a number of producers, including Nissan, which produces the Leaf, the world's top-selling electric car, with over 200,000 units sold by December 2015. An electric car is propelled by electric motors, which are powered by electrical energy stored in rechargeable batteries. The electric car has been around for a long time, since the 1880s, so strictly speaking, it is not a new product. Indeed it was one of the main types of automobiles until it was driven out of the market by the mass production of gasoline-powered cars by Henry Ford and the sharp drop in their prices. The recent revival of the electric car since 2008 was driven by technological advances in batteries, high global oil prices at the time, and environmental concerns — gasoline-powered cars are a major source of local air pollution as well as greenhouse gases. Electric cars are better for the environment than gasoline-powered cars because they do not emit tailpipe pollutants. Furthermore, their environmental benefits are expected to grow over time as electricity generation shifts to greener sources — e.g. from coal to natural gas.[2]

Although there are quite a few companies that make electric cars, Tesla Motors has become synonymous with electric cars. Also, entrepreneur Elon Musk, a co-founder and the driving force behind the company, has become synonymous with Tesla Motors. Prior to his involvement in Tesla, Musk had created a number of successful companies, most notably PayPal, a worldwide online payments system. Musk's overarching goal is to mass produce electric cars, and to reduce their costs to levels that are comparable to gasoline-powered cars. Tesla has evolved from a maker of luxury sports cars, the Tesla Roadster, which had a base price of US$100,000 in 2010, to the still-expensive but

[1] https://en.wikipedia.org/wiki/Electric_car

[2] Contrary to popular opinion, electric cars are not pollution-free. The amount of pollution they produce depends on the source of their power — electricity. For example, if the electric cars get their electricity from coal-fired power plants, they would contribute more pollution than if they got their electricity from cleaner power plants. http://www.slate.com/articles/technology/technology/2013/09/how_green_is_a_tesla_electric_cars_environmental_impact_depends_on_where.html

more affordable Tesla S sedans, which sold for a base price of US$70,000 in 2015. The number of Tesla S sold surpassed 100,000 units in 2015.[3] In addition to the high price, a couple of related technical issues — limited range and infrastructure for recharging batteries — hinder the mass production of electric cars. It remains to be seen whether Musk can fulfill his audacious dream of becoming the Henry Ford of electric cars, but let us all root for him, for the sake of the environment.

An even more audacious green entrepreneur is the Dutch inventor Boyan Slat, who has devised an ingenious system for cleaning up plastic waste from the world's oceans. Slat was born on 27 July 1994, and he came across his big idea — his Thomas Edison moment — in 2011, when he was amazingly only 16. Perhaps not so amazingly since young minds are often the most creative minds. His passive cleanup system uses ocean currents to gather and trap plastic debris, of which there are massive amounts floating around the Pacific, Atlantic and Indian oceans. Over the past three decades, millions of tons of plastic have contaminated the oceans, and around 10% of the almost 300 million tons that is produced each year eventually ends up in oceans.[4] Despite initial lack of interest and widespread skepticism, Slat sold his idea to the public, which is easier to do in this age of the internet and social media, and he eventually secured enough funding to start his startup, aptly named The Ocean Cleanup. The company's first operational ocean-cleaning system is set to be deployed in waters off the Japanese island of Tsushima in 2016.[5]

The Ocean Cleanup is a perfect storm of entrepreneurship, environmentalism, and technology. Slat's innovative idea attracted thousands of volunteers, especially after his TEDx talk *How*

[3] Among electric cars, only the Nissan Leaf has sold more units.

[4] http://www.bbc.com/news/magazine-29631332

[5] http://www.techtimes.com/articles/57413/20150603/boyan-slat-20-year-old-holland-plan-clean-up-oceans.htm

the Oceans Can Clean Themselves went viral. The strong wave of popular enthusiasm led to a crowdfunding campaign which raised US$2.2 million and provided The Ocean Cleanup with the seed money to finance its pilot projects, including Tsushima.[6] Slat's plan for cleaning up the oceans still has plenty of critics and it is unclear whether it will work. But if it does, the environmental benefits will be enormous. It can reduce the time needed to rid the oceans of a given amount of plastic debris from thousands of years to a few years, and it may even dent the Great Pacific Garbage Patch, a huge flotsam of plastic waste halfway between California and Hawaii. Slat epitomizes the new generation of green entrepreneurs who combine concern for the environment with pursuit of profit. Financial sector reform, and deregulation and other government reforms that free up entrepreneurship, will give the world many more Slatses. The future of mankind, no less, depends on it.

[6] Crowdfunding refers to the process of raising money to finance a new business from many donors using an online platform. It is an IT-enabled mechanism for funding new companies, especially those that promote a cleaner environment or another public good.

TOWARD A BETTER CAPITALISM AND TOWARD A BETTER WORLD

68

Given the growing mountain of serious problems plaguing the world economy, it is easy to be pessimistic about its future prospects. The world's banks seem prone to catastrophic crisis, as evident in the Global Financial Crisis which almost brought the world economy to its knees and precipitated a repeat of the Great Depression. The world was perilously close to an economic and financial meltdown which would have caused untold human misery and suffering. Moreover, the income gap between the rich and the poor seems to be growing ever wider. While the top 0.01% is drowning in a sea of money, 99.99% of us are struggling just to make ends meet. Extreme poverty continues to enslave large swathes of mankind, especially in Africa but also elsewhere. The prospects for gainful unemployment are growing increasingly bleak for youths, in advanced and developing countries alike. Climate change threatens the very future of mankind. And the list goes on and on.

It is all too easy to blame capitalism for this growing mountain of problems and all other ills of the world. After all, since the defeat of communism and socialism, capitalism has become the dominant global economic system and ideology. With the exception of North Korea,

> **It is all too easy to blame capitalism for this growing mountain of problems and all other ills of the world. After all, since the defeat of communism and socialism, capitalism has become the dominant global economic system and ideology.**

Cuba, and a few other impoverished, destitute, time-warped hold-outs, capitalism now governs the production of goods and services across the world. Capitalism is widely blamed for the deterioration of income inequality in both advanced and developing countries. A long-held popular allegation is that capitalism exploits workers to the benefit of capitalists. Another criticism leveled by many is that capitalism destroys the environment and causes global warming. The common refrain is that capitalists pollute, contaminate and irreparably degrade the air, water and ground in their blind pursuit of profit. Yet another criticism is that capitalism replaces workers with machines, and thus causes unemployment. And so forth and so forth.

While it is unfair to blame capitalism for all of mankind's problems, even the most ardent advocates of capitalism would acknowledge that capitalism is far from a perfect system. The Volkswagen emission scandal that erupted in late 2015 and dominated news headlines around the world is but one example of capitalism's imperfections. The car maker had tampered with its engines so that emissions controls were activated only during laboratory emissions testing at the US Environmental Protection Agency (EPA). The cheating enabled Volkswagen to meet US regulatory standards during testing, but the 11 million vehicles affected worldwide emitted up to 40 times more than the permitted levels of nitrogen oxide in real-world driving. What was shocking about the scandal was that Volkswagen is one of the largest and most respected companies from Germany, a country known for high quality and reliable products. The scandal underlines the clear need for the government to rein in the excesses of capitalist greed.

More broadly, the government has a vital role to play under capitalism. For example, good

"

While it is unfair to blame capitalism for all of mankind's problems, even the most ardent advocates of capitalism would acknowledge that capitalism is far from a perfect system. The Volkswagen emission scandal that erupted in late 2015 and dominated news headlines around the world is but one example of capitalism's imperfections.

"

infrastructure such as roads, ports and electricity reduce the cost of doing business for all firms and industries. Likewise, good public education systems turn out skilled, productive workers and benefit the entire economy. Be that as it may, the government can only be a supporting actor, but never the lead actor in a market economy; the role player who grabs rebounds and plays tough defense, not the MVP who scores 30 points a game. Not that being a good supporting actor is easy. In fact, most governments are terrible at grabbing rebounds and playing tough defense. This explains why so many countries, especially developing countries, are mired in a seemingly permanent stagnation. The resulting lack of economic opportunities breeds discontent and resentment, and creates an army of angry young men with raging hormones. Such men are easy pickings for the IS (Islamic State), al Qaeda, and other similar outfits.

The MVP is, of course, the innovative, risk-taking, profit-seeking entrepreneur who comes up with new products, services, technologies, business models, and ideas — Steve Jobs and his buddies in the garage in California. It is precisely because the star player in the capitalist game is the private entrepreneur rather than the risk-averse, desk-bound government bureaucrat that capitalism is incomparably more productive than socialism. By far the biggest contribution of the government is to create a level playing field for vigorous Schumpeterian competition among private firms, with new, superior products and technologies driving out old, inferior ones. In order for capitalism to be socially beneficial Schumpeterian competition based on performance rather than socially harmful crony capitalism based on connections, a government that can serve as an honest and competent referee is simply indispensable.

> **"**
> The MVP is, of course, the innovative, risk-taking, profit-seeking entrepreneur who comes up with new products, services, technologies, business models, and ideas — Steve Jobs and his buddies in the garage in California. It is precisely because the star player in the capitalist game is the private entrepreneur rather than the risk-averse, desk-bound government bureaucrat that capitalism is incomparably more productive than socialism.
> **"**

315

Unfortunately, today's 21st century capitalism is so far removed from such ideal visions of Adam Smith that the great economist would roll in his grave if he could see its grossly mutated and degraded version. Above all, across the world, in rich and poor countries, the visible, in many cases suffocating, hand of the government is replacing and squeezing the very life out of the private sector, rendering it stagnant and lifeless. Instead of supporting the MVP and helping the team win the game, it is as if the bit player is taking over the game, with disastrous results for the team. The core essence of entrepreneurial capitalism — the benign kind that creates new products, companies and industries, generates wealth and jobs, and propels human progress — is risk-taking. Excessive regulation and meddling by the government, not just bribes and corruption, acts as a heavy tax on risk-taking and entrepreneurial activity. Even more insidiously, the unhealthily cozy ties between government and business are altering the basic rules of the game. All too often nowadays, the winners of the capitalist game are those with the closest links to the government, not those with the best products and technologies.

Besides the stifling embrace of the government, the emergence of financial capitalism poses another grave threat to entrepreneurial capitalism in the 21st century. Finance no longer serves the real economy, but itself. Prior to the Global Financial Crisis, Wall Street spent a lot of its time and energy cooking up socially dubious but privately profitable financial innovations. Other than 500% bonuses for fat cat investment bankers and hedge fund managers, it is difficult to see who benefits from this kind of "innovation." The global crisis, just like the stock market crash of October 1929 that precipitated the Great Depression, highlights the enormous cost of

> **"**
>
> The core essence of entrepreneurial capitalism — the benign kind that creates new products, companies and industries, generates wealth and jobs, and propels human progress — is risk-taking. Excessive regulation and meddling by the government, not just bribes and corruption, acts as a heavy tax on risk-taking and entrepreneurial activity.
>
> **"**

finance for the sake of finance. Far too much funds stay within the financial system, fueling the trading of stocks and bonds and thus inflating their prices instead of fueling productive activity. This is good news for the rich who own the bulk of financial assets but bad news for new startups and smaller companies which promote economic dynamism and generate large numbers of jobs.

The kind of finance that the world needs is not such self-serving finance, but finance that lubricates the wheels of business, economic activity and growth, the kind that creates iPhones, not the kind that transforms junk subprime mortgages into "profitable" financial assets. In short, the world needs more Mike Markkulas to pick and grow more Apples. But picking and growing an Apple is hard work, especially when there is always the easy option of MBS (mortgage-backed securities) and CDO (collateralized debt obligations). Tougher regulation and an end to unconditional bailouts will make Wall Street less lazy and actually work for its money, like the rest of us. They will also return finance to its economy-serving roots. No more free lunch for Wall Street! True, banks and the financial industry are too important to fail since businesses cannot start or grow without finance. But it is equally true that Wall Street has veered far away from its original mission of lubricating economic activity. Far worse, its greed-fueled frenzy of speculation and bogus innovations, made possible by the government's guarantee to bail it out if its recklessness landed it in trouble, almost bankrupted the global economy.

Fortunately for the world, capitalism can be fixed and it can move back toward the benign, original version envisioned by Adam Smith from its currently grossly deformed and destructive

> **The kind of finance that the world needs is not such self-serving finance, but finance that lubricates the wheels of business, economic activity and growth, the kind that creates iPhones, not the kind that transforms junk subprime mortgages into 'profitable' financial assets.... Tougher regulation and an end to unconditional bailouts will make Wall Street less lazy and actually work for its money, like the rest of us. They will also return finance to its economy-serving roots.**

form. Capitalism is broken not because it is inherently a lousy system, but because of misguided government interventions. Therefore, undoing those interventions will get capitalism back on track. First and foremost, governments around the world should go back to their roles as supporting actors, and allow the Steve Jobses, Elon Musks and Ted Turners of the world to take center stage again. Governments should cut back excessive regulations, provide good public services, and do other useful things, but they should not be in the business of doing business. The sooner governments wake up to that reality and do everything within their powers to reduce the tax on risk-taking and thus encourage entrepreneurship, the better. The business of government is to make it easy for business to do business, not to do business itself.

Returning the financial industry to its roots of serving the economy rather than serving itself is another priority for fixing capitalism. In particular, reducing the large amount of government subsidies, both explicit and implicit, will encourage banks to revert their attention to financing entrepreneurial activity. Imposing tougher regulations and tougher conditions on future bailouts will discourage banks from taking excessive risk, such as lending huge amounts of mortgage to homebuyers with poor credit rating. Lax monetary policy and one-way interest rates that have a habit of going down but rarely up are, in effect, another subsidy for the financial industry. Subsidies encourage banks to pile into financial assets and away from financing the real economy. They also push up the pay of finance professionals, and lure the best and brightest into finance, as opposed to, say, scientific research on climate change. For example, solar power and renewable energy development would benefit hugely from an infusion of more talent.

> **"**
>
> Capitalism is broken not because it is inherently a lousy system, but because of misguided government interventions. Therefore, undoing those interventions will get capitalism back on track.... Governments should cut back excessive regulations, provide good public services, and do other useful things, but they should not be in the business of doing business. The sooner governments wake up to that reality and do everything within their powers to reduce the tax on risk-taking and thus encourage entrepreneurship, the better.
>
> **"**

Broadly speaking, the analysis of this book suggests that there are three types of capitalism — entrepreneurial capitalism, crony or connection-based capitalism, and financial capitalism. Entrepreneurial capitalism is epitomized by the likes of Steve Jobs, Elon Musk, and Boyan Slat, visionary, profit-seeking, risk-taking individuals creating new, socially valuable products, services, and technologies, private greed promoting the social good, as envisioned by Smith. The everyday capitalist who quits his safe 9 to 5 salaried job to take a big risk, and start his own business, embodies entrepreneurial capitalism in a less glamorous but no less important way. Crony capitalism refers to politicians and businessmen scratching each other's back. Under crony capitalism, a successful firm is a special interest group with close ties to the government. Critically, the source of its success is not superior performance, but favors from the government. Finally, the Global Financial Crisis highlights the enormous destructive potential of financial capitalism, or the finance for the sake of finance, as opposed to finance that serves the real economy. Under financial capitalism, banks and other financial institutions trade financial assets with each other rather than lend to firms and entrepreneurs

Clearly, not all capitalisms are created equal, and some capitalisms are better than others. In particular, entrepreneurial capitalism is patently superior to crony capitalism or financial capitalism, certainly for the social good. There is a huge difference between profits based on creating the iPhone on one hand, and profits based on connections with the government or profits based on socially harmful "innovations" that only benefit the financial industry. Admittedly, the difference between the three is not always clear cut. For example, a financier who invents

> " Broadly speaking, the analysis of this book suggests that there are three types of capitalism — entrepreneurial capitalism, crony or connection-based capitalism, and financial capitalism.... Clearly, not all capitalisms are created equal, and some capitalisms are better than others. In particular, entrepreneurial capitalism is patently superior to crony capitalism or financial capitalism, certainly for the social good. "

319

a socially useful financial product straddles both financial and entrepreneurial capitalism. An entrepreneur who produces a good product *and* exploits good ties with the government is an entrepreneurial capitalist *and* crony capitalist. But the big problem with today's capitalism is that there is far too little entrepreneurial capitalism and far too much crony and financial capitalism. To change the script, the government has to do a much better of refereeing the capitalist game.

It is easy to take the blessings of capitalism for granted and to focus only on its supposed flaws. But a reformed and revitalized capitalism, based on less meddlesome government and more supportive financial system, can do so much for mankind. Just two examples — the stunning rise of China as an economic giant and the plethora of life-enriching IT services from Silicon Valley — underline the transformative power of entrepreneurial capitalism. Capitalism is part of the solution, not part of the problem. What the world needs is more, not less capitalism. Take the environment, for example. The demand for cleaner environment implies profit opportunities, and will give rise to a whole range of new products, companies and industries. Tesla electric cars are just one example of a wave of green innovations on the horizon. Green entrepreneurs like Slat are indispensable for protecting our environment and saving our Earth before it is too late to turn back the environmental clock.

Likewise, entrepreneurship is the key to generating more employment opportunities and ending Third World poverty. The best way to help others is to become a successful entrepreneur and thus create jobs. It is individually risky — far safer and easier to work in a 9 to 5 job — but socially invaluable. In fact, an economy without risk-taking entrepreneurship, an economy with

“

It is easy to take the blessings of capitalism for granted and to focus only on its supposed flaws. But a reformed and revitalized capitalism, based on less meddlesome government and more supportive financial system, can do so much for mankind.... Capitalism is part of the solution, not part of the problem. What the world needs is more, not less capitalism. Take the environment, for example. The demand for cleaner environment implies profit opportunities, and will give rise to a whole range of new products, companies and industries.

”

only 9 to 5ers, is like a stagnant pool of water. No dynamism, no progress, no life. The best way for governments to help their citizens is to create a more conducive environment for entrepreneurship. More entrepreneurial capitalism means more economic growth and dynamism, and less poverty, unemployment, despair, anger and frustration. It also means far fewer government workers doing no work and far fewer potential recruits for the IS. Despite the gloom and doom of the growing legion of pessimists about mankind's future, there is every reason to hope that tomorrow will be better than today. Setting capitalism free to work its wonderful growth-promoting, job-creating, poverty-reducing magic will make that hope — that tomorrow will be better than today — come true.

"

The best way for governments to help their citizens is to create a more conducive environment for entrepreneurship. More entrepreneurial capitalism means more economic growth and dynamism, and less poverty, unemployment, despair, anger and frustration.... Setting capitalism free to work its wonderful growth-promoting, job-creating, poverty-reducing magic will make that hope — that tomorrow will be better than today — come true.

"

INDEX

324

329

331

Printed in the United States
By Bookmasters

Printed in the United States
By Bookmasters